PAPER IN MOTION
A Collection of Origami Vehicles

Marc Kirschenbaum

Fit to Print Publishing, Inc.
New York, New York

Paper in Motion
Copyright © 2019
Fit To Print Publishing, Inc.

All rights reserved. No part of this publication may be reproduced, stored in a retrieval system or transmitted in any form or by any means, electronic, mechanical, photocopying, recording or otherwise, without the permission of the copyright holder.

ISBN 978-1-951146-02-3

The diagrams in this book were produced with Macromedia's Freehand, and image processing was done with Adobe Photoshop. The Backtalk family of typefaces was used for the body text and the cover uses Florida Serial with PT Sans. Ellen Cohen assisted with the cover design and provided valuable artistic assistance.

Contents

Introduction	5
Symbols and Terminology	6
Boats	
Ship in a bottle	10
Sailboat	17
Bikes	
Penny-farthing	29
Bicycle	38
Cars	
Prehistoric Car	55
Classic Car	70
Dune Buggy	86
Aircraft	
Biplane	90
Catching a Plane	103
Monoplane	116
Helicopter	133
Chopper	141
Spacecraft	
Satellite	145
Spaceship	153
Materials and Methods	160

Introduction

Vehicles are more than just a means of getting from one place to the next. They are an embodiment of aesthetics and novel mechanics. It is not uncommon to see artists capture the beauty of these glorious machines. Origami also has a balance of artistic expression and sophisticated engineering. This makes paper folding an ideal art form to realize these technological marvels.

The challenge of origami is translating specific topologies onto the fixed starting point of a single square sheet of paper. The *Biplane*, for instance has wing sections that loop together, and the *Bicycle* has a frame with even more looped sections. Additional appendages must be generated from the paper to accommodate for all these sections with holes. This creates additional complexity to the folding sequence.

Unlike animals and flowers that have a specific look, having man-made objects as artistic subject matter affords extra room for interpretation. The *Satellite* is a compilation of various spacecraft configurations. Various elements of automobiles of the 1930's appear in the *Classic Car*. Models like the *Spaceship* and *Prehistoric Car* are completely fictitious.

Most of the pieces employ color patterns from showing both sides of the paper. The *Ship in a Bottle* uses color to define the silhouette of the boat against the bottle. For the *Helicopter*, the paper goes into a zig-zag formation to allow for a lighter colored windshield, rotor and landing gear.

A common element among this collection is the difficulty level. Most of the sequences will challenge the most seasoned folders. If you are looking for something to get your feet wet with, the *Chopper* and *Dune Buggy* are simpler than the rest of the models. Collectively, these vehicles will provide many hours of folding fun. Enjoy!

Symbols and Terminology

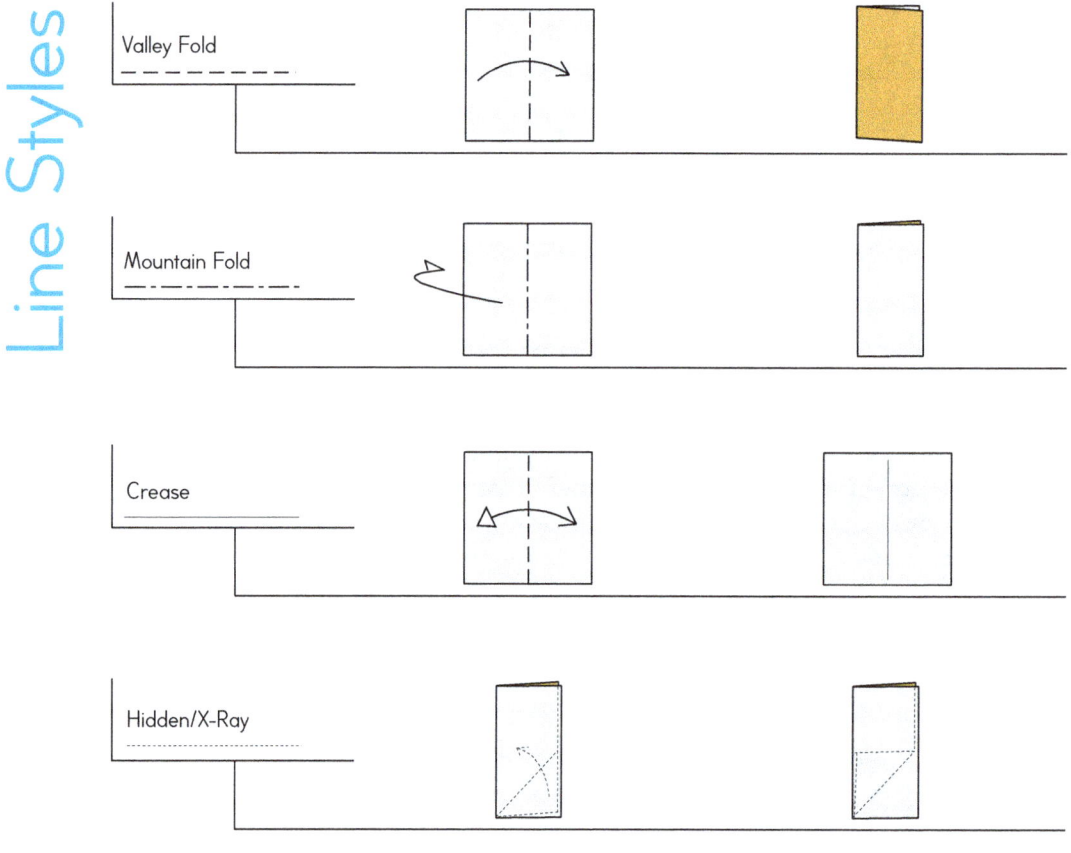

Line Styles

- Valley Fold
- Mountain Fold
- Crease
- Hidden/X-Ray

Arrows

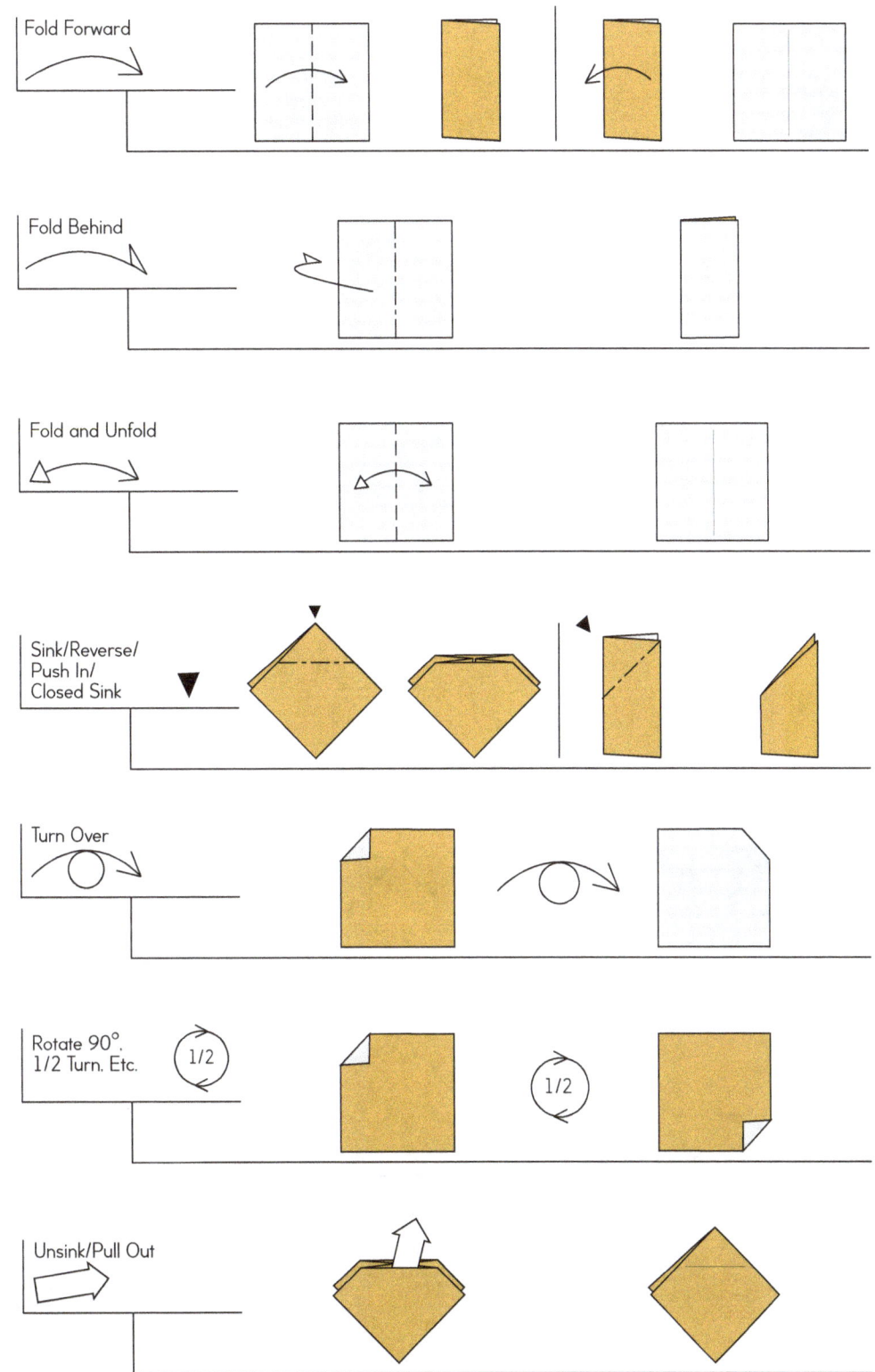

Maneuvers

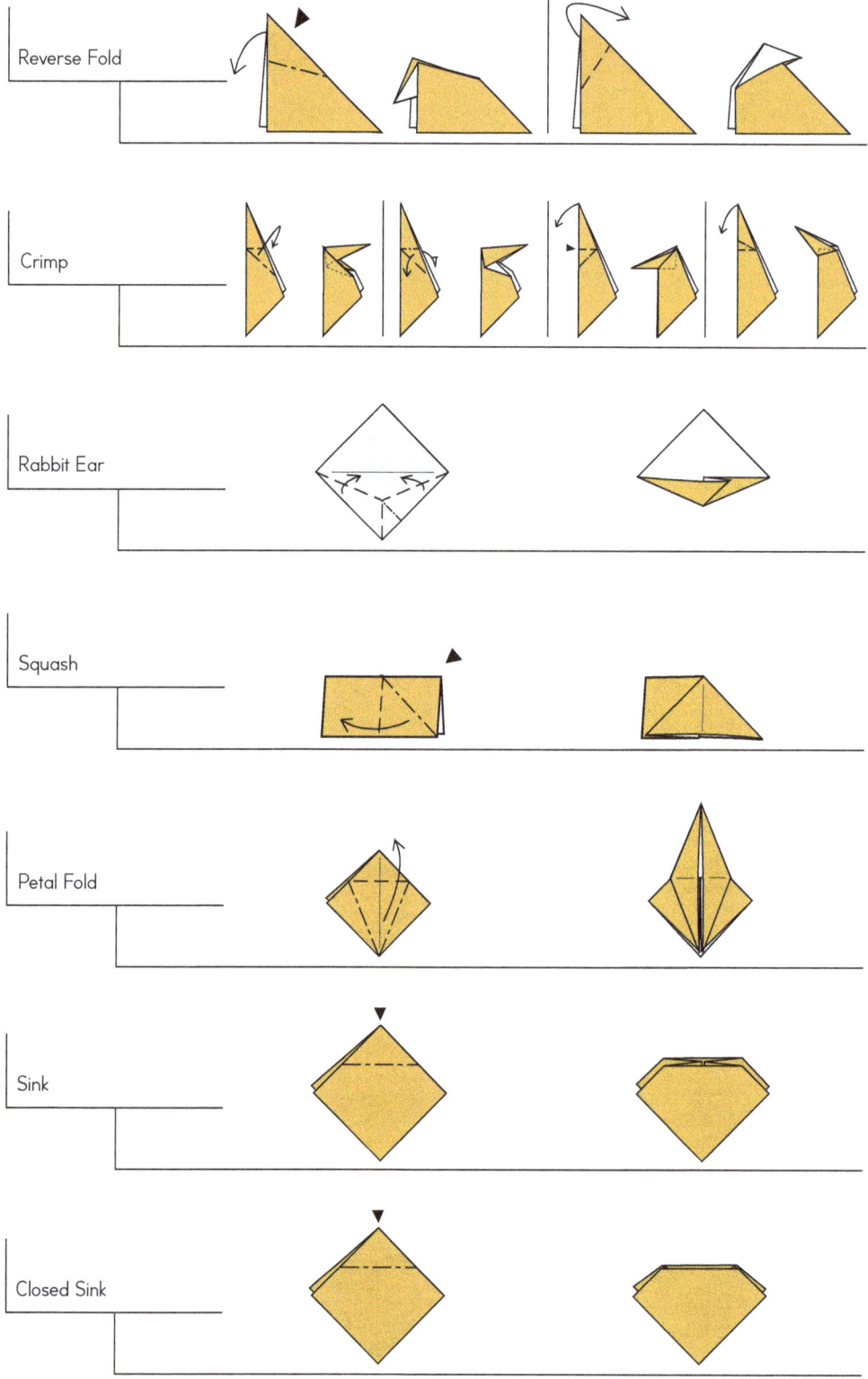

- Reverse Fold
- Crimp
- Rabbit Ear
- Squash
- Petal Fold
- Sink
- Closed Sink

Sink Triangularly

Pleat

Swivel

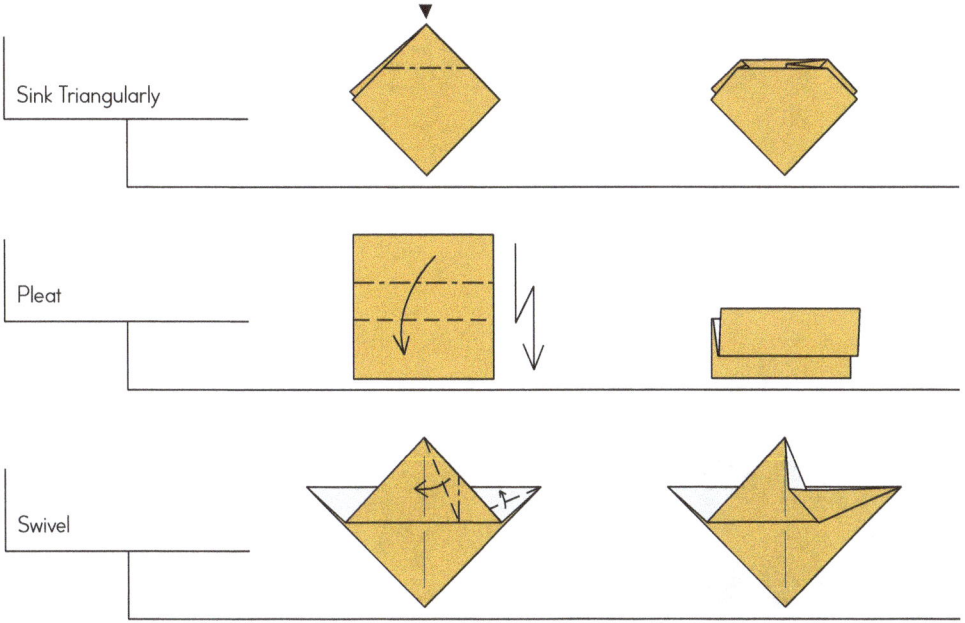

Ship in a Bottle

Origami artist Sy Chen is a master at creating origami pieces with clever use of negative space. This *Ship in a Bottle* captures that style in the way the elements of the boat are not connected. This simplicity of form also makes this model one of the easier to fold in this collection. There are some interesting folds in this sequence to connect the 1/3rd based geometries and the folds based on 22.5-degree angles. When this model first debuted, Mr. Chen gave it his approval.

ship in a bottle

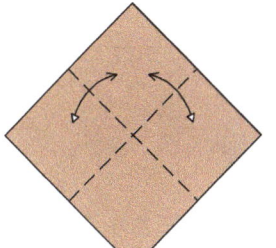

1. Precrease in half both ways.

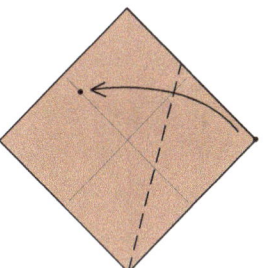

2. Valley fold the corner over to meet the crease.

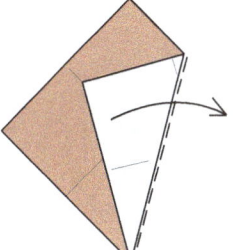

3. Unfold.

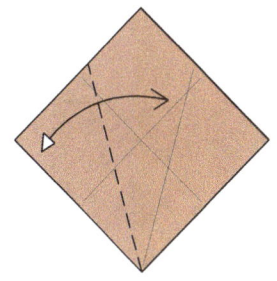

4. Repeat the precrease in the opposite direction.

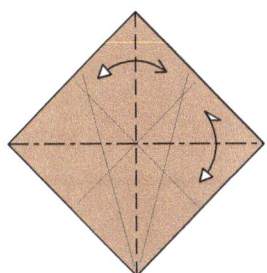

5. Precrease the diagonals with a valley fold and mountain fold as indicated.

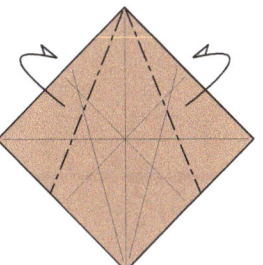

6. Mountain fold the sides along the angle bisectors.

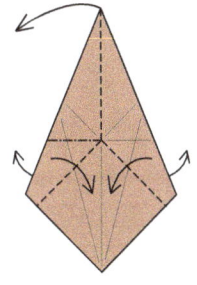

7. Rabbit ear, allowing the back corners to swing outwards.

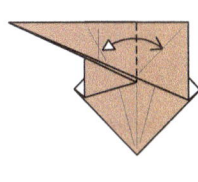

8. Precrease, by swinging the center flap back and forth.

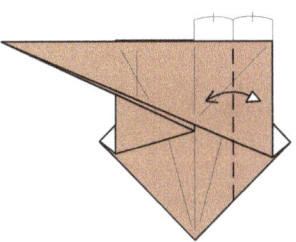

9. Precrease in half.

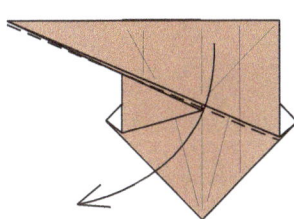

10. Swing down one layer.

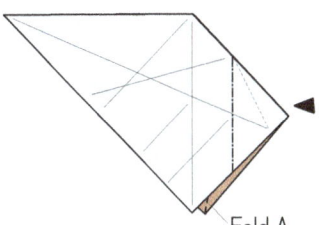

11. Reverse fold asymmetrically, noting fold A lies along the crease from step 2.

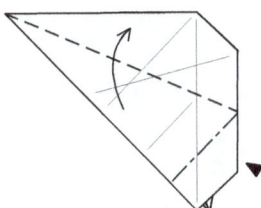

12. Form an asymmetrical squash fold.

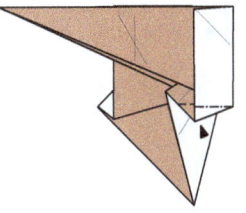

13. Reverse fold.

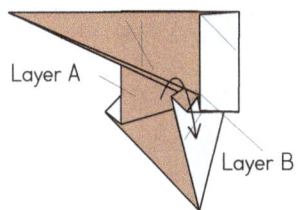

14. Bring layer A on top of layer B.

11

— ship in a bottle —

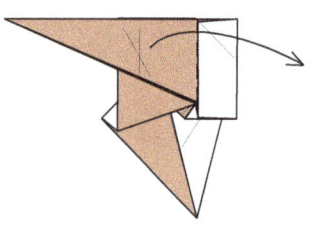

15. Swing the center flap over.

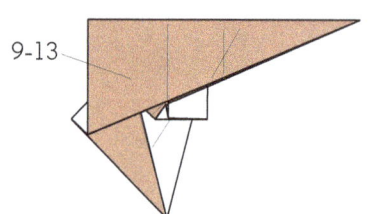

16. Repeat steps 9-13 in mirror image.

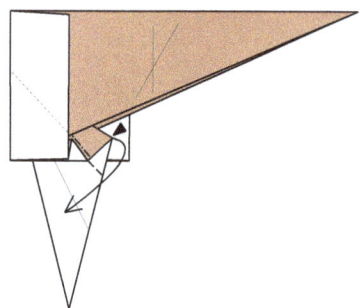

17. Reverse fold.

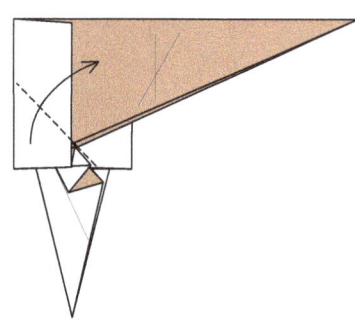

18. Lightly lift the corner up.

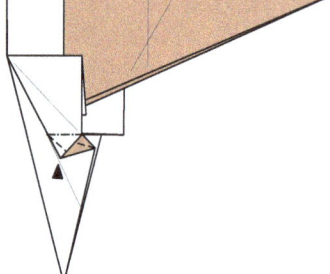

19. Reverse fold.

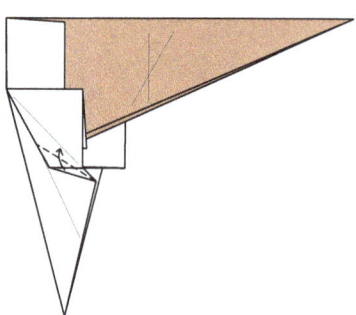

20. Valley fold along the angle bisector.

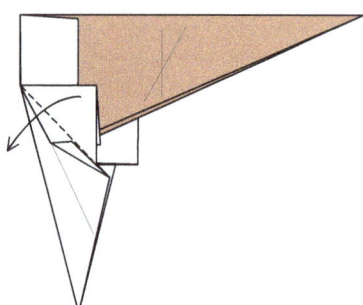

21. Swing back down.

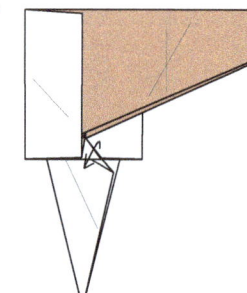

22. Bring the trapped corner to the surface.

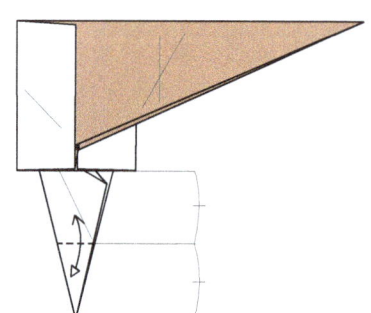

23. Precrease the flap in half.

ship in a bottle

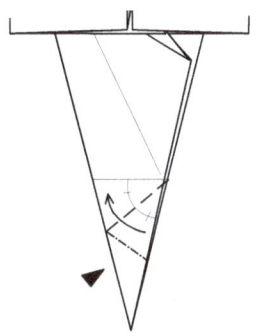

24. Squash fold.

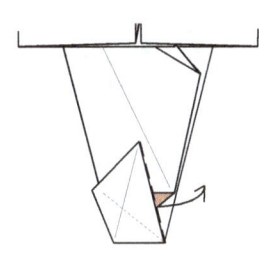

25. Swivel the hidden layer out to make the top flap symmetrical.

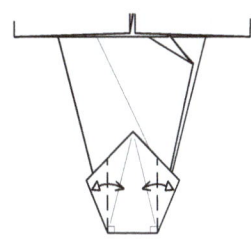

26. Lightly precrease the top flap.

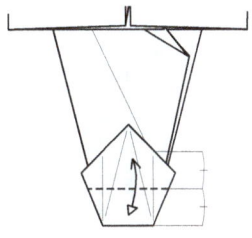

27. Precrease again.

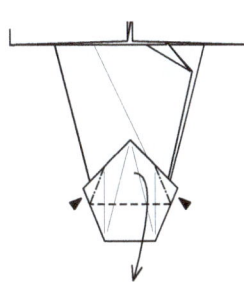

28. Petal fold.

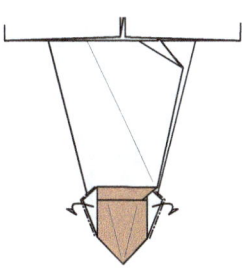

29. Wrap around a single layer at each side.

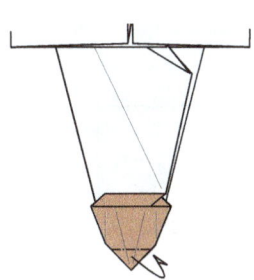

30. Mountain fold the corner, and tuck it into the pocket behind.

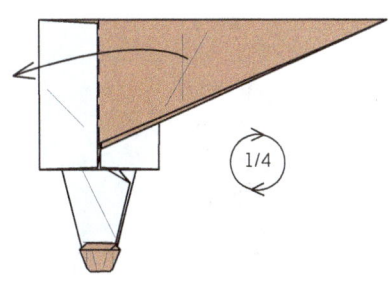

31. Swing over the center flap. Rotate 1/4 turn.

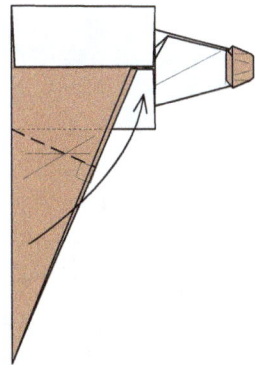

32. Valley fold up, noting the fold is aligned with the hidden corner below.

13

ship in a bottle

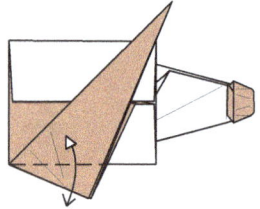

33. Precrease.

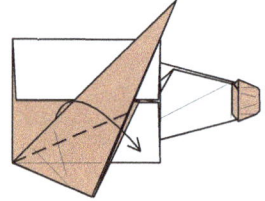

34. Valley fold down.

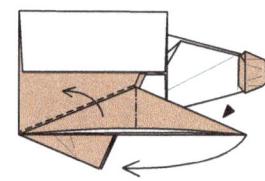

35. Squash fold, leaving one layer at top, and two at the bottom.

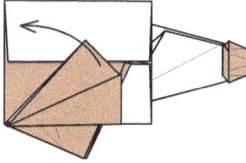

36. Pull out the pleat and flatten.

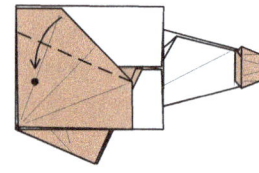

37. Valley fold the corner to lie on the crease.

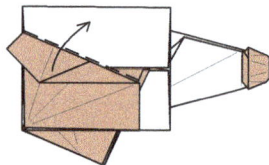

38. Unfold.

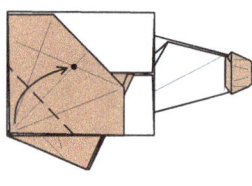

39. Valley fold to the intersection of creases.

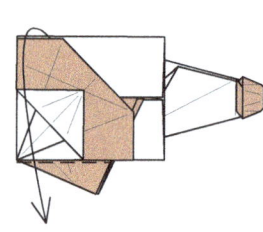

40. Swing the top section down.

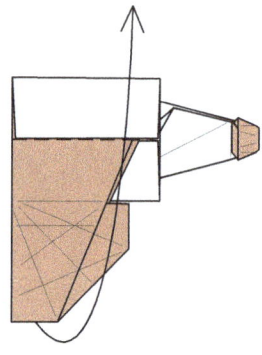

41. Swing upwards.

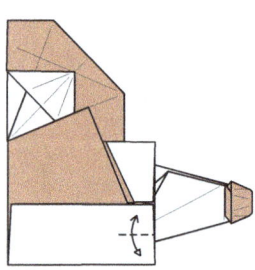

42. Lightly precrease in half.

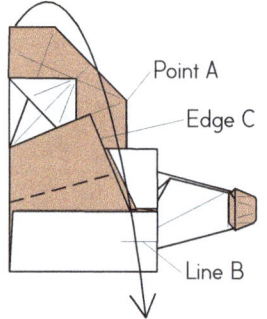

43. Valley fold down, such that point A meets line B, and edge C is straight.

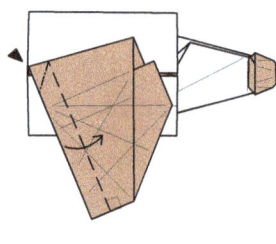

44. Swivel the edge over.

ship in a bottle

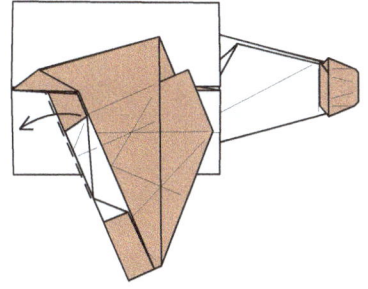

45. Valley fold one layer through.

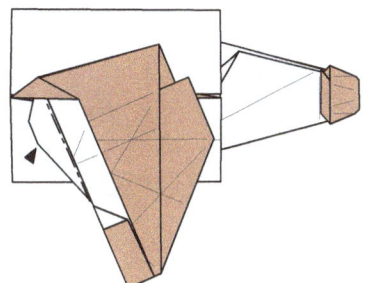

46. Sink triangularly (closed at top, open at bottom).

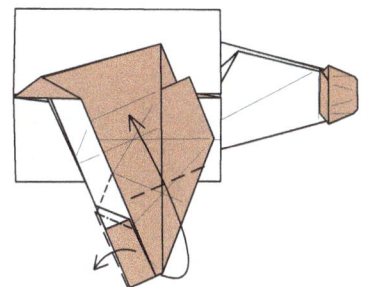

47. Valley fold to the crease, while swiveling out the side.

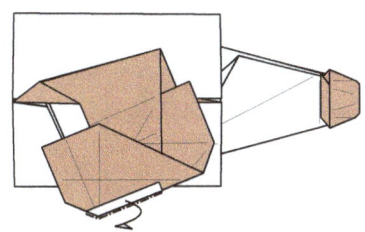

48. Wrap a single layer around.

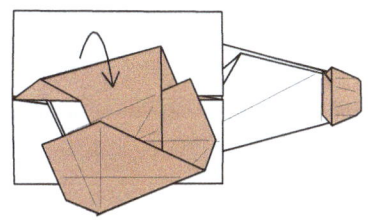

49. Bring the single layer on top of the colored flap.

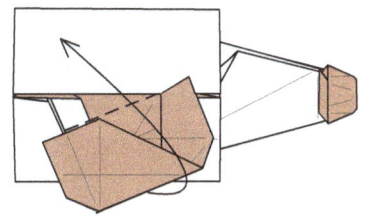

50. Swing upwards.

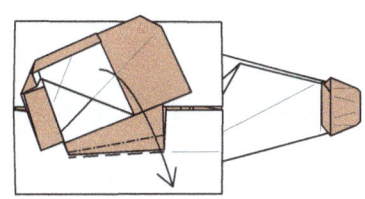

51. Pivot the center structure down until the side edges are straight.

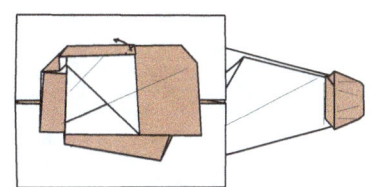

52. Valley fold the tiny corner up.

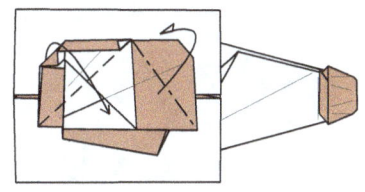

53. Mountain fold at the right, and lightly valley fold at the left.

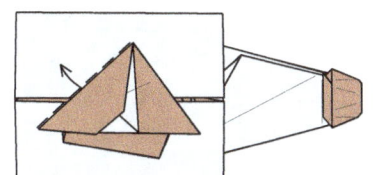

54. Release the trapped paper.

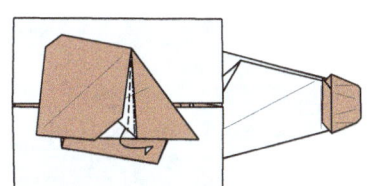

55. Swivel the white section under.

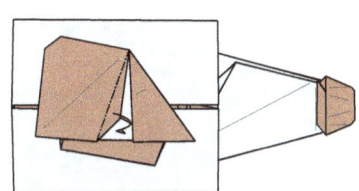

56. Mountain fold.

15

ship in a bottle

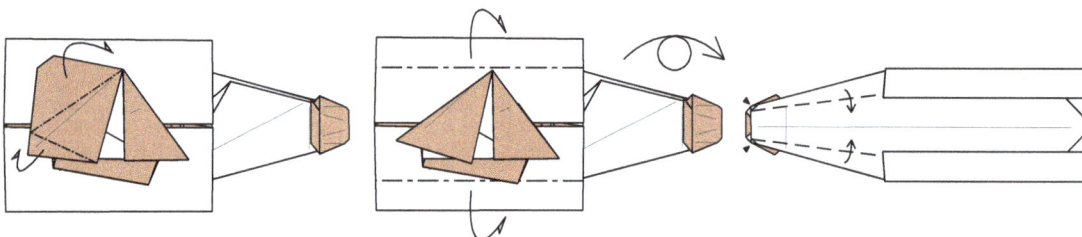

57. Shape the flap with mountain folds.

58. Mountain fold the sides and turn over.

59. Swivel in the sides, allowing tiny squashes to form at the left.

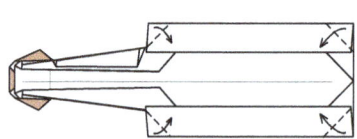 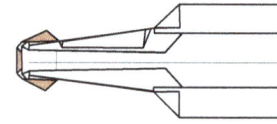 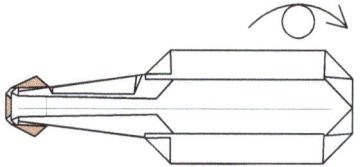

60. Valley fold the four corners in.

61. Mountain fold the flaps into the pockets.

62. Turn over.

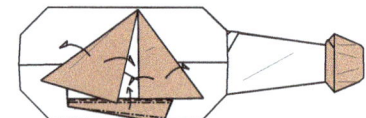

63. Round the sails and boat to taste.

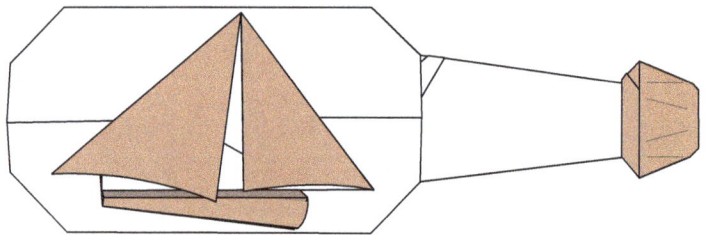

64. Completed *Ship in a Bottle*.

16

Sailboat

This *Sailboat* was an entry for an informal competition of boats for an OrigamiUSA Convention. Most of the design is straightforward, except for where the mast meets the boat. The model must rapidly shrink from the base of the sail to the mast, and then get wide again quickly to form the boat section. To facilitate this, lots of sink folds are needed. Despite this extra complexity, this boat is missing a chunk of its bottom!

sailboat

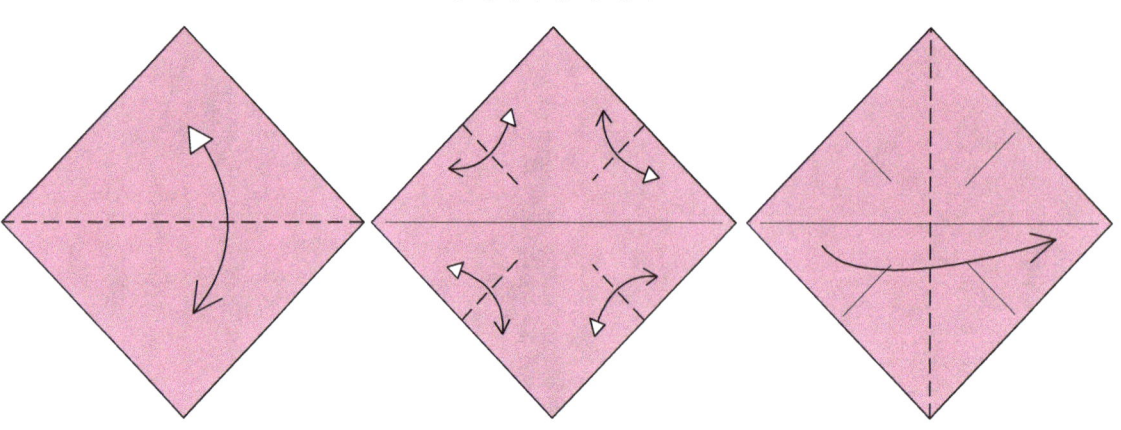

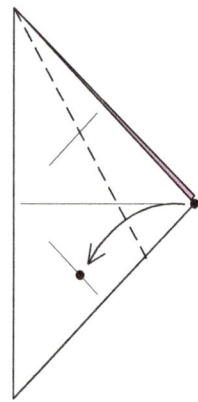

4. Valley fold, such that the corner hits the crease.

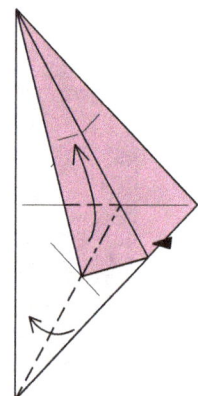

5. Swivel over.

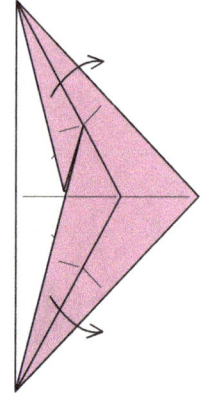

6. Unfold the top section.

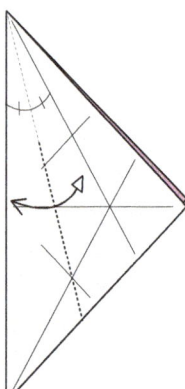

7. Precrease along the angle bisector, while avoiding creasing the top.

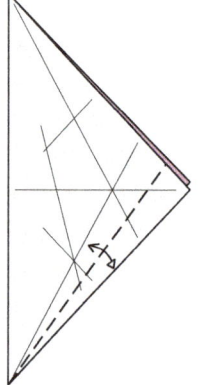

8. Precrease along the angle bisector.

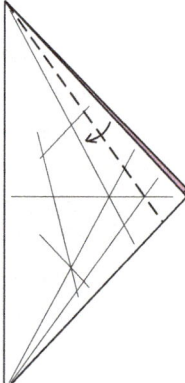

9. Valley fold along the angle bisector.

sailboat

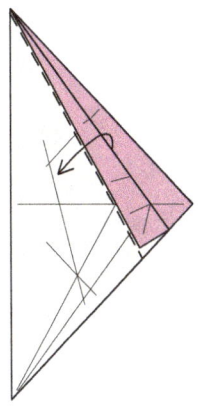 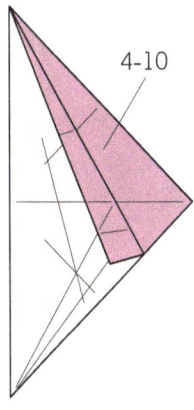 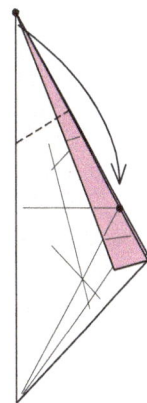

10. Valley fold along the existing crease.

11. Repeat steps 4-10 behind.

12. Valley fold to the indicated point.

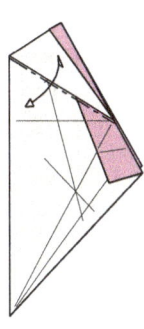 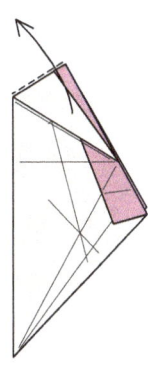 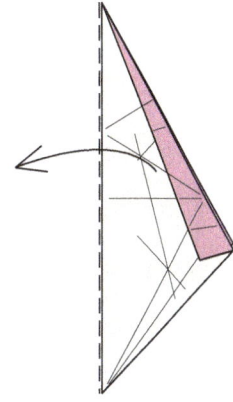

13. Precrease with a mountain fold.

14. Swing the flap up.

15. Unfold along the center.

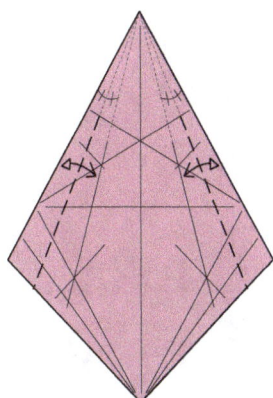 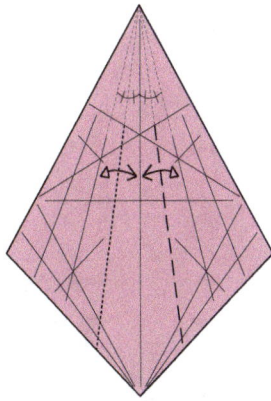 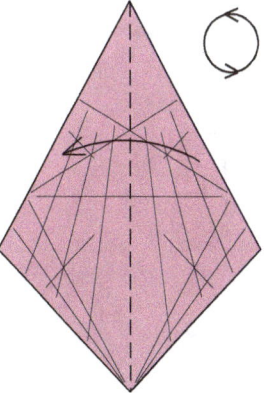

16. Precrease along the outer angle bisectors, while avoiding creasing the top.

17. Precrease along the inner angle bisectors, while avoiding creasing the top.

18. Valley fold in half. Rotate the model so that the left edges are straight.

19

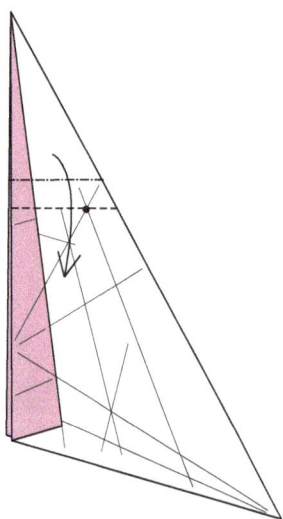

19. Pleat fold, noting the indicated intersection. The mountain fold is along an existing crease.

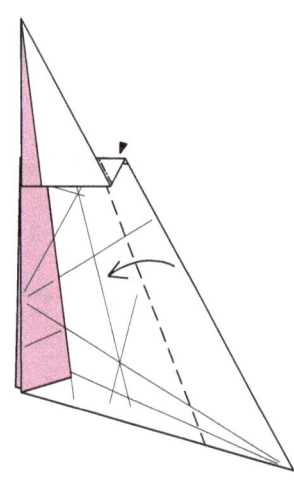

20. Swivel fold along the existing crease.

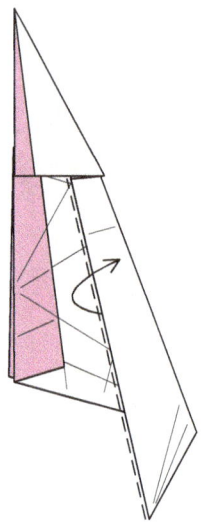

21. Wrap a single layer around to the surface (like a closed sink).

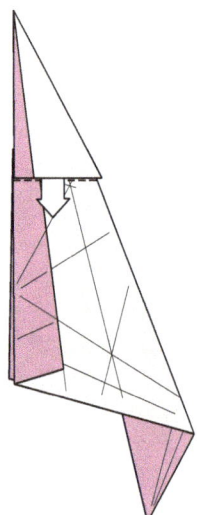

22. Unsink a single layer.

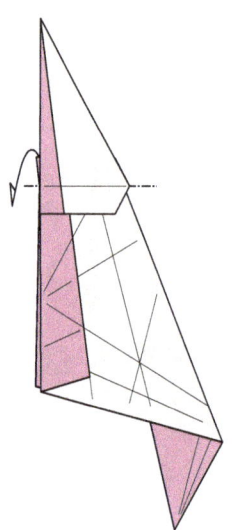

23. Fold down the flap from behind, making the model symmetrical.

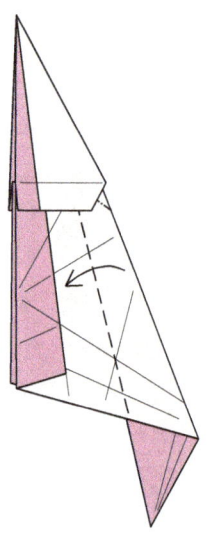

24. Swivel fold along the existing crease.

sailboat

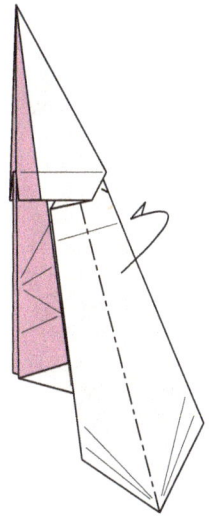
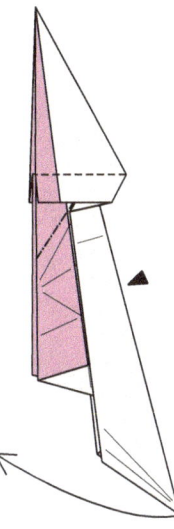
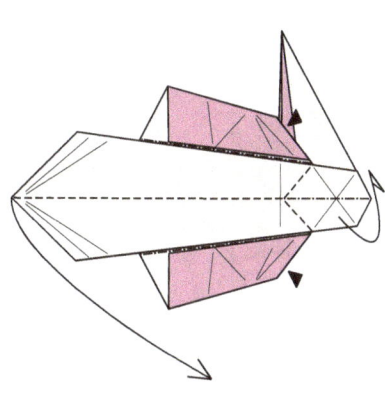

25. Mountain fold, allowing a swivel to form behind.

26. Squash fold the long flap.

27. Rabbit ear the flap down, while mountain folding part of the flap up. Allow the colored sections to squash flat.

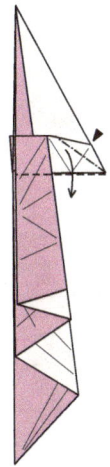
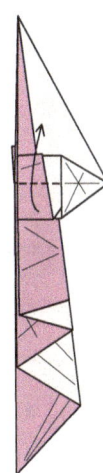
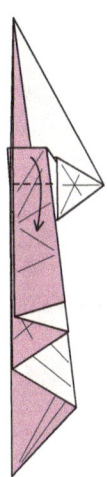
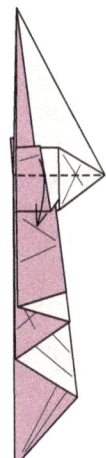

28. Valley fold one flap down, allowing the corner to squash flat.

29. Swing the trapped flap up.

30. Fold the flap back down.

31. Swing the next flap down.

sailboat

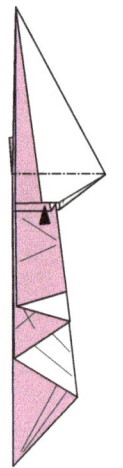 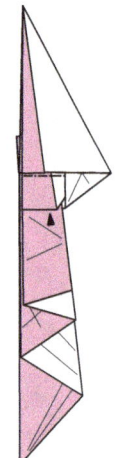 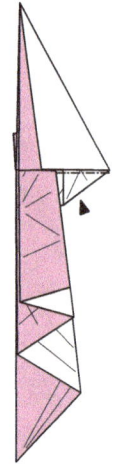 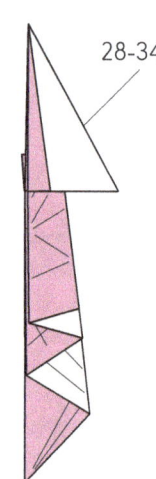

28-34

32. Closed reverse fold.

33. Closed reverse fold the next flap.

34. Closed sink the next flap.

35. Repeat steps 28-34 behind.

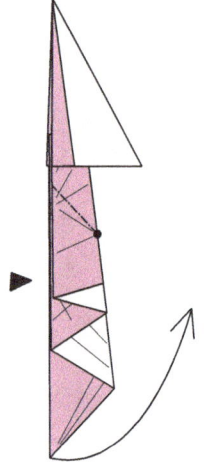 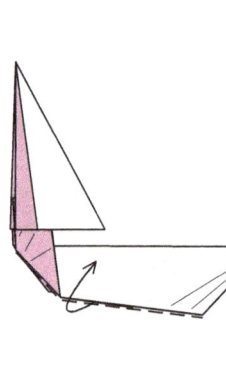 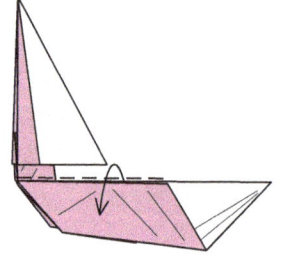 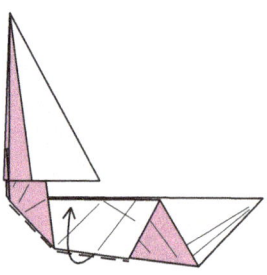

36. Reverse fold up (note the indicated intersection), so that the resulting edge lies straight.

37. Wrap around all of the inner layers to the surface.

38. Wrap around the inner layers to the surface.

39. Wrap around again.

sailboat

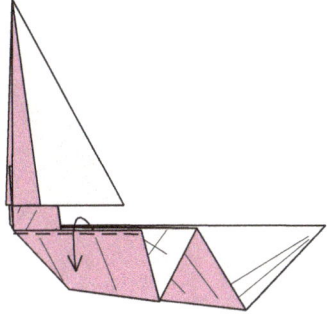

40. Wrap around the remaining layer.

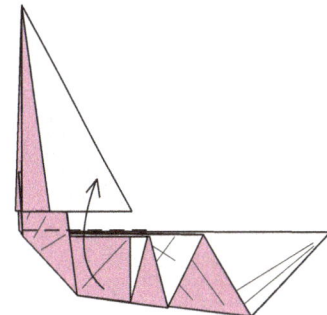

41. Repeat steps 37-40 behind.

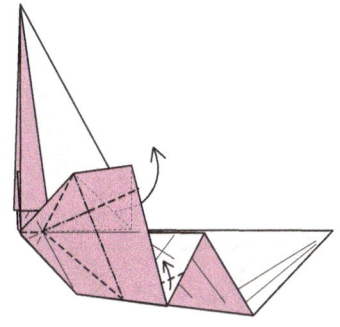

42. Swing up one flap.

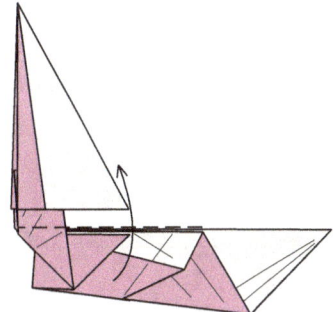

43. Fold the flap back down while collapsing, using mostly existing creases. The hidden original corner gets folded in half.

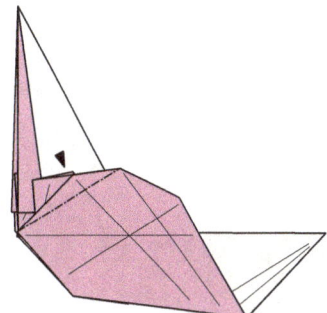

44. Swing the flaps upwards.

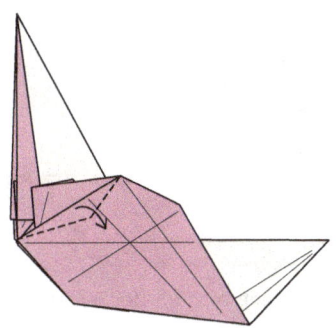

45. Sink the corner (this has to be an open sink).

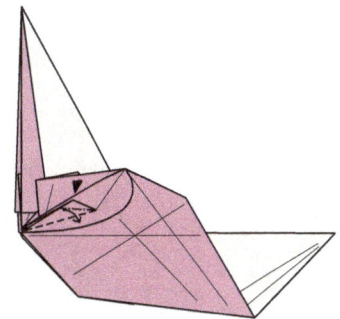

46. Pull down one layer to reveal the inside of the sink. The top will not lie flat.

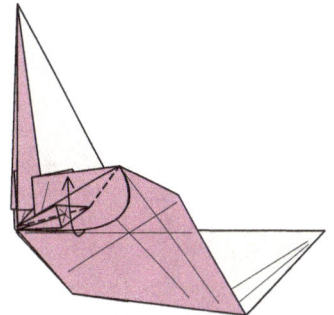

47. Spread squash.

48. Close the model back up.

sailboat

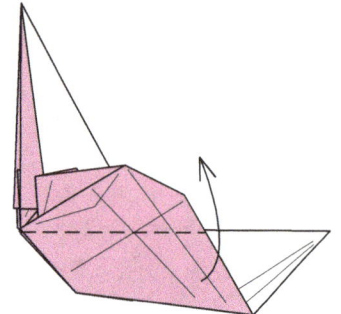

49. Valley fold one flap up.

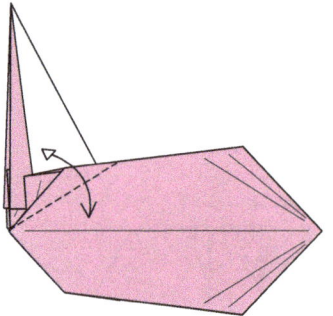

50. Precrease, matching the folded edge on the flap behind.

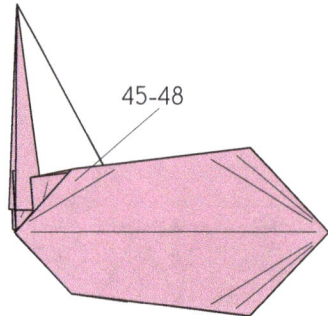

51. Repeat steps 45-48 on the indicated flap.

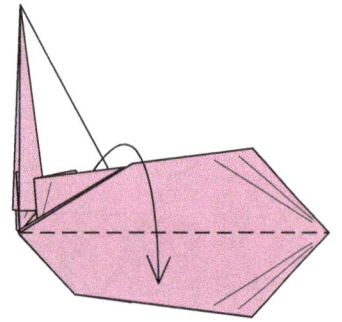

52. Swing all of the flaps down.

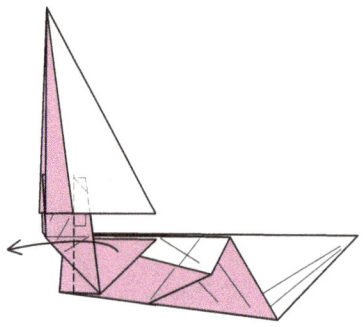

53. Valley fold over, starting where the mast meets the sail. A swivel will form inside.

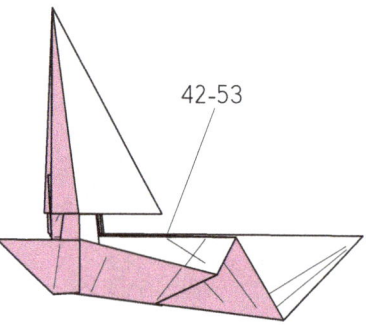

54. Repeat steps 42-53 behind.

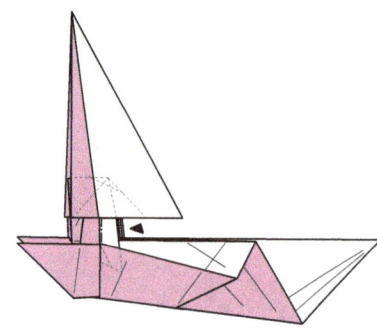

55. Sink the white flap, so that it is flush with the colored edge. You will have to sink part of the hidden flap under the sail to accomplish this.

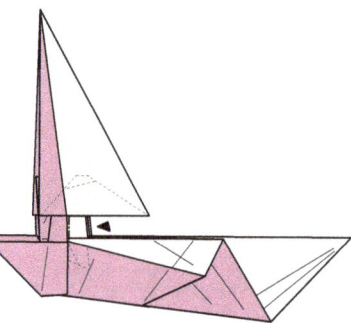

56. Sink the next white flap, again sinking a hidden flap to facilitate this.

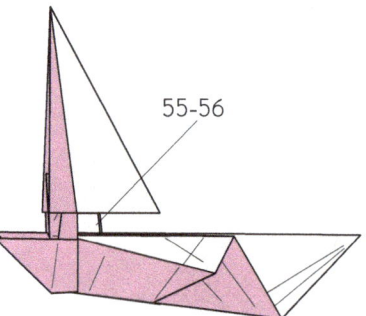

57. Repeat steps 55-56 behind.

sailboat

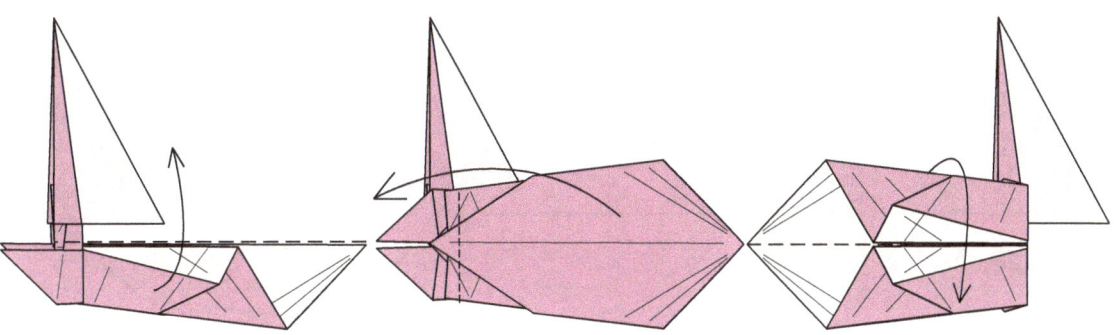

58. Spread apart the bottom section.

59. Valley fold over as far as possible.

60. Close the bottom section.

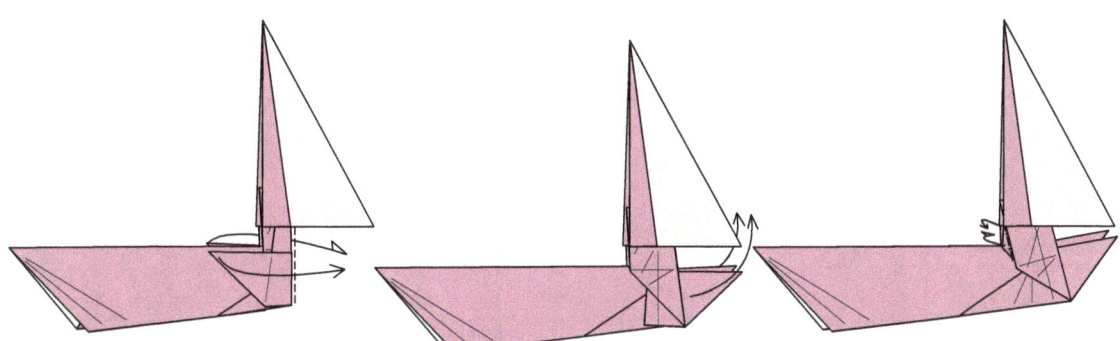

61. Fold the side flaps to the right, undoing the internal swivel folds.

62. Pull the side flaps up, undoing a pleat at each side. The sides will be slightly concave.

63. Mountain fold a protruding corner at each side.

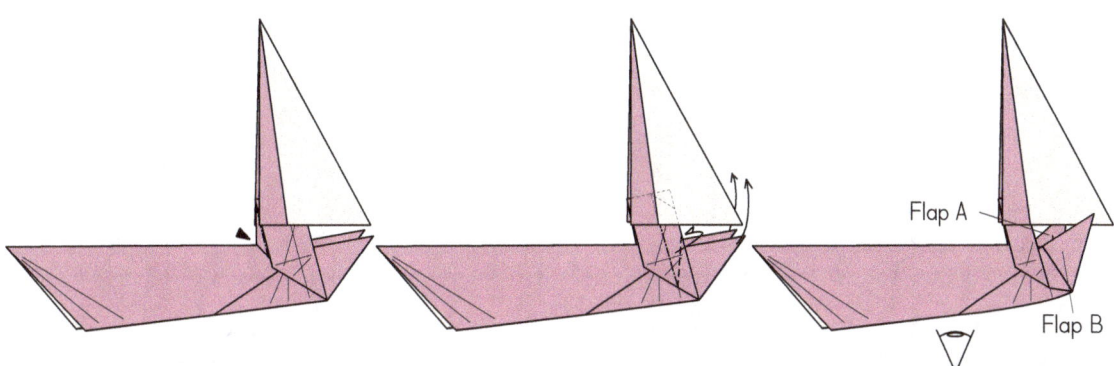

64. Sink the protruding corner.

65. Mountain fold the edges behind, swiveling at the top and bottom. The flaps will stick out even further.

66. Tuck flap A into Flap B. The bottom will spread apart flat.

sailboat

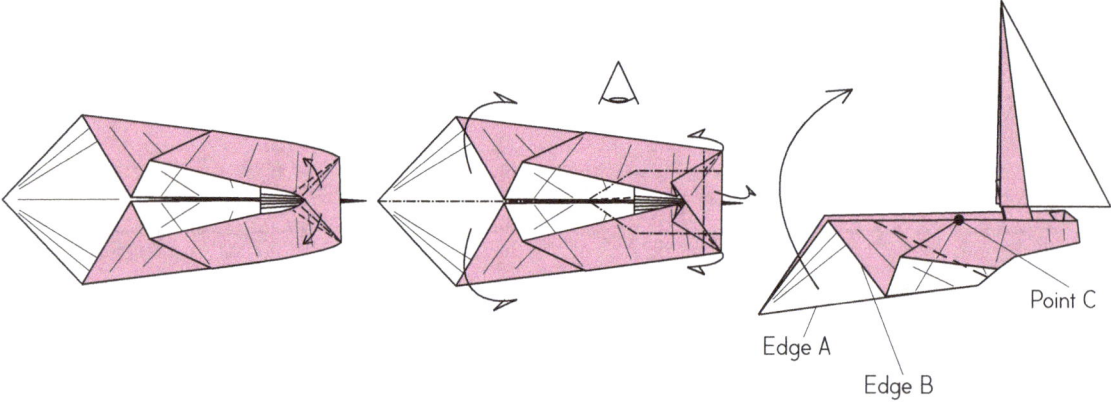

67. View from previous step. Insert pleats to further flatten out the bottom.

68. Form the right side into a boxlike structure, reverse folding the corners. The left side just gets folded in half.

69. View from previous step. Valley fold, such that edge A hits point C, and edge B lies straight.

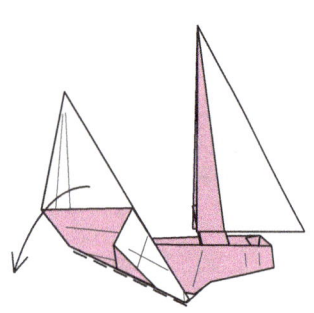 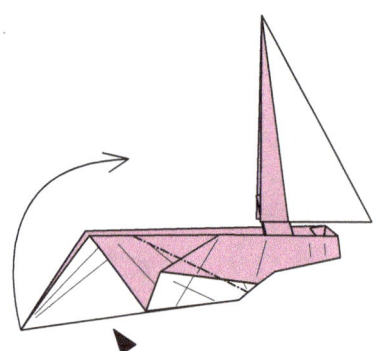 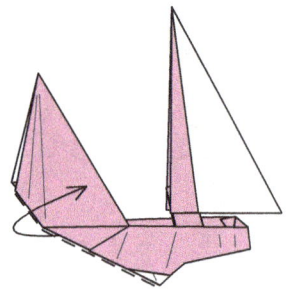

70. Unfold the flap down.

71. Reverse fold the flap along the existing crease.

72. Wrap around the inner layers to the outside.

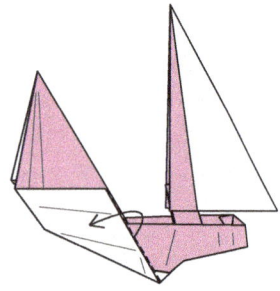 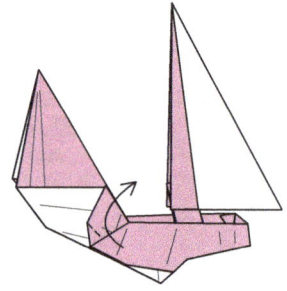 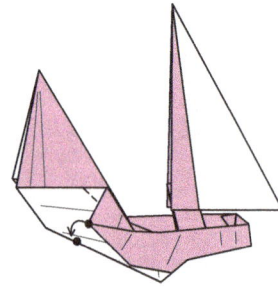

73. Wrap around a layer to the outside.

74. Slide the flap up.

75. Slide the flap down to meet the bottom edge.

sailboat

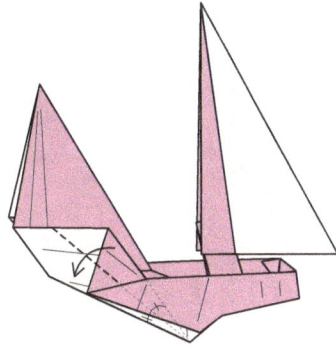

75. Valley fold the flap along the angle bisector.

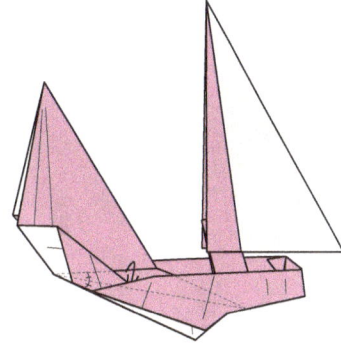

76. Valley fold the next flap along the angle bisector.

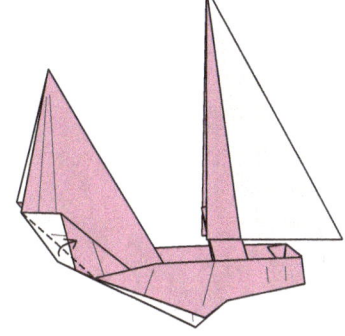

77. Valley fold the corner.

78. Mountain fold the white edge into the model.

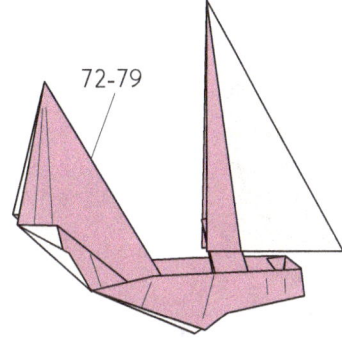

79. Repeat steps 72-79 behind.

80. Mountain fold the remaining white edge inside.

81. Slide the outside layers of the mast slightly over to the right.

82. Reverse fold the tip.

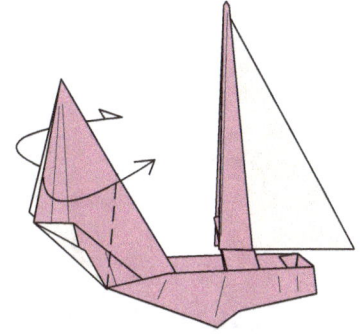

83. Outside reverse fold the flap so that the raw edges are vertical.

sailboat

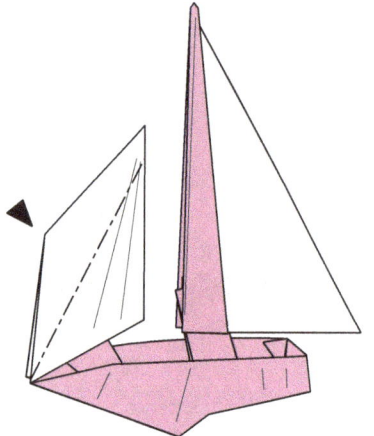

84. Closed sink the flap. There are no reference points for this fold.

85. Reverse fold the colored portion of the flap.

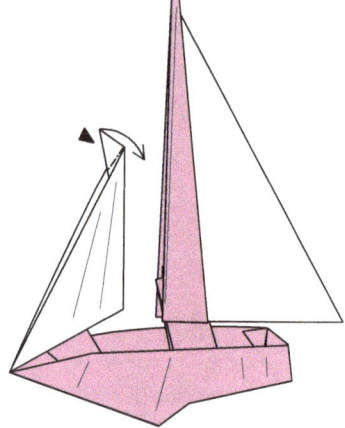

86. Reverse fold again.

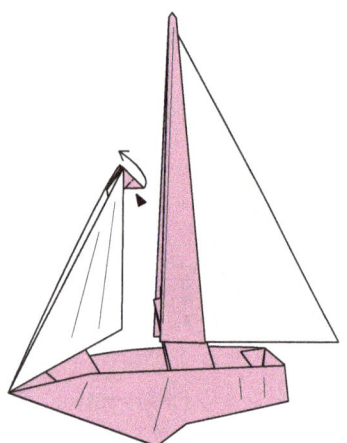

87. Reverse fold the flap again.

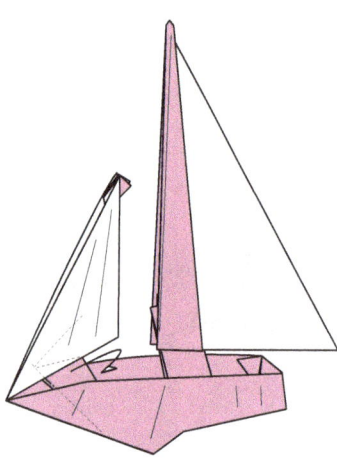

88. Mountain fold the layer between the sail as much as possible, creating an internal swivel.

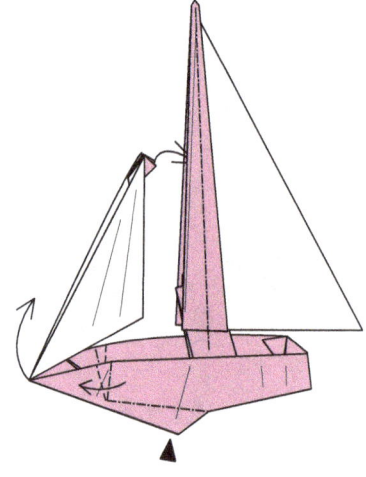

89. Crimp the sides while flattening the bottom. Pinch the sides of the mast, and tuck the colored tip of the front sail into the mast. Shape the model to taste.

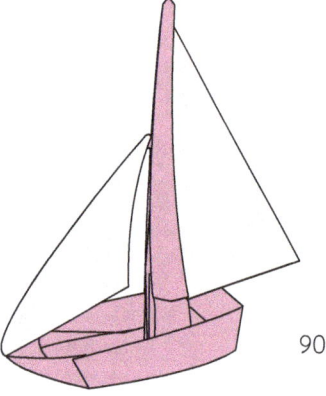

90. Completed *Sailboat*.

Penny-farthing

Both the *Bicycle* and this *Penny-farthing* share the same sequence for the wheels and were designed concurrently. This one is far easier to fold, as the frame does not have a complex web of struts. In real life however, this would be a much tougher bike to ride. To make this model stand, you will need to create an armature with modeling wire.

penny-farthing

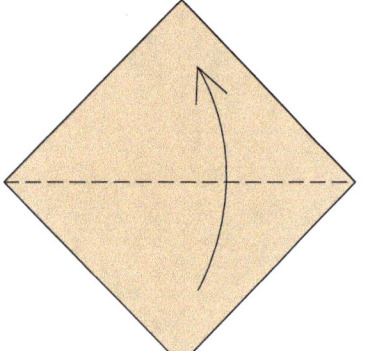 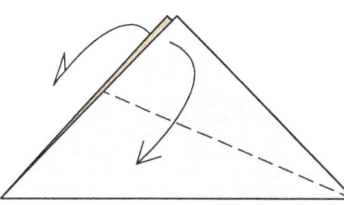 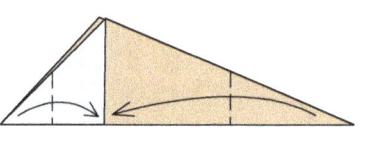

1. This will be the color of the bike's frame. Valley fold in half.

2. Valley fold both sides down.

3. Valley fold the corners in.

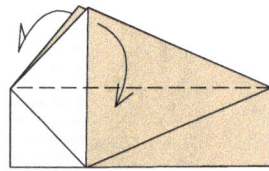 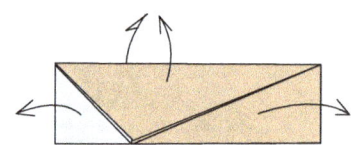

4. Valley fold the sides down.

5. Unfold to step 2.

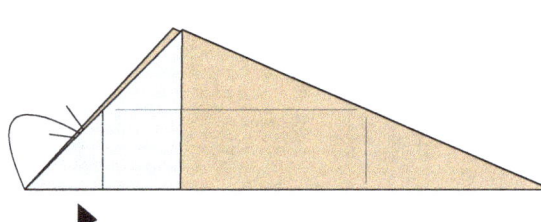 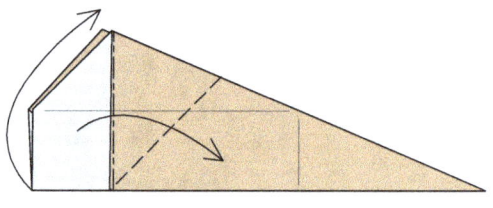

6. Reverse fold the corner in.

7. Crimp downwards.

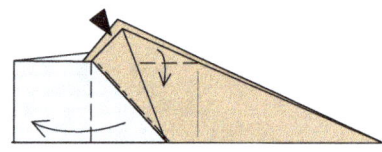 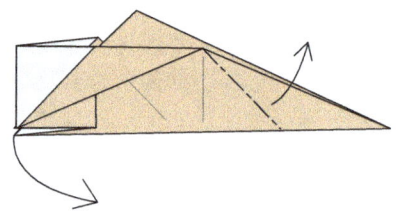

8. Swivel the flap over.

9. Pull out the original corner, while sliding up the top edge.

penny-farthing

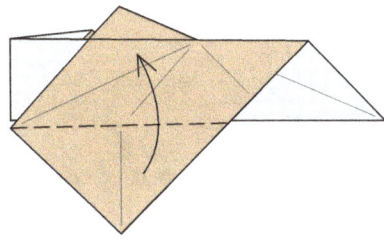

10. Valley fold up.

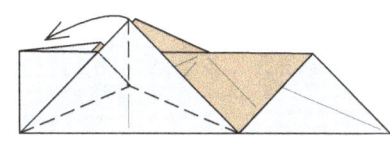

11. Rabbit ear the flap.

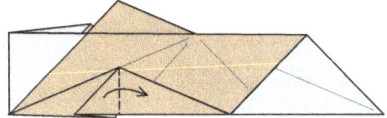

12. Swing the flap over.

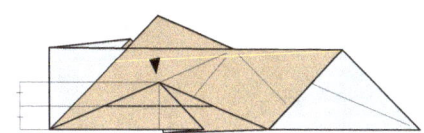

13. Sink the flap in half.

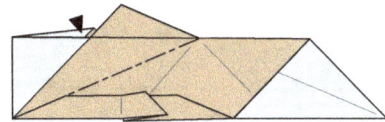

14. Sink along the angle bisector (precrease first).

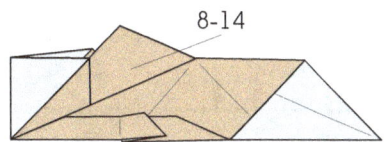

15. Repeat steps 8–14 behind.

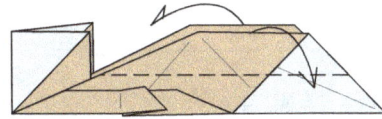

16. Valley fold the sides down.

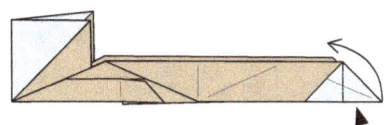

17. Reverse fold the corner in.

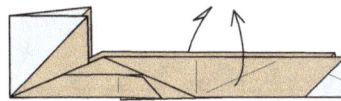

18. Raise the sides up.

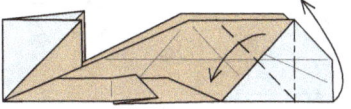

19. Crimp downwards.

penny-farthing

20. Swivel the corner over at each side.

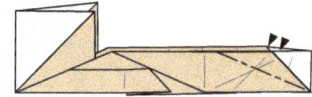

21. Sink along the angle bisectors (precrease first).

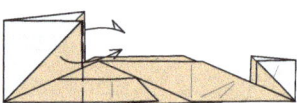

22. Swing the side flaps over.

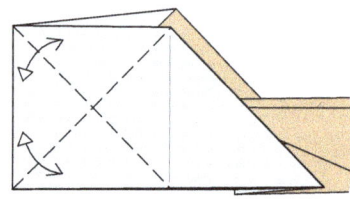

23. Precrease through all layers.

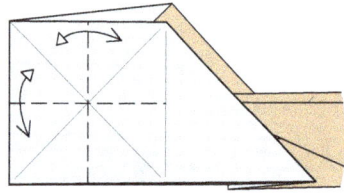

24. Precrease through all layers.

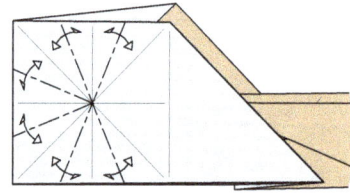

25. Precrease through all layers with mountain folds.

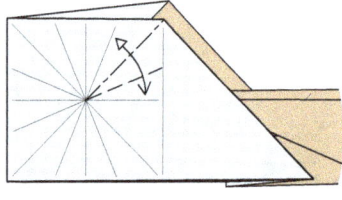

26. Precrease the top layer by pleating and unfolding.

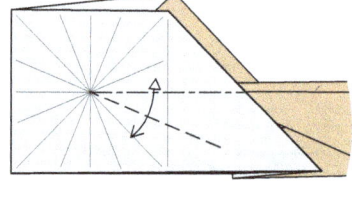

27. Precrease the top layer by pleating and unfolding.

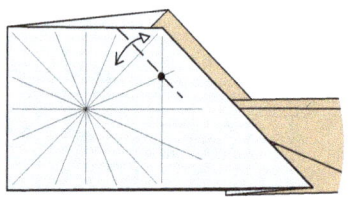

28. Precrease the top layer through the indicated intersection.

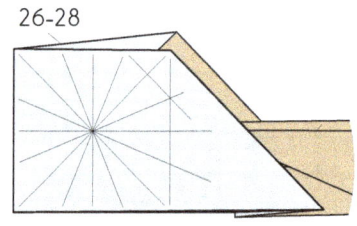

26-28

29. Repeat steps 26-28 behind.

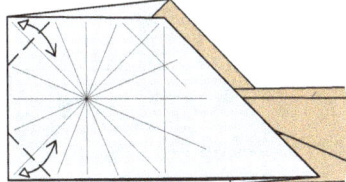

30. Precrease through all layers.

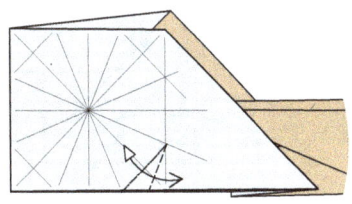

31. Precrease through all layers by forming a pleat.

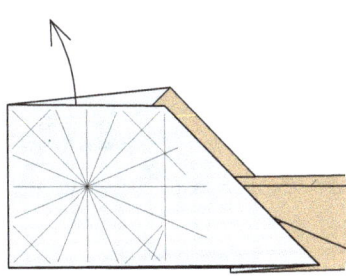

32. Pull out the hidden corner.

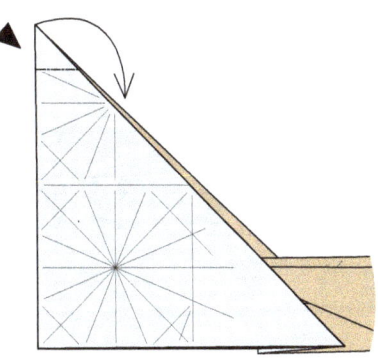

33. Reverse fold the corner.

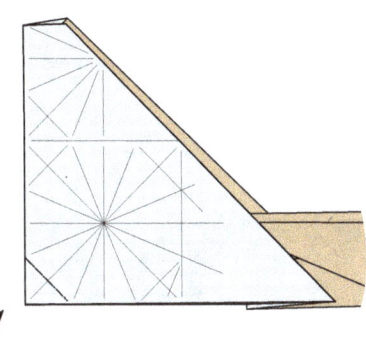

34. Closed sink the corner.

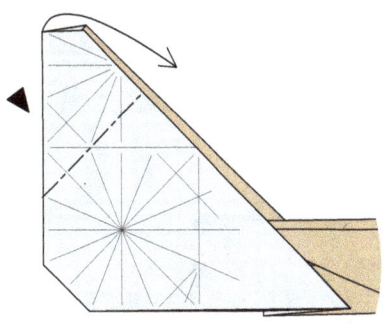

35. Reverse fold down

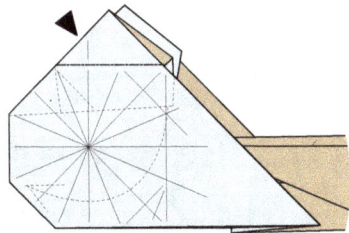

36. Pull the hidden flap down, allowing a pleat to form inside.

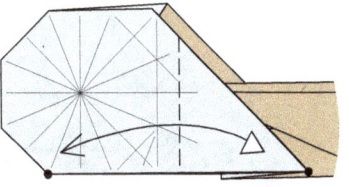

37. Precrease towards the indicated crease.

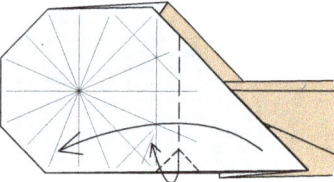 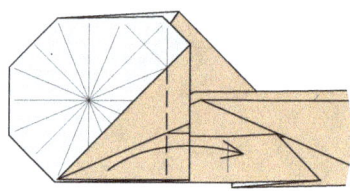

38. Valley fold down again, incorporating a reverse fold on the top layer only.

39. Lightly valley fold over.

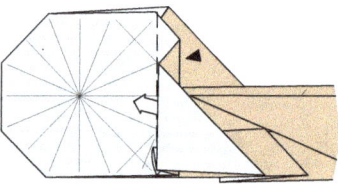 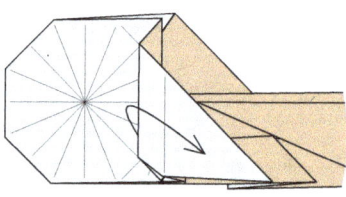

40. Sink the edge through.

41. Pull the single layer to the surface (closed sink).

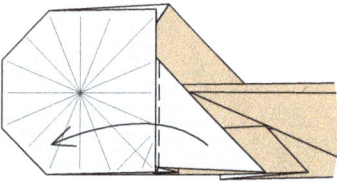 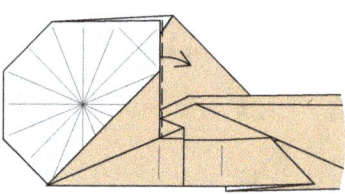

42. Swing the flap over.

43. Pull the flap from behind over. A small hidden crimp will get released.

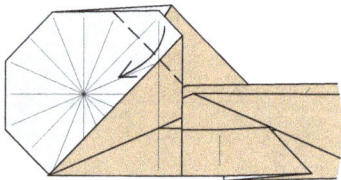 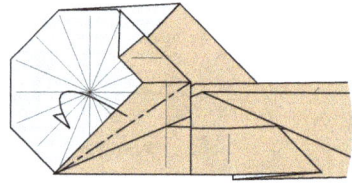

44. Valley fold along the existing crease.

45. Swivel the single layer behind.

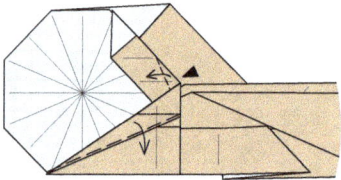 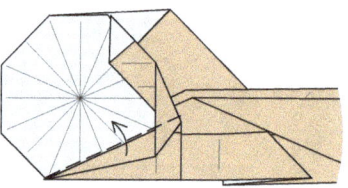

46. Swivel the edge over, allowing the corner to spread squash.

47. Swing over the edge.

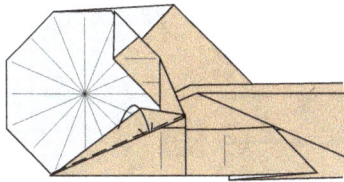

48. Tuck the flap into the lowest pocket.

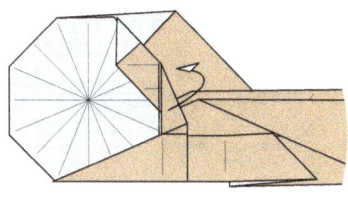

49. Mountain fold behind, allowing the hidden crimp to come undone.

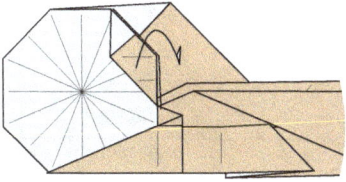

50. Wrap the single layer around.

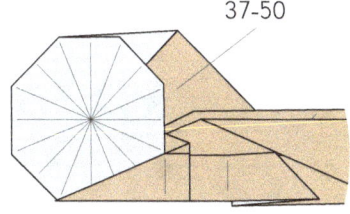

51. Repeat steps 37-50 behind.

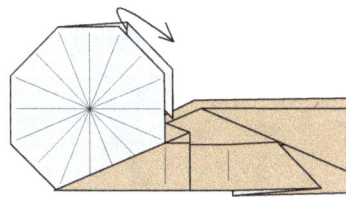

52. Pull out the trapped corner on the rear layer.

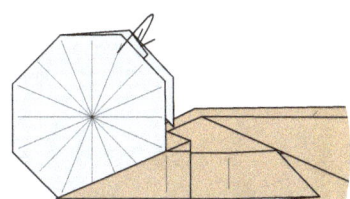

53. Tuck the hidden flap into the pocket.

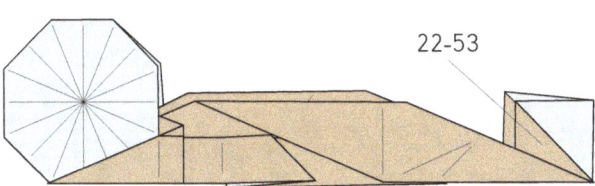

54. Repeat steps 22-53 in mirror image.

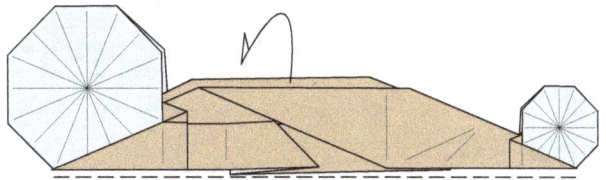

55. Open out along the center. The ends will not lie flat.

penny-farthing

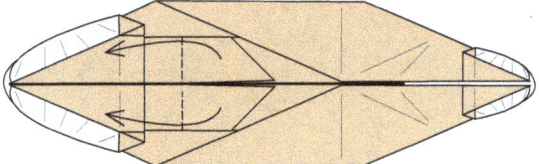

56. Swing the top flaps over.

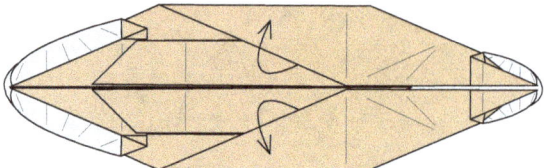

57. Bring the layers around to the surface.

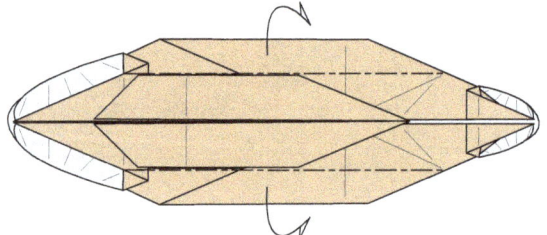

58. Mountain fold the sides to align with the top layer.

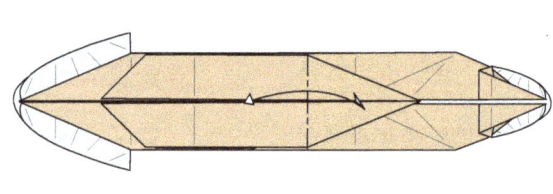

59. Precrease through all layers with a mountain fold.

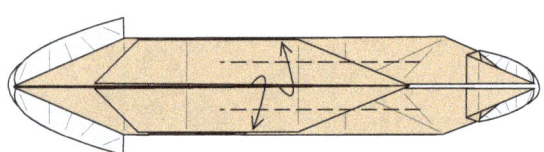

60. Valley fold all of the layers outwards. The model will not lie flat.

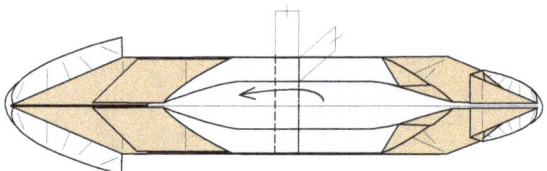

61. Pleat the flap. The mountain fold lies along an existing crease.

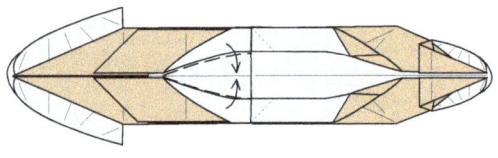

62. Swivel the sides in.

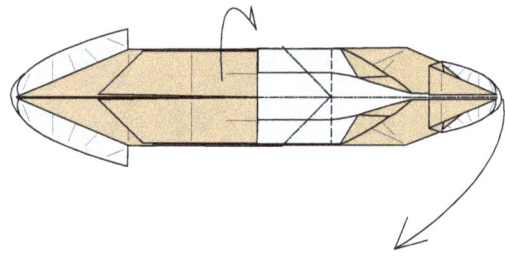

63. Rabbit ear the side down while lightly mountain folding in half.

penny-farthing

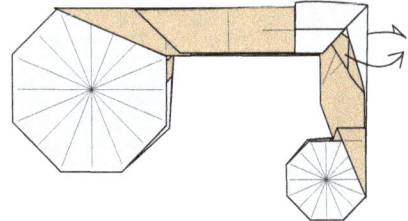 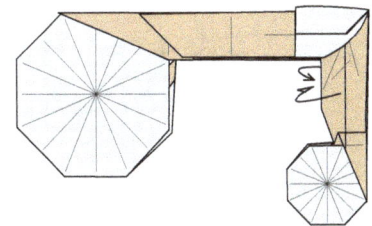

64. Slide the layers over at each side. The corner will not lie completely flat.

65. Swivel the sides in.

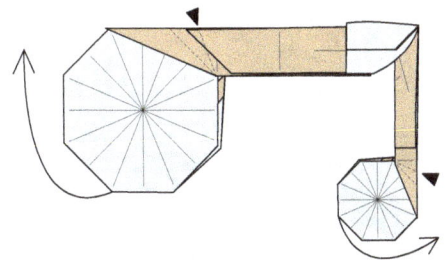 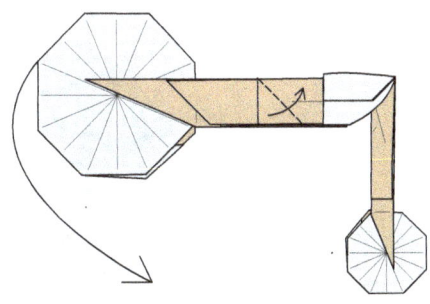

66. Crimp along the hidden creases at each side.

67. Crimp the side down.

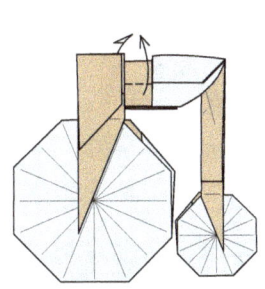 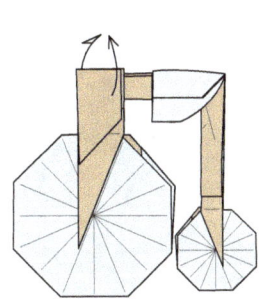 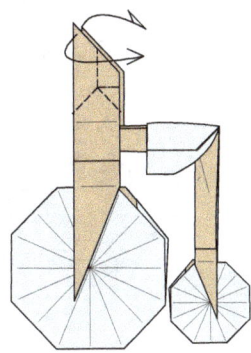

68. Swivel the sides up.

69. Swing the flaps up.

70. Rabbit ear the flaps.

 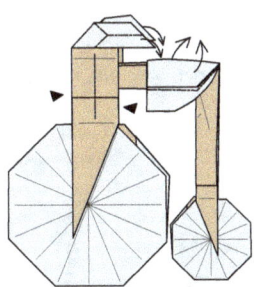 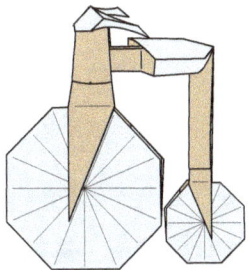

71. Wrap around a single layer on the flaps.

72. Lift the sides of the seat up. Round out the handlebars and front section.

73. Completed *Penny-farthing*.

Bicycle

Once you have mastered the *Penny-farthing* you can use your wheel-making skills on this *Bicycle*. The frame on this has far more appendages to create all the looped sections. You will need to feel comfortable shifting some layers to ensure these flaps align correctly. To make this model stand, you will need to create an armature with modeling wire.

bicycle

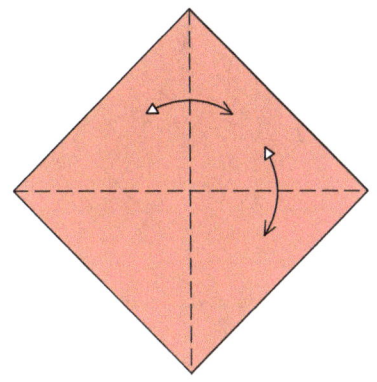

1. This will be the color of the bike's frame. Precrease the diagonals.

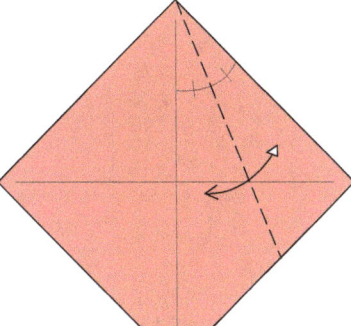

2. Precrease along the angle bisector.

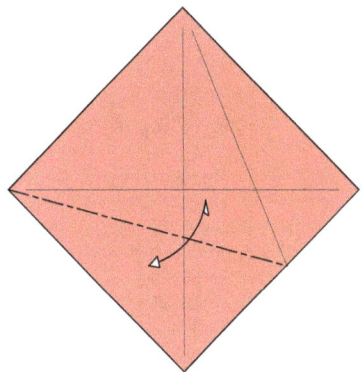

3. Precrease from the corner to the bottom of the last crease.

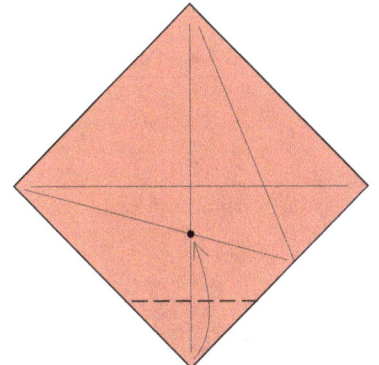

4. Valley fold towards the indicated intersection.

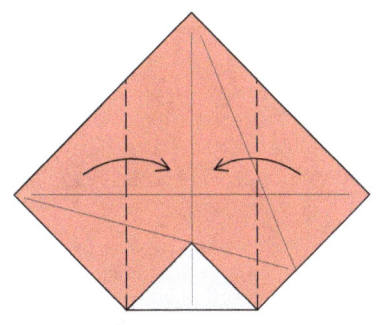

5. Valley fold the sides inwards.

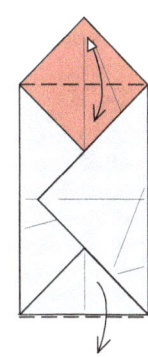

6. Open out the bottom flap and precrease at the top to match.

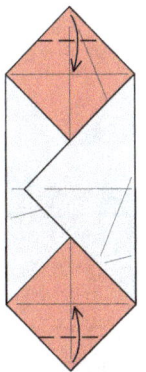

7. Valley fold the corners to meet the creases.

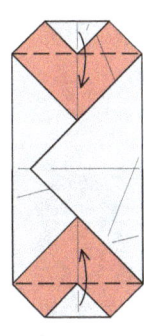

8. Valley fold along the existing creases.

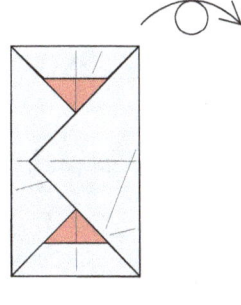

9. Turn over.

39

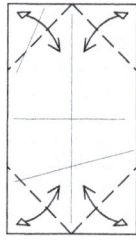
10. Precrease the four corners.

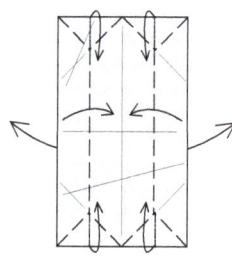
11. Valley fold the sides to the center while incorporating reverse folds.

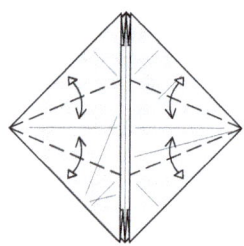
12. Precrease along the angle bisectors.

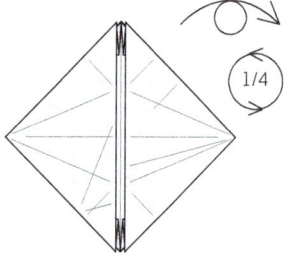
13. Turn over and rotate.

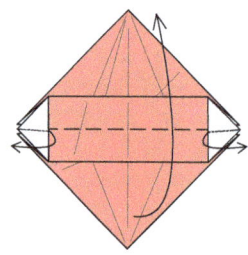
14. Valley fold in half while pulling out the corners.

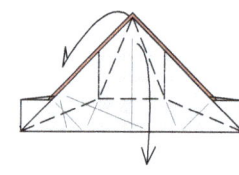
15. Collapse the outer flaps down.

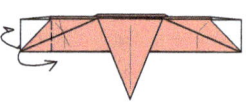
16. Swing the side flaps over.

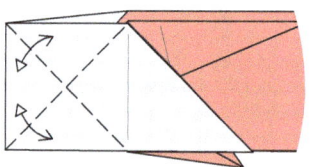
17. Precrease through all layers.

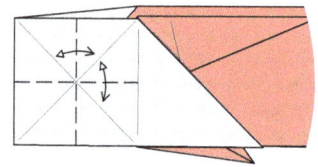
18. Precrease through all layers.

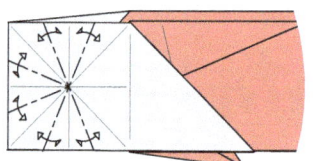
19. Precrease through all layers with mountain folds.

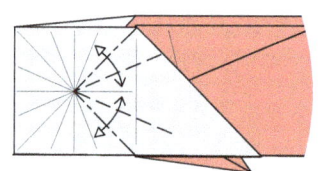
20. Precrease the top layer by pleating and unfolding.

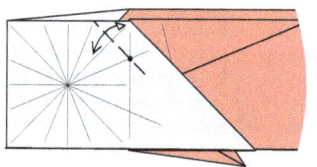
21. Precrease the top layer through the indicated intersection.

bicycle

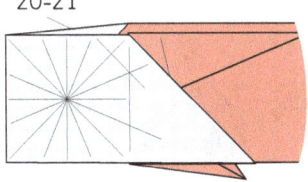

22. Repeat steps 20-21 behind.

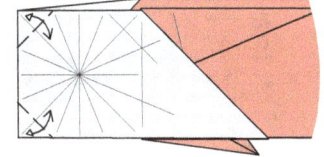

23. Precrease through all layers.

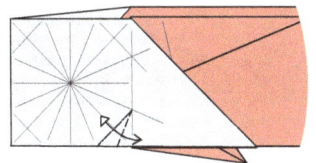

24. Precrease through all layers by forming a pleat.

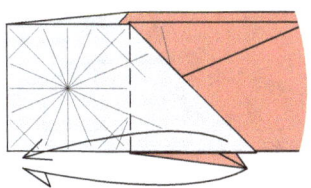

25. Swing the flaps back.

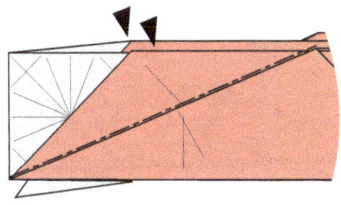

26. Sink the two edges (precrease first).

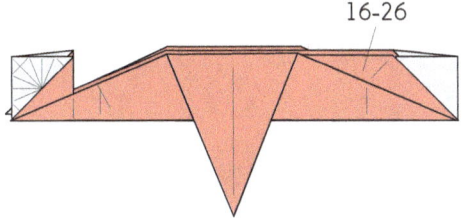

27. Repeat steps 16-26 in mirror image.

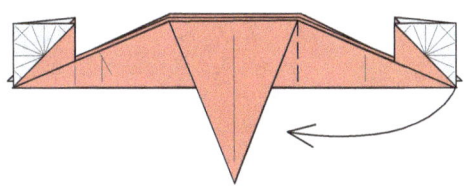

28. Valley fold through all layers.

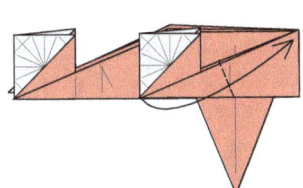

29. Valley fold towards the corner.

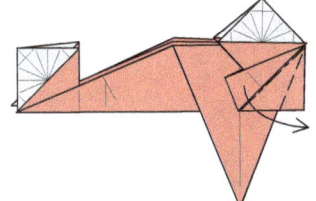

30. Pleat the flap down.

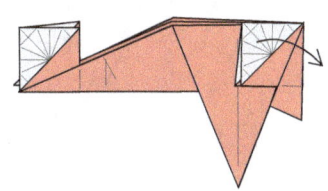

31. Unfold the pleat.

41

bicycle

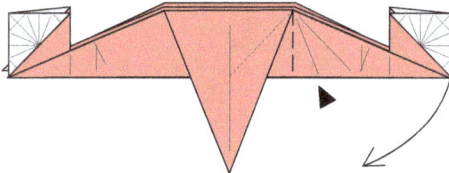

32. Crimp the flap down, spreading the layers evenly.

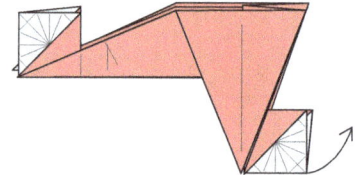

33. Unfold the crimp.

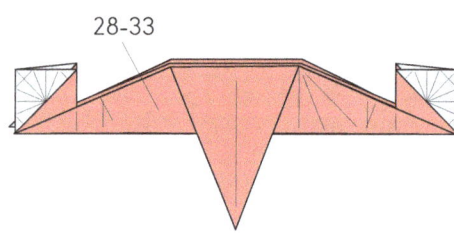

34. Repeat steps 28-33 in mirror image.

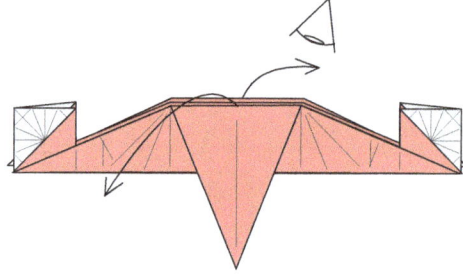

35. Spread apart the center pleats.

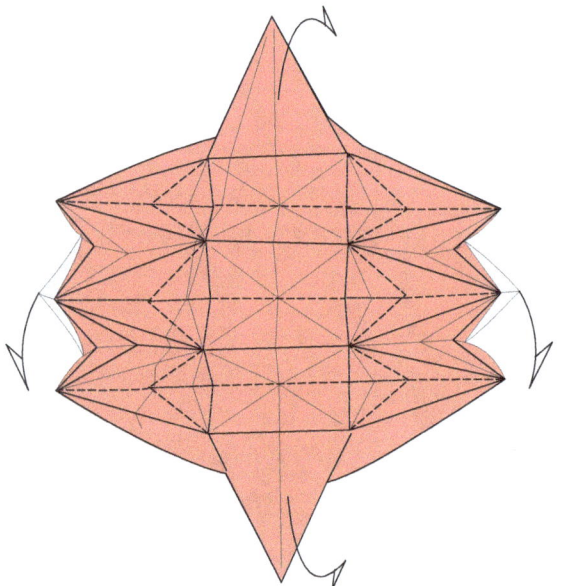

36. Crimp the sides down and flatten.

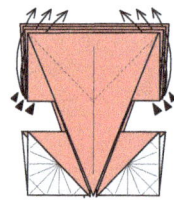

37. Reverse fold the three sets of corners upwards.

bicycle

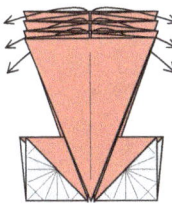 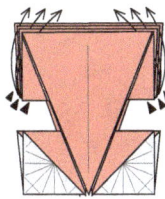 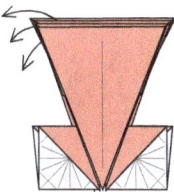

38. Reverse fold the corners back down.

39. Reverse fold the three sets of corners in.

40. Undo the reverse folds on one side only.

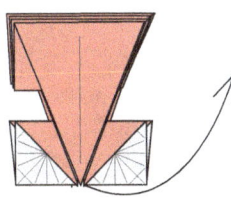 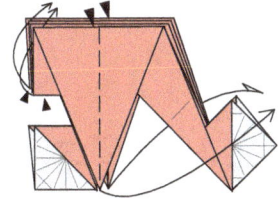 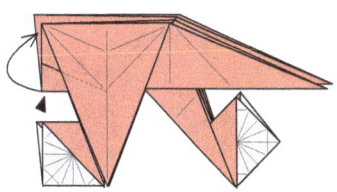

41. Spread apart the inner pleats (created by the reverse folds from step 39), pulling the flap over.

42. Pull the outer flaps over, allowing them to fold in half and squashing at the left.

43. Reverse fold the center flap.

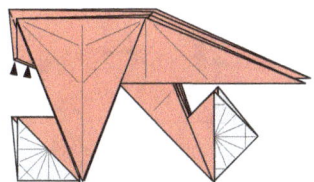 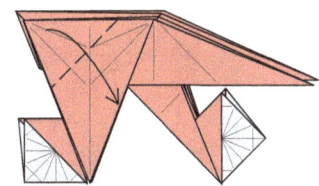 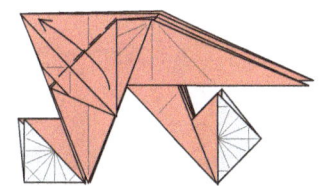

44. Form two reverse folds.

45. Lightly valley fold down, allowing the center flap to stretch flat.

46. Swing the flap back up.

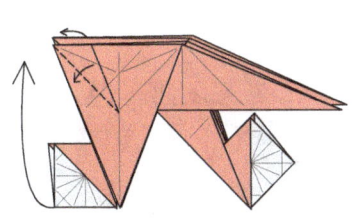 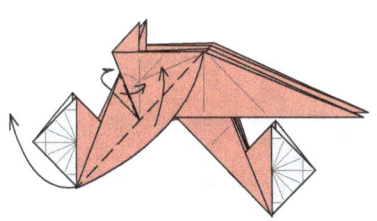 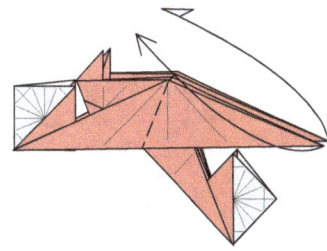

47. Crimp the double layer at each side, allowing the front flap to raise up. The model will not lie flat.

48. Form another set of crimps at each side, allowing the front to raise more and flatten.

49. Swing the side flaps up as far as possible.

bicycle

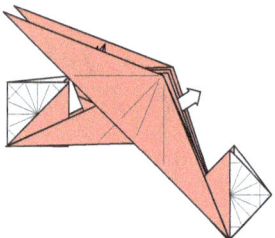

50. Unsink at the center set of layers.

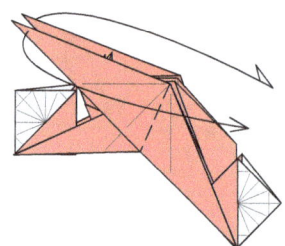

51. Swing the outer flaps over.

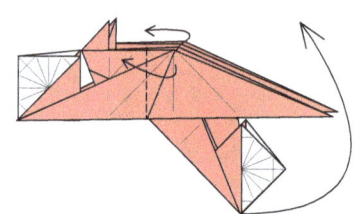

52. Crimp the back section up, spreading the layers evenly.

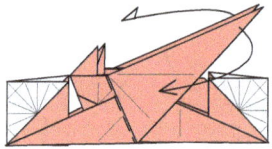

53. Swing the outer flaps over.

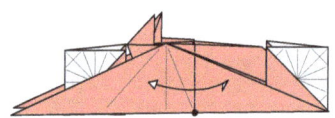

54. Precrease through all layers.

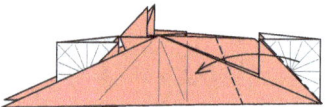

55. Pleat towards the last crease.

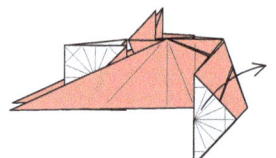

56. Unfold the pleat.

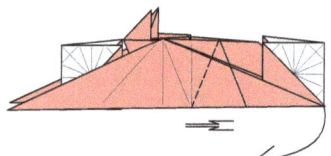

57. Crimp down using the existing creases as a guide.

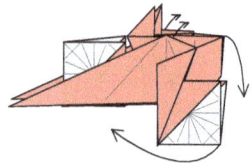

58. Rotate the back section down, opening out the top crimps.

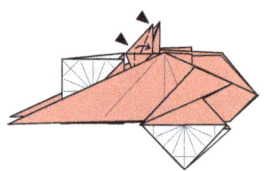

59. Reverse the two points along the angle bisectors.

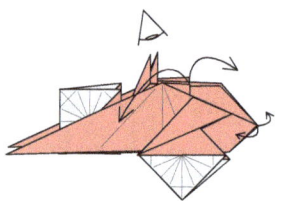

60. Open out along the center, releasing the trapped paper at the right corner.

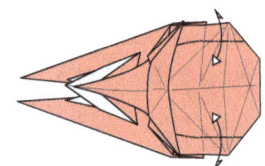

61. View from previous step. Precrease with mountain folds as far as possible.

44

bicycle

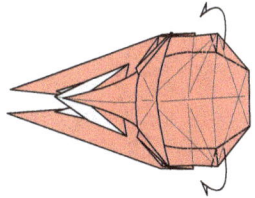

62. Rabbit ear the sides behind, aligning to the folded edge below.

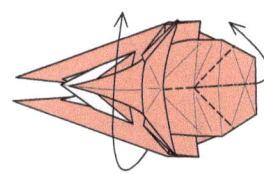

63. Fold the model back in half while incorporating a reverse fold.

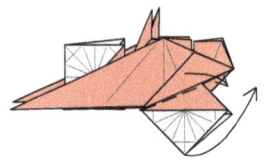

64. Pull the bottom flap over, allowing the sides to open out.

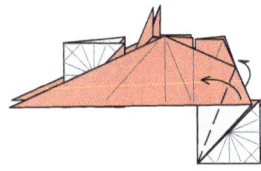

65. Valley fold the flaps over.

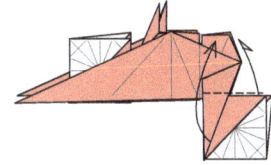

66. Swing the flaps up as far as possible.

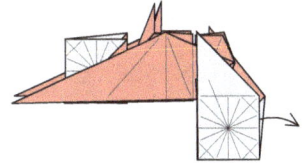

67. Pull out the hidden corner.

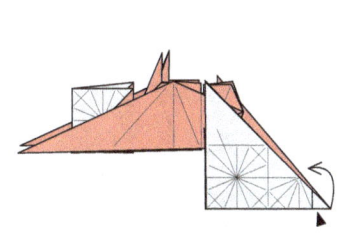

68. Reverse fold the corner.

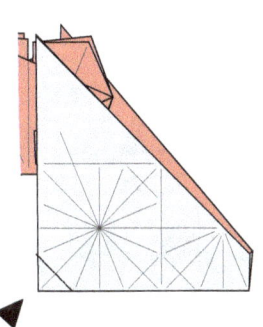

69. Closed sink the corner.

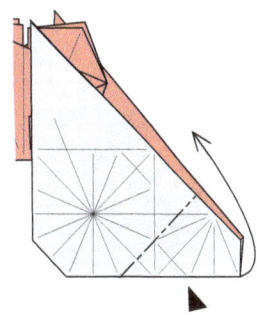

70. Reverse fold up.

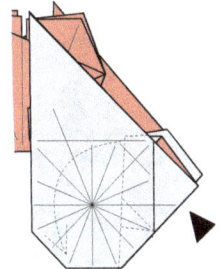

71. Pull the hidden flap down allowing a pleat to form inside.

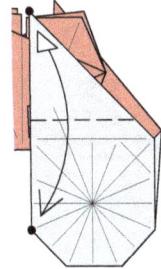

72. Precrease towards the indicated crease.

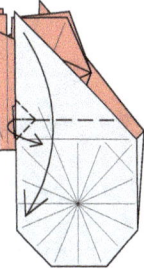

73. Valley fold down again, incorporating a reverse fold on the top layer only.

bicycle

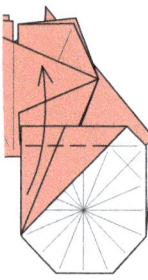

74. Lightly valley fold up.

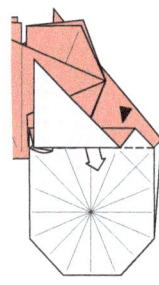

75. Sink the edge through.

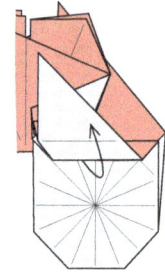

76. Pull the single layer to the surface (closed sink).

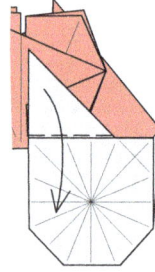

77. Swing the flap down.

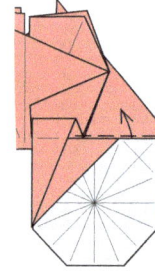

78. Pull the flap from behind up. A small hidden crimp will get released.

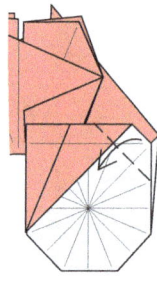

79. Valley fold along the existing crease.

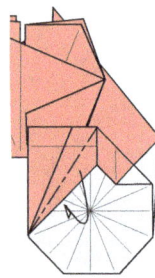

80. Swivel the single layer behind.

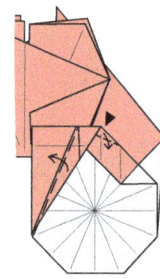

81. Swivel the edge over, allowing the corner to spread squash.

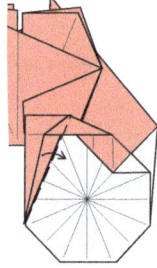

82. Swing over the edge.

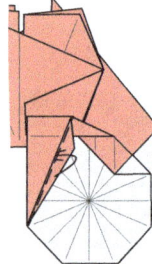

83. Tuck the flap into the lowest pocket.

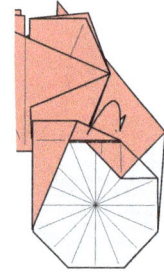

84. Mountain fold behind, allowing the hidden crimp to come undone.

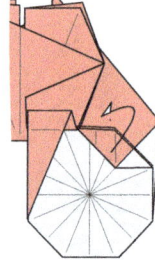

85. Wrap the single layer around.

bicycle

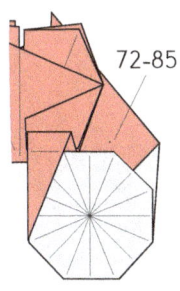
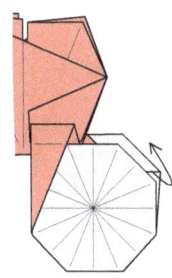
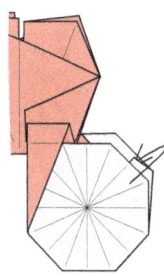

86. Repeat steps 72-85 behind.

87. Pull out the trapped corner on the rear layer.

88. Tuck the hidden flap into the pocket.

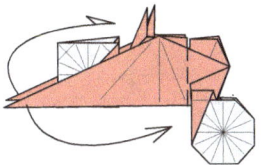
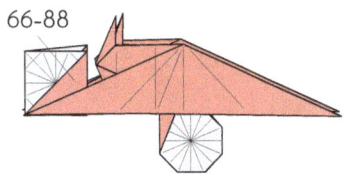
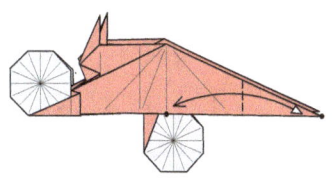

89. Swing the two side flaps over.

90. Repeat steps 66-88 on the front flap (noting that this flap is rotated).

91. Valley fold the top flap to the indicated crease.

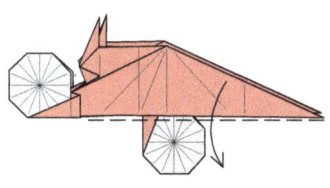
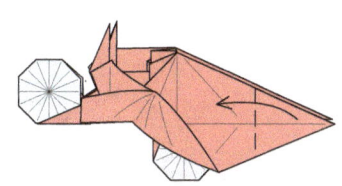
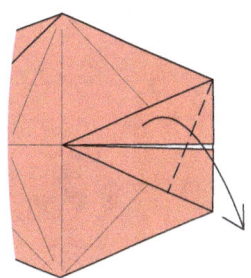

92. Open out the top flap. It will not lie completely flat.

93. Valley fold along the existing crease.

94. Valley fold so that the lower edge is aligned.

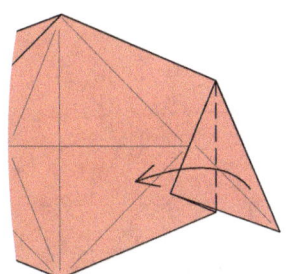
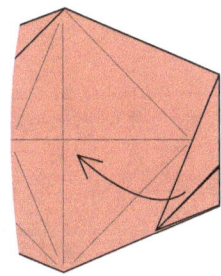
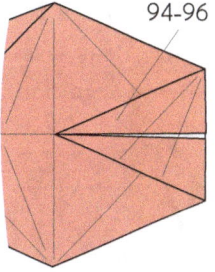

95. Valley fold along the angle bisector.

96. Unfold the pleat.

97. Repeat steps 94-96 in mirror image.

bicycle

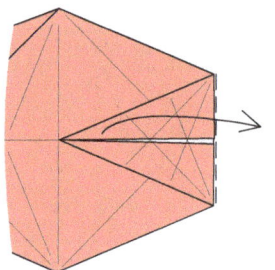

98. Swing the flap over.

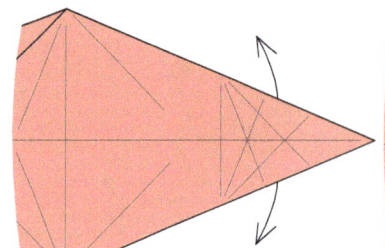

99. Open out the single layers from behind.

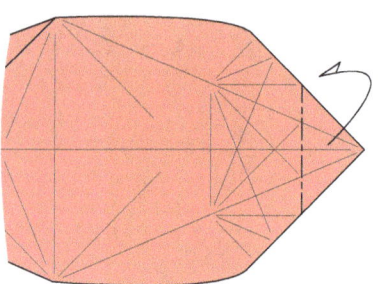

100. Mountain fold along the existing crease.

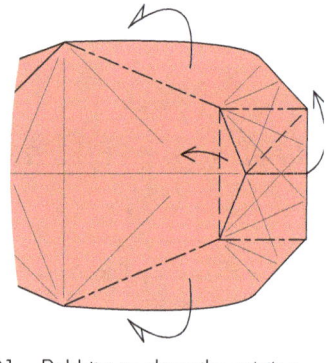

101. Rabbit ear along the existing creases while folding the sides back in.

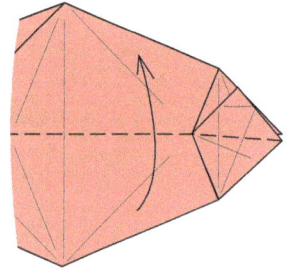

102. Close the flap back up.

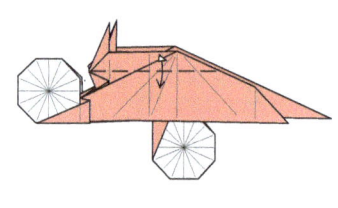

103. Precrease the edge down as far as possible.

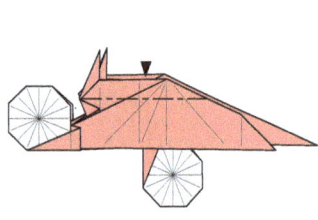

104. Closed sink the edge in.

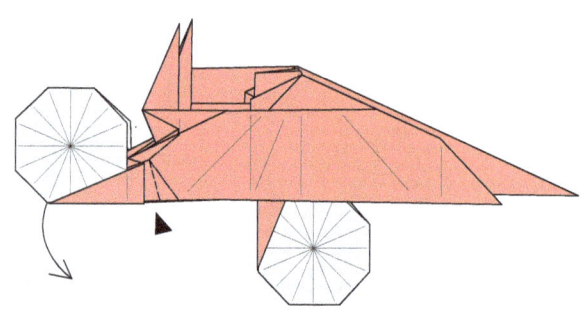

105. Crimp the front down, allowing the top edges to swivel in.

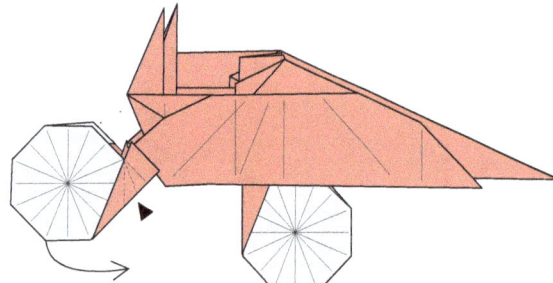

106. Crimp down along the hidden creases.

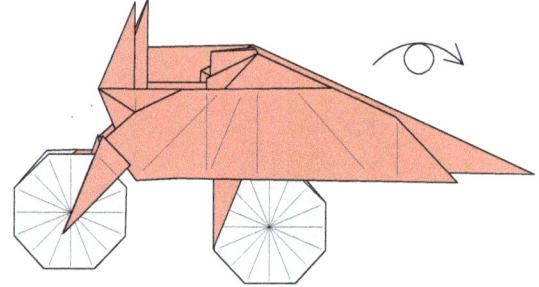

107. Turn over.

bicycle

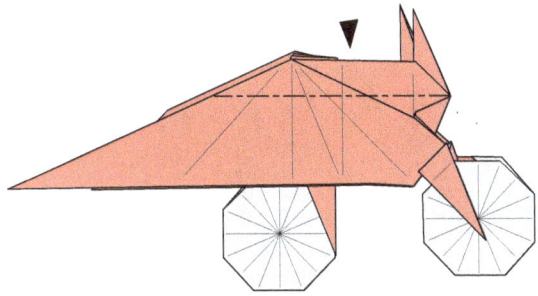

108. Closed sink to align with the flap behind.

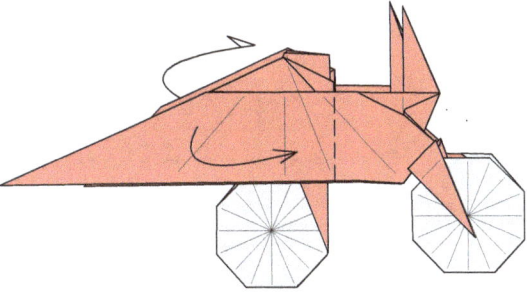

109. Swing over the side flaps.

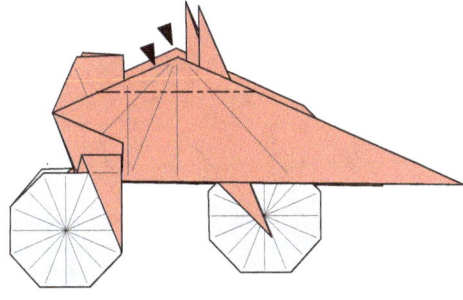

110. Closed sink the two corners to align with the edges below.

111. Open out the top layer. The corner will not lie flat.

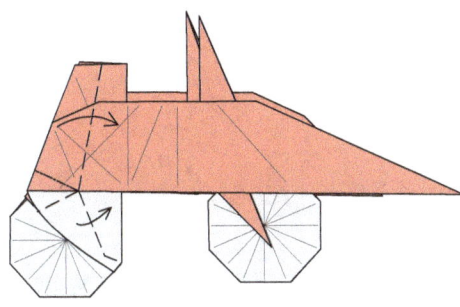

112. Close the layer back over while incorporating a rabbit ear.

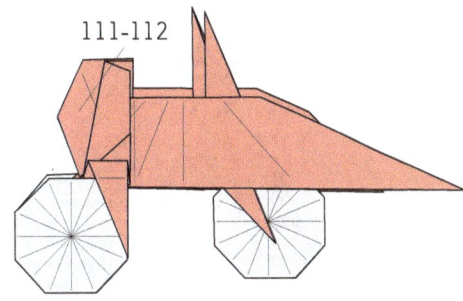

111-112

113. Repeat steps 111-112 behind.

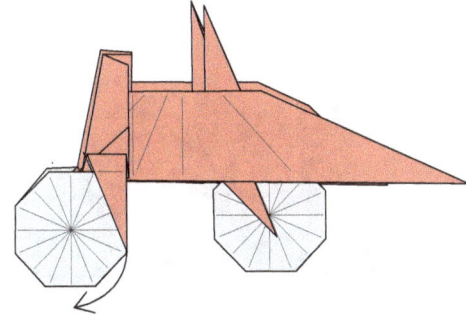

114. Rotate the flap while swiveling in the thick edges.

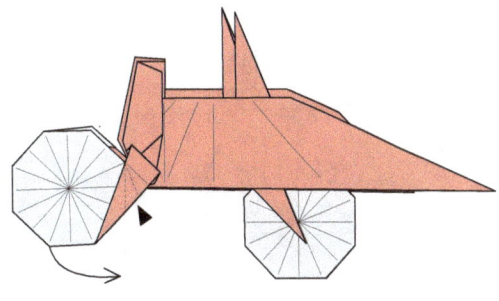

115. Crimp down along the hidden creases.

bicycle

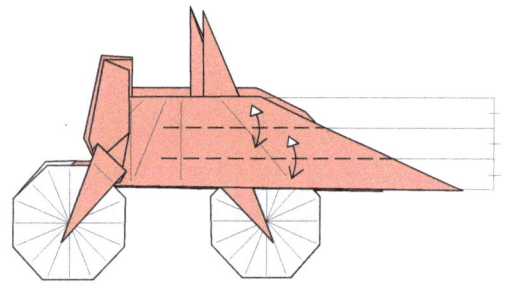

116. Precrease the top flap into thirds.

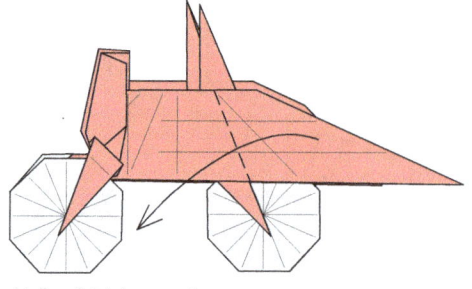

117. Valley fold the top flap over.

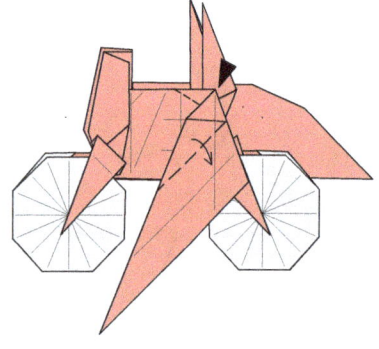

118. Valley fold along the existing crease, allowing a squash to form at the top.

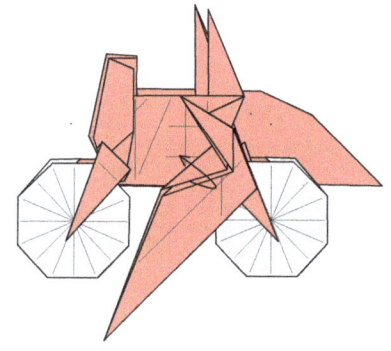

119. Pull the layer around to the surface.

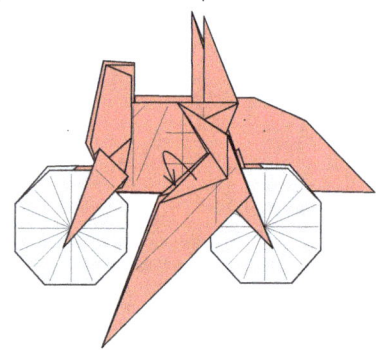

120. Swivel the edge around into the interior of the flap.

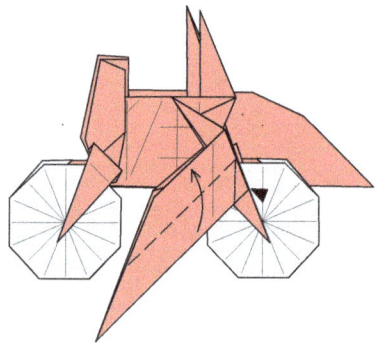

121. Valley fold along the existing crease, allowing a squash to form at the bottom.

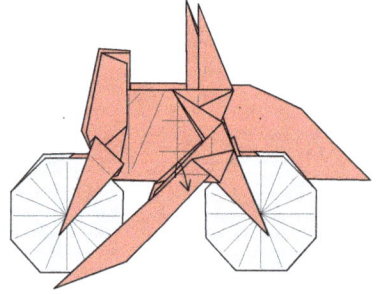

122. Pull a layer around to the surface (closed sink).

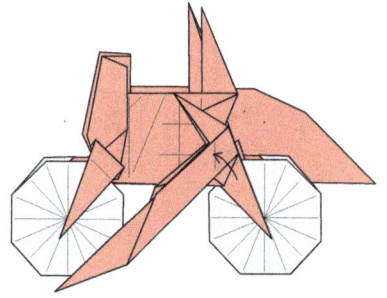

123. Bring the indicated flap to the surface.

bicycle

124. Turn over.

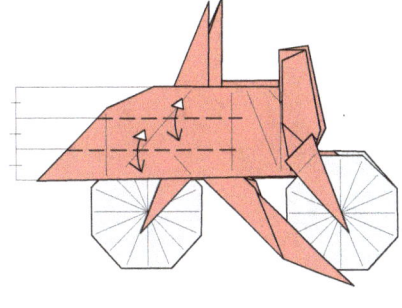

125. Precrease the top flap into thirds.

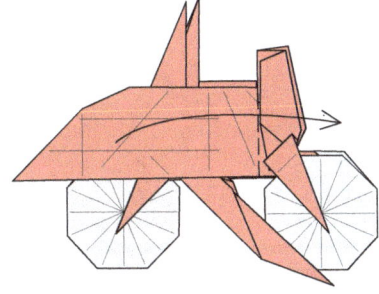

126. Swing the flap over.

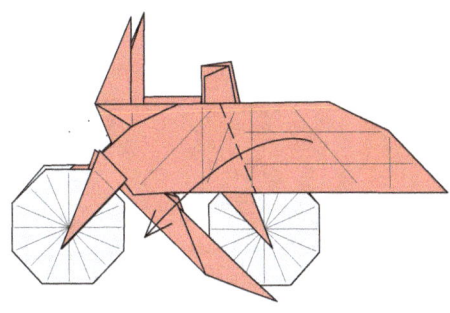

127. Valley fold the flap down.

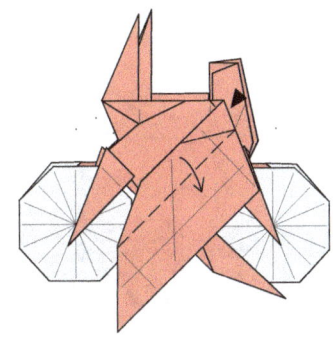

128. Valley fold along the existing crease, allowing a squash to form at the top.

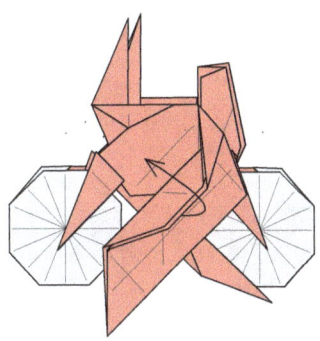

129. Pull the layer around to the surface.

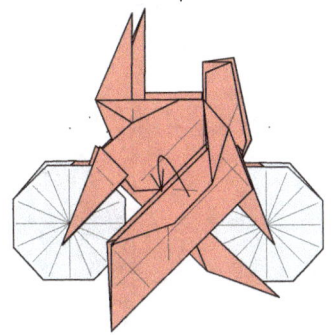

130. Swivel the edge around into the interior of the flap.

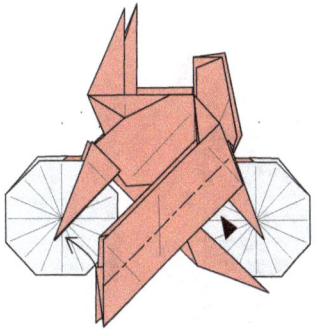

131. Closed sink along the existing crease, pulling the hidden flap up.

bicycle

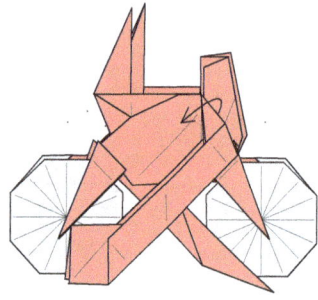

132. Bring the indicated section to the surface.

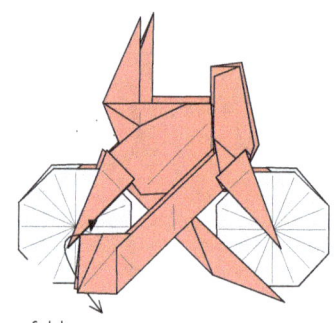

133. Reverse fold.

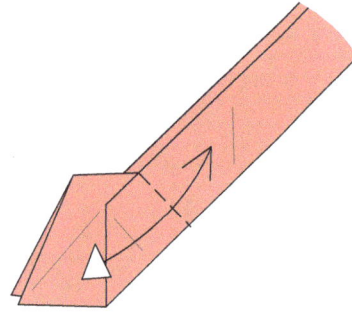

134. Precrease.

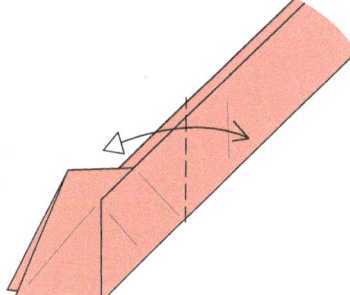

135. Precrease along the angle bisector.

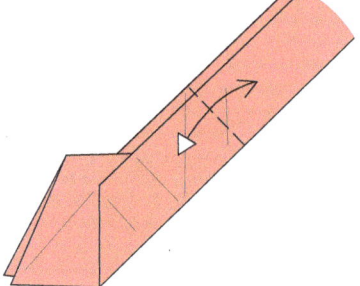

136. Precrease again.

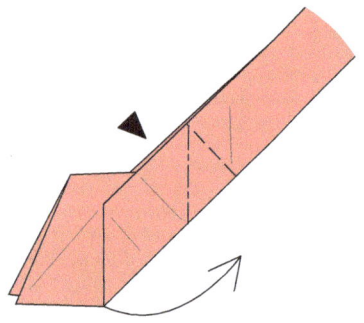

137. Crimp along the existing creases.

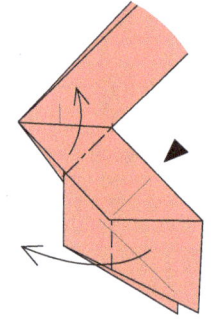

138. Swivel the flap over.

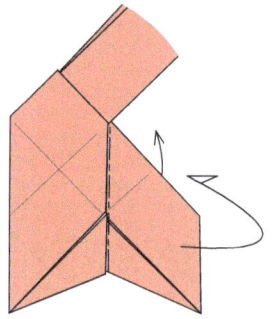

139. Repeat the same swivel behind.

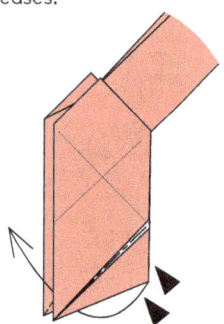

140. Reverse fold the two corners at the same time.

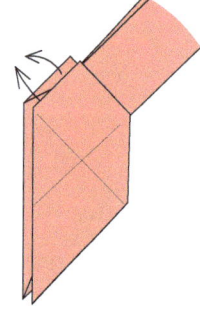

141. Pull out the trapped layers.

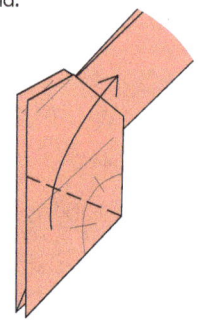

142. Valley fold the top flap up.

bicycle

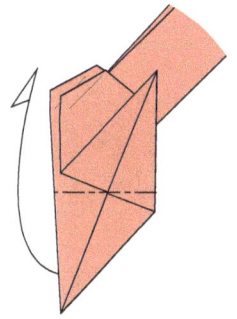

143. Mountain fold.

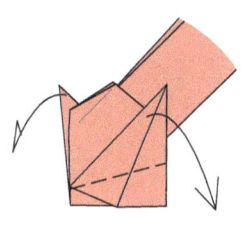

144. Fold the flaps in opposite directions.

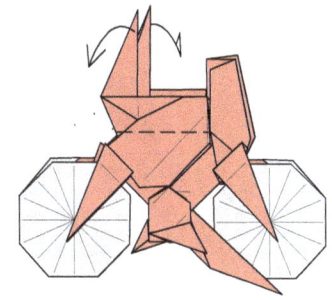

145. Valley fold the top sections as far as possible, allowing hidden swivels to form.

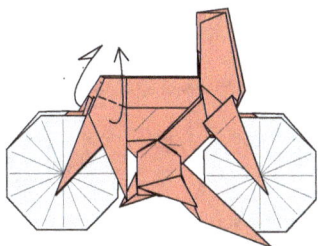

146. Valley fold the side flaps up.

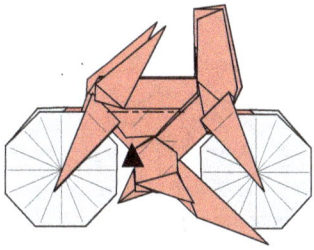

147. Sink the center layers to align with the outer edge.

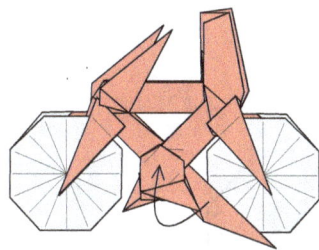

148. Bring the back flap to the front.

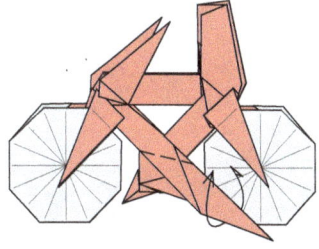

149. Outside reverse fold.

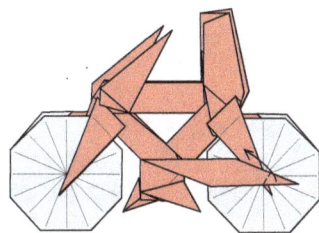

150. Valley fold the tip.

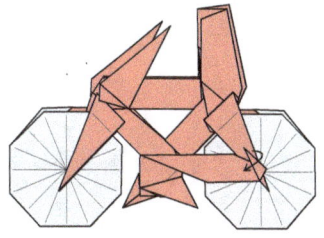

151. Tuck the tip into the flap.

bicycle

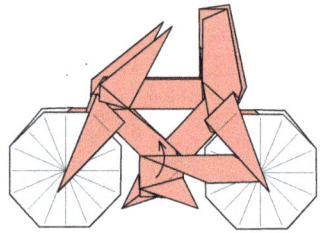

152. Tuck the flap between the pedal assembly.

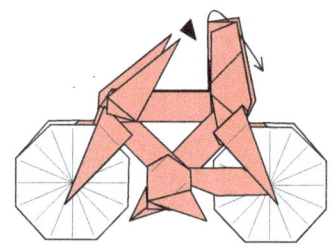

153. Reverse fold.

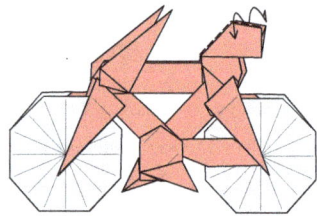

154. Wrap around a single layer at each side.

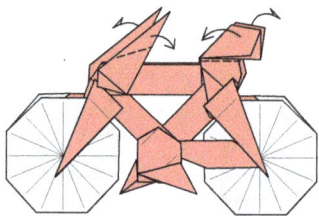

155. Open out the seat. Round out the handlebars.

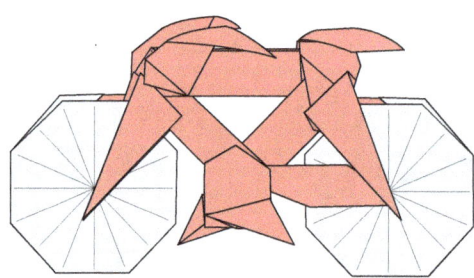

156. Completed *Bicycle*.

Prehistoric Car

An OrigamiUSA design competition originally called for a vehicle but was quickly changed to a prehistoric model design challenge. This *Prehistoric Car* satisfied both design requirements, making for an unusual entry amongst all the dinosaur fossils. Equally satisfying is that a prehistoric base (the classic Bird Base) was utilized to make this vehicle.

prehistoric car

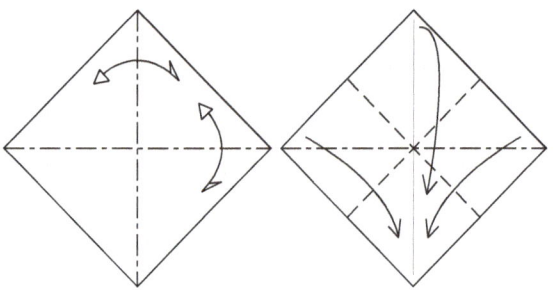
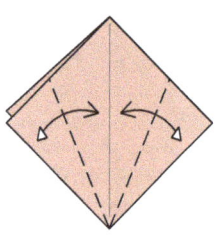
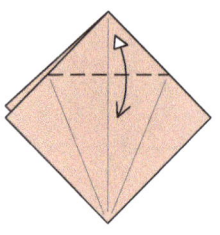

1. Precrease with mountain folds.
2. Collapse down.
3. Precrease along the angle bisectors.
4. Precrease the top.

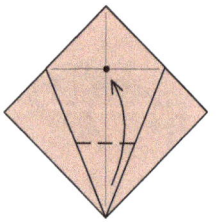
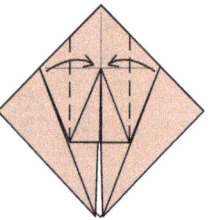
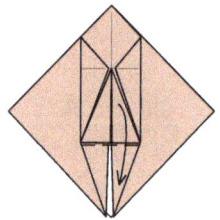

5. Reverse fold the sides.
6. Valley fold to the indicated intersection.
7. Valley fold to the center.
8. Swing the flap down.

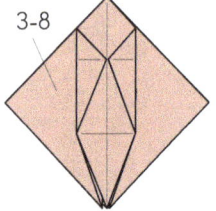
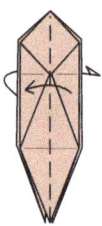
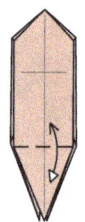
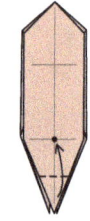

9. Repeat steps 3-8 behind.
10. Swing over a flap at each side.
11. Precrease.
12. Valley fold up.

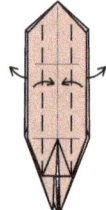

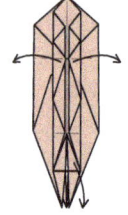
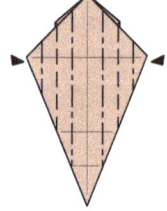

13. Valley fold to the center, allowing the flaps from behind to flip outwards.
14. Valley fold the corners to the center.
15. Unfold the pleats and swing down the bottom flap.
16. Sink the sides in and out along the existing creases.

prehistoric car

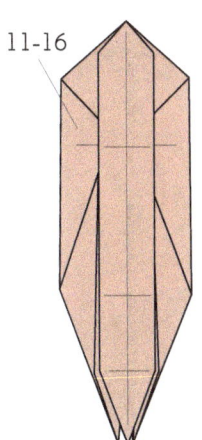
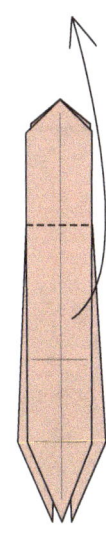
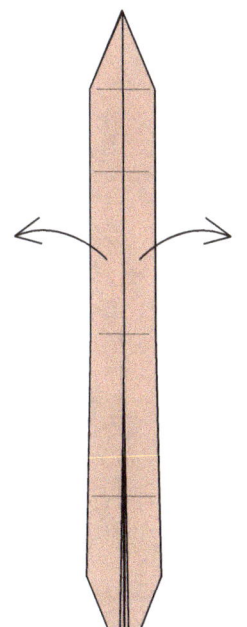
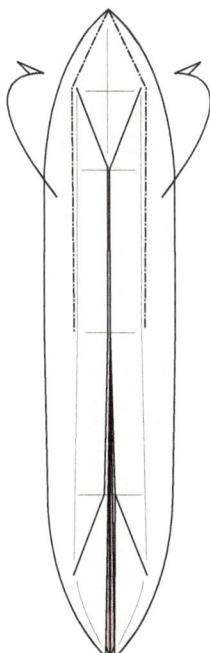

17. Repeat steps 11-16 behind.

18. Swing up one flap.

19. Open out the top layer.

20. Mountain fold the edges behind at the top only.

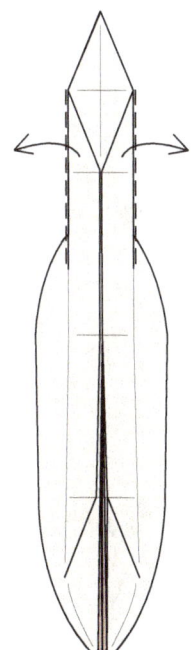
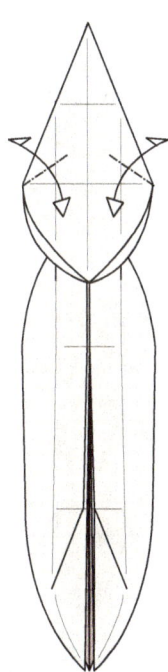
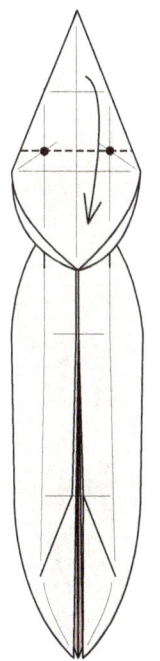
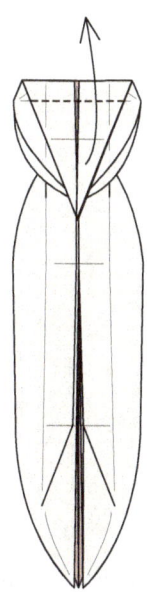

21. Open out the sides.

22. Precrease along the angle bisectors.

23. Valley fold through the indicated intersections.

24. Valley fold to align with the crease below.

prehistoric car

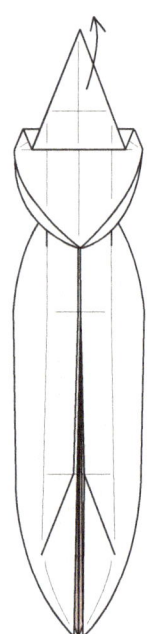

25. Unfold the pleat.

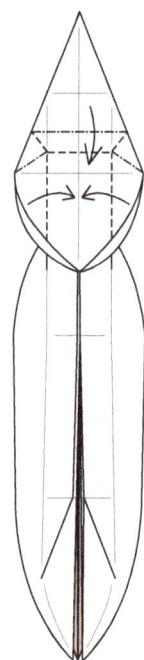

26. Swivel in the sides.

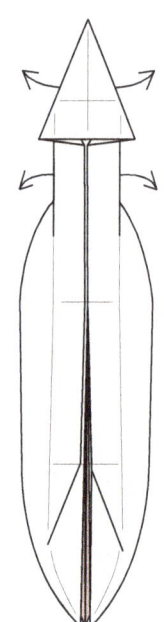

27. Pull out a single layer from each side.

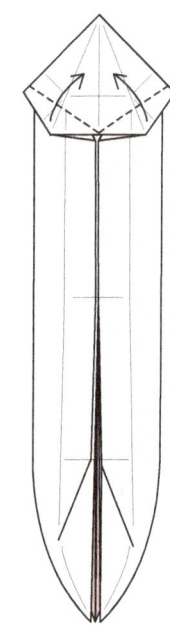

28. Swing the flaps up.

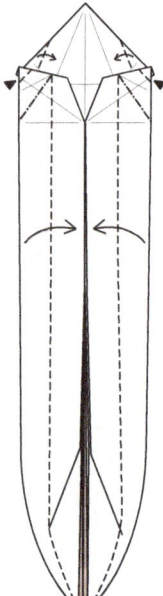

29. Valley fold the sides back in, allowing squashes to form at the corners.

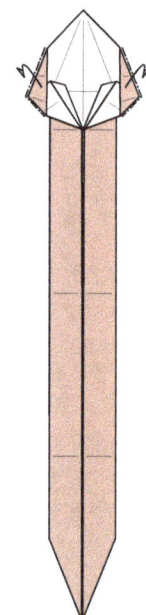

30. Wrap around a single layer at each side.

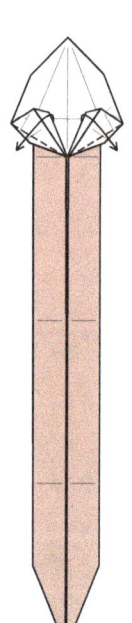

31. Swing down the flaps.

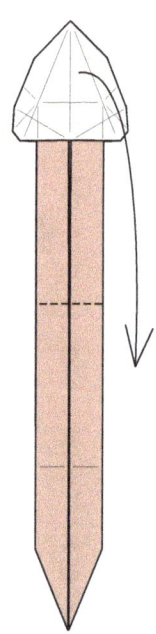

32. Swing down the large flap.

prehistoric car

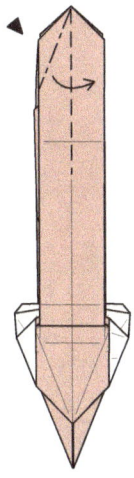
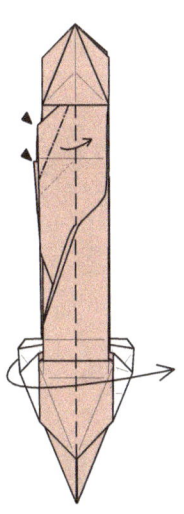
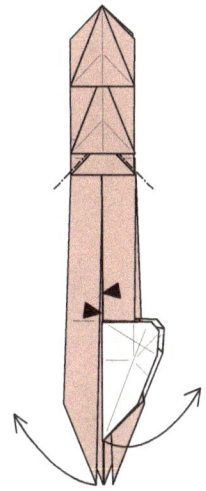

33. Swing over part of the top layer and spread squash the corner.

34. Valley fold the remainder of the flap in half, forming another spread squash and a reverse fold.

35. Reverse fold the two flaps outwards.

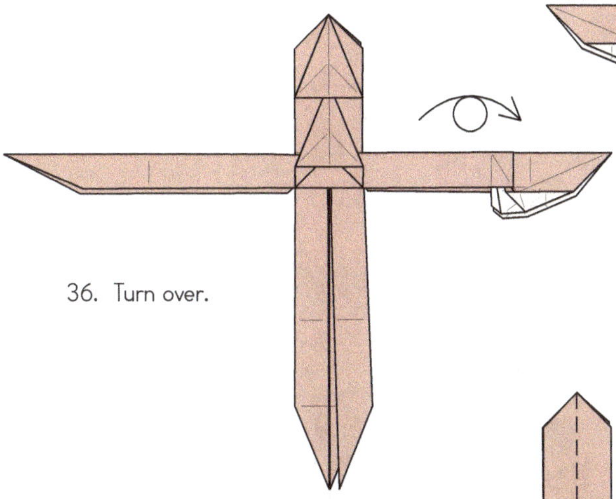

36. Turn over.

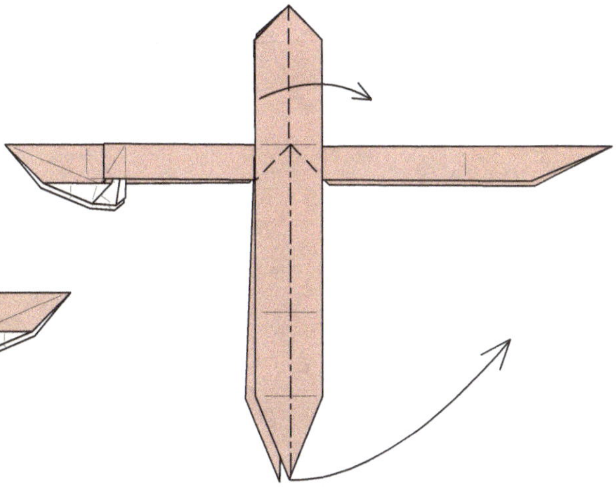

37. Valley fold while incorporating a reverse fold.

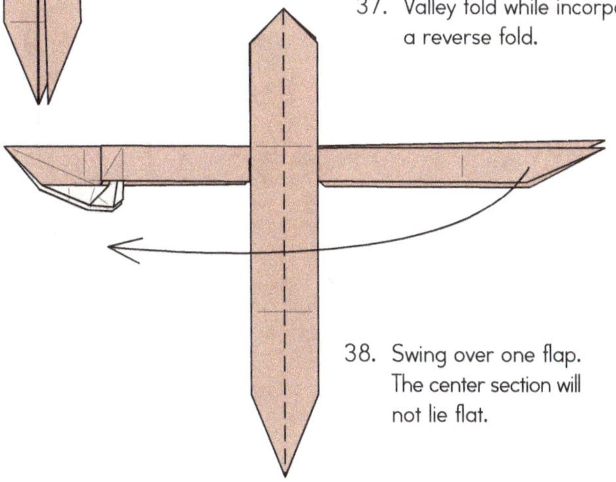

38. Swing over one flap. The center section will not lie flat.

59

prehistoric car

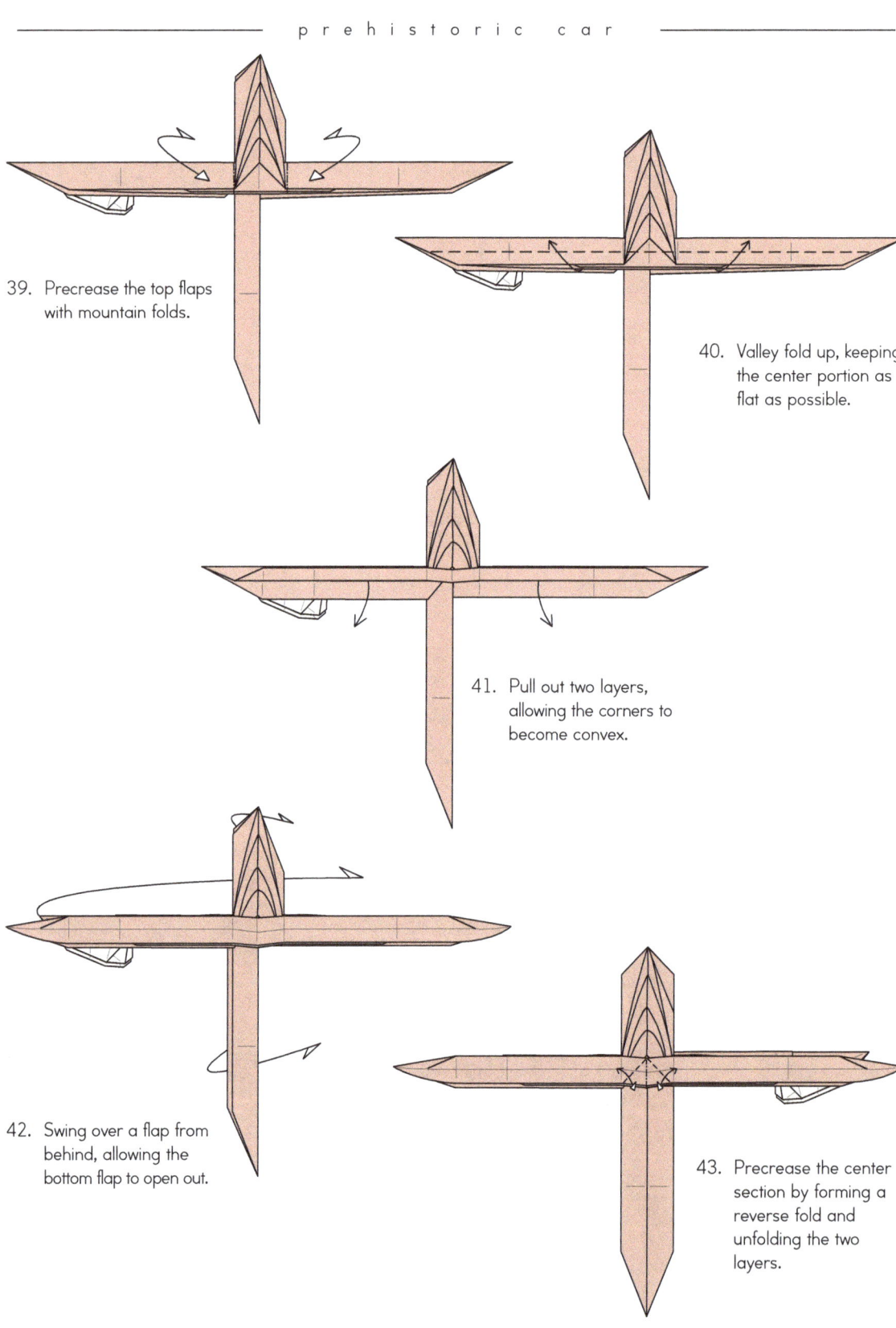

39. Precrease the top flaps with mountain folds.

40. Valley fold up, keeping the center portion as flat as possible.

41. Pull out two layers, allowing the corners to become convex.

42. Swing over a flap from behind, allowing the bottom flap to open out.

43. Precrease the center section by forming a reverse fold and unfolding the two layers.

prehistoric car

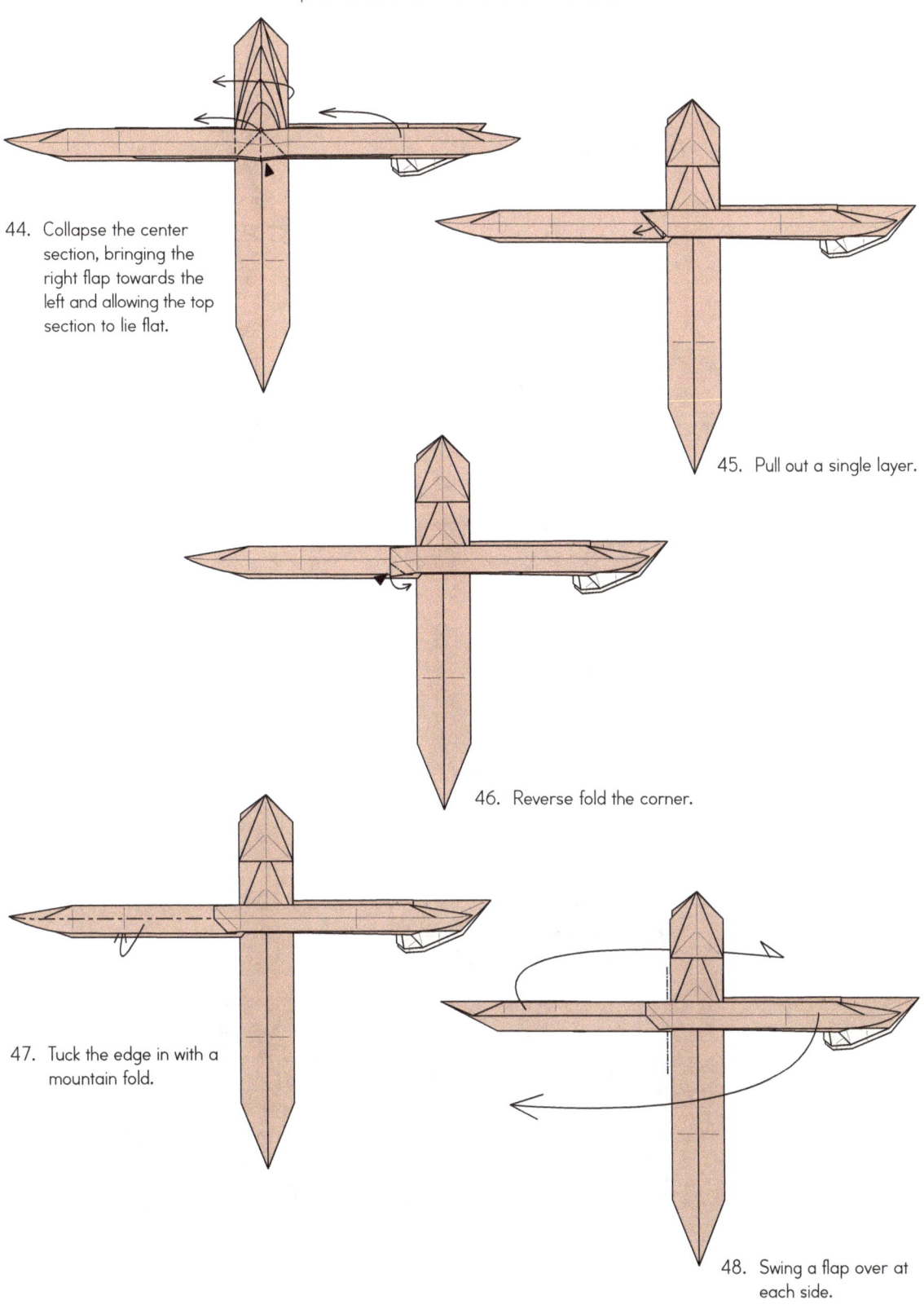

44. Collapse the center section, bringing the right flap towards the left and allowing the top section to lie flat.

45. Pull out a single layer.

46. Reverse fold the corner.

47. Tuck the edge in with a mountain fold.

48. Swing a flap over at each side.

61

prehistoric car

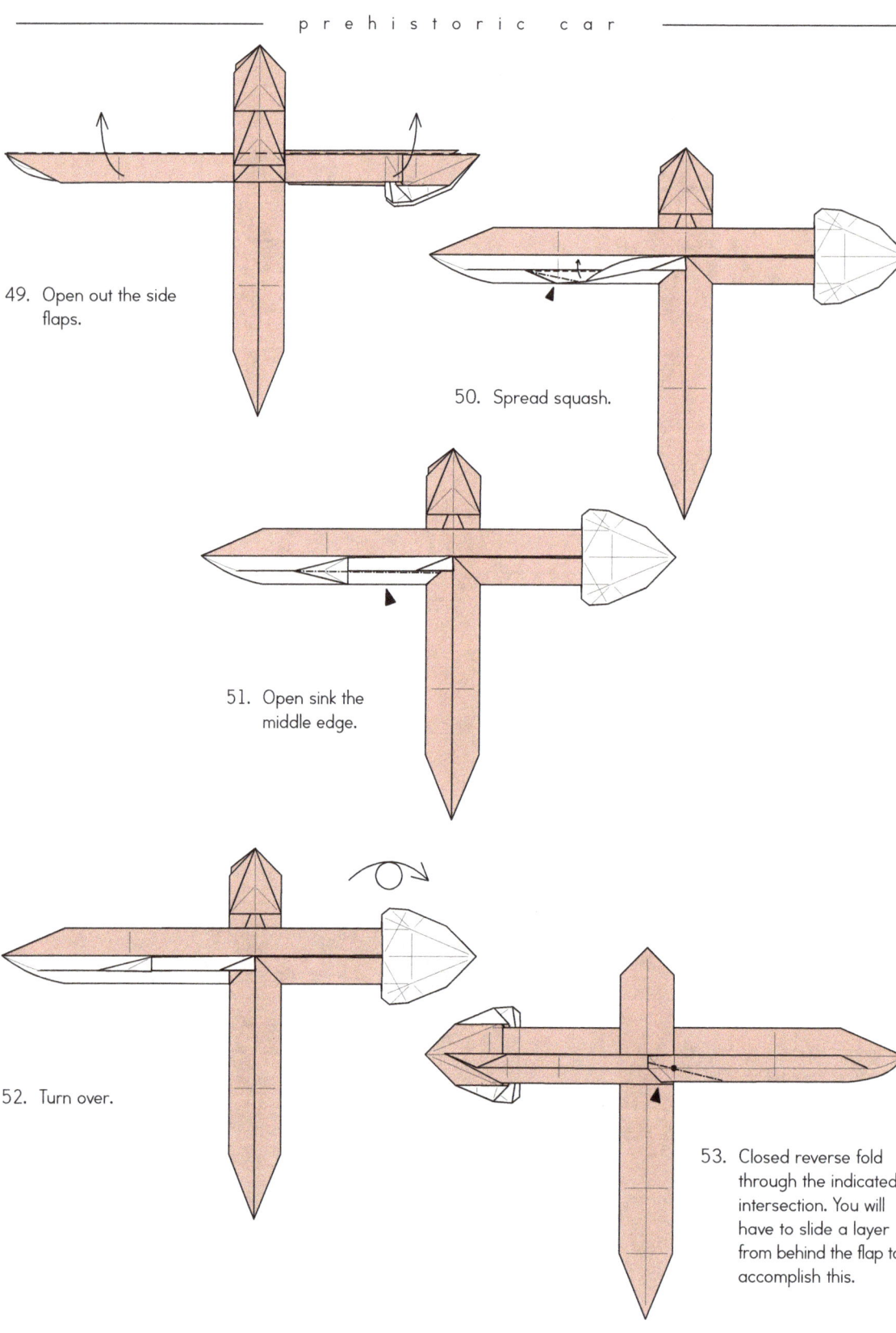

49. Open out the side flaps.

50. Spread squash.

51. Open sink the middle edge.

52. Turn over.

53. Closed reverse fold through the indicated intersection. You will have to slide a layer from behind the flap to accomplish this.

prehistoric car

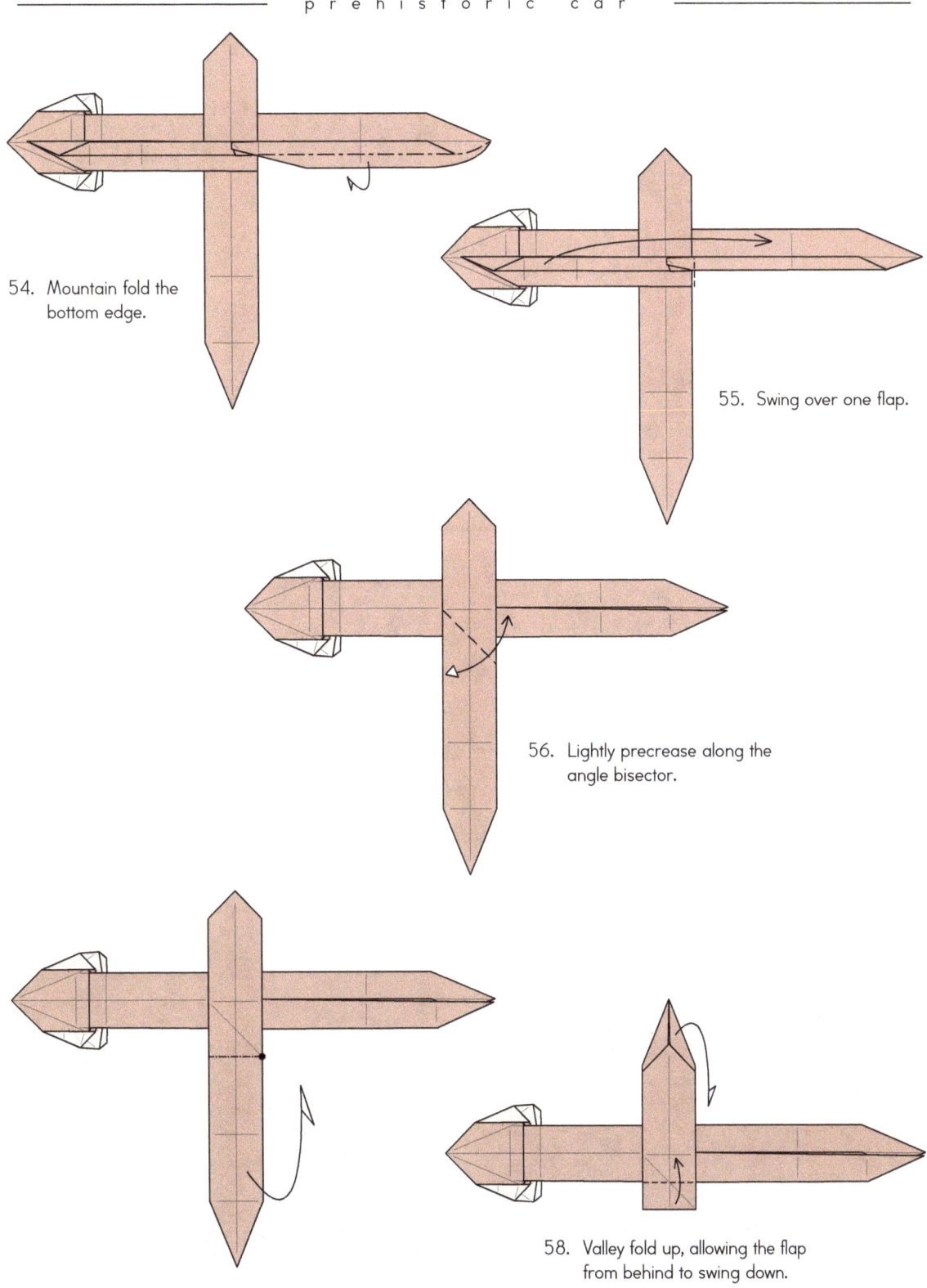

54. Mountain fold the bottom edge.

55. Swing over one flap.

56. Lightly precrease along the angle bisector.

57. Mountain fold the bottom flap.

58. Valley fold up, allowing the flap from behind to swing down.

prehistoric car

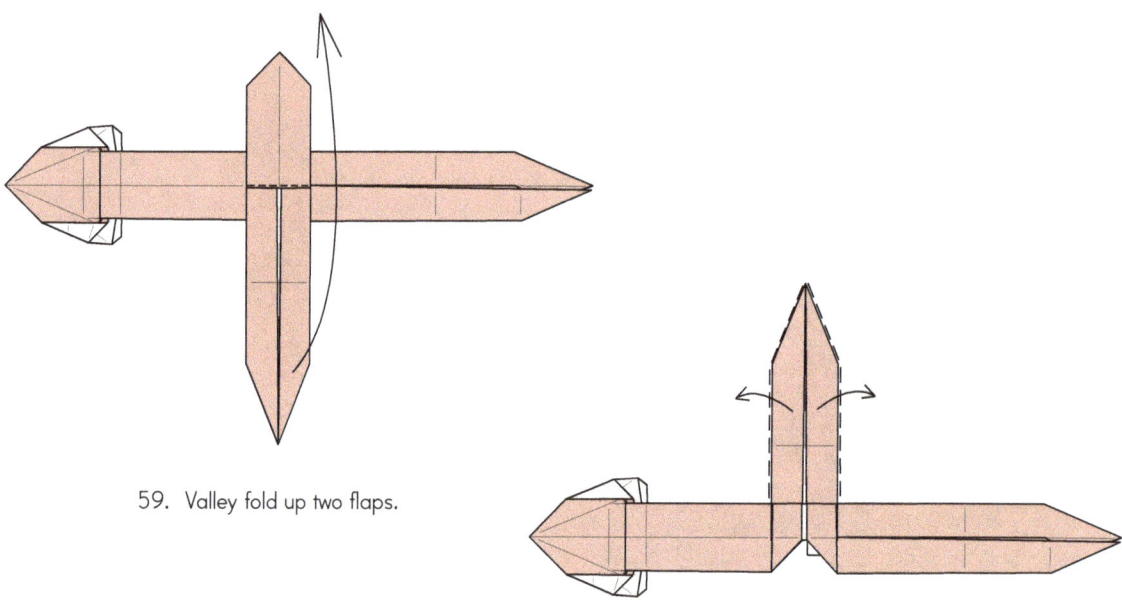

59. Valley fold up two flaps.

60. Swivel fold two layers out at each side. The top will not lie flat.

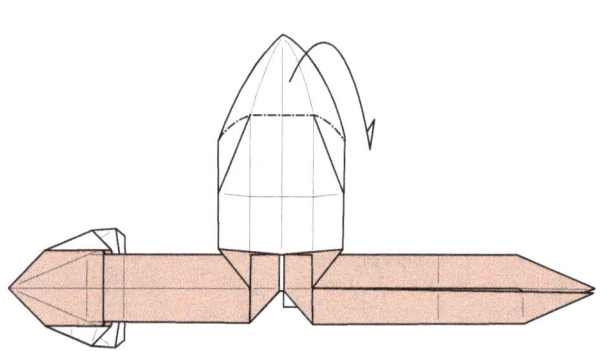

61. Wrap the top edge around to flatten.

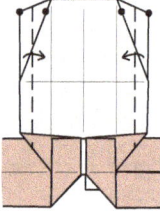

62. Valley fold the sides in to meet the indicated edges.

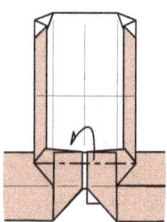

63. Tuck the edge in, swiveling at the corners.

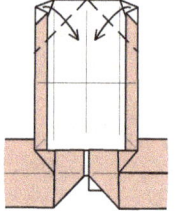

64. Valley fold the sides to the center.

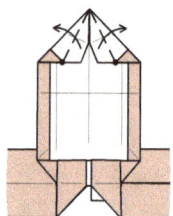

65. Valley fold the sides out, noting the dotted points.

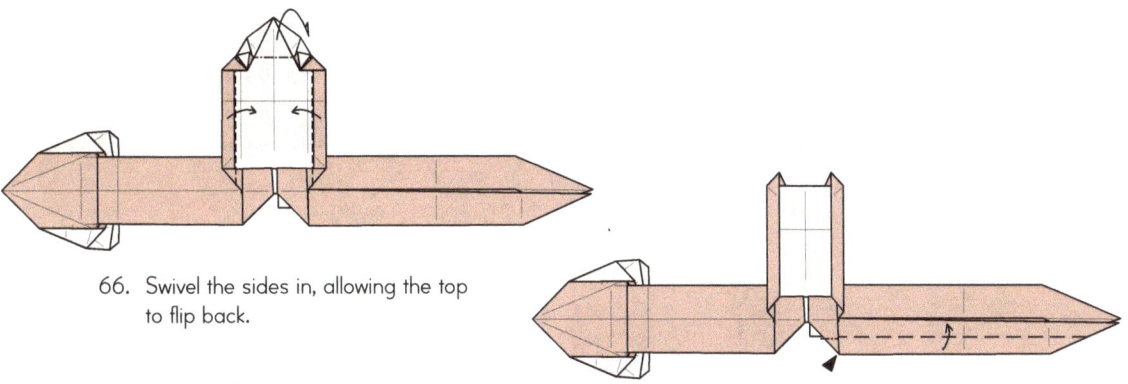

66. Swivel the sides in, allowing the top to flip back.

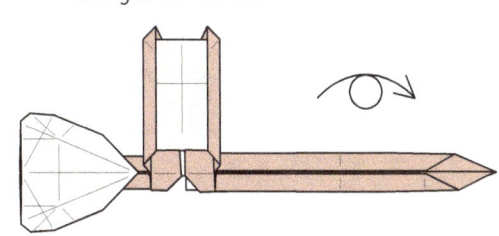

67. Valley fold the flap in half, reverse folding at the corner.

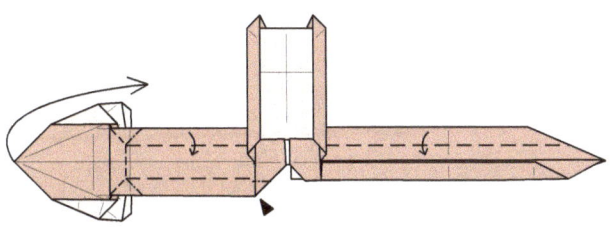

68. Valley fold the sides in, reverse folding a corner and forming swivel folds at the left side.

69. Turn over.

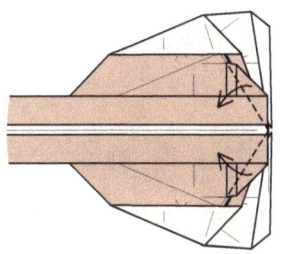 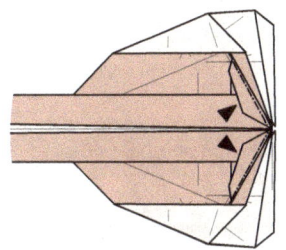 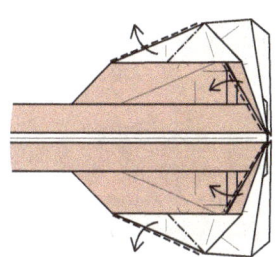

70. Valley fold the edges over as far as possible.

71. Closed sink the corners.

72. Swivel the edges outwards.

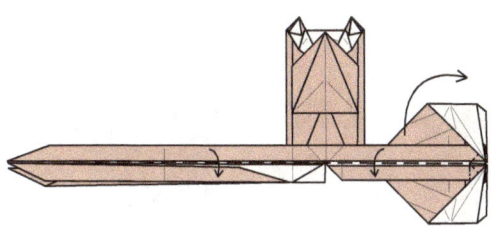

73. Valley fold the flap in half, forming a rabbit ear at the right. The flap will rotate.

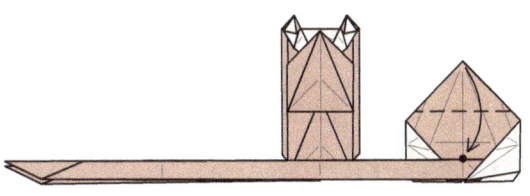

74. Valley fold the corner to the nearest edge.

prehistoric car

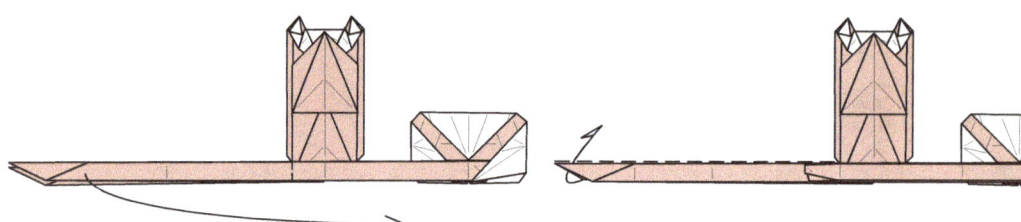

75. Swing over a flap as far as possible.

76. Swing up a flap from behind.

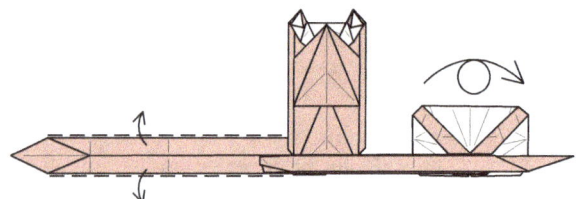

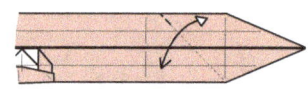

77. Open out the side layers. The flap will not lie flat at its base. Turn over.

78. Precrease, pinching only near the top edge.

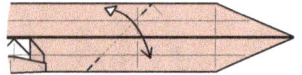

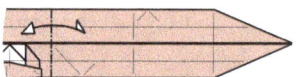

79. Pinch again, starting from the previous crease.

80. Precrease again.

81. Precrease with a mountain fold.

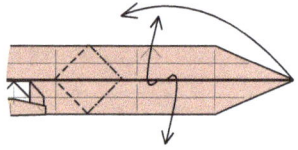

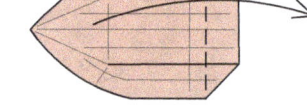

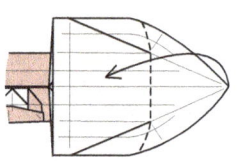

82. Swivel over two layers at each side. The flap will be convex.

83. Valley fold the flap over.

84. Flatten the flap with valley folds.

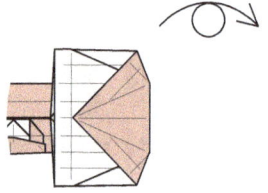

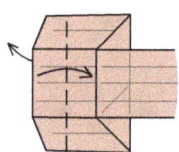

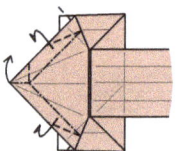

85. Turn over.

86. Valley fold to the edge, flipping the flap out from behind.

87. Mountain fold along the existing creases, forming a rabbit ear at the corner and swiveling the sides.

prehistoric car

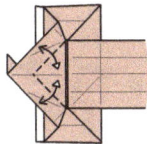

88. Precrease.

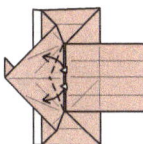

89. Precrease along the angle bisectors.

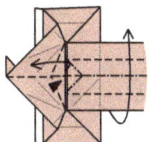

90. Pleat the flap while singing the center. Reverse fold at the left.

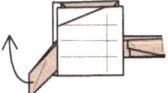

91. Pull the flap up, releasing the trapped layer from the previous reverse fold.

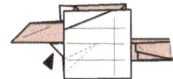

92. Sink the triangular section, forming a sink on the inside to facilitate this.

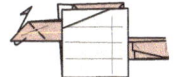

93. Mountain fold the tip.

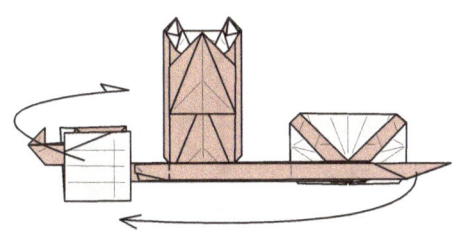

94. Flip the two flaps over.

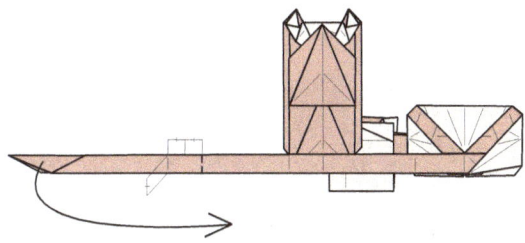

95. Valley fold, noting the distance from the indicated crease.

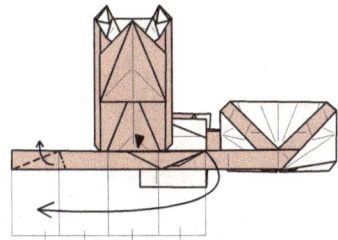

96. Spread squash the flap over, starting from one-fourth the width of the flap.

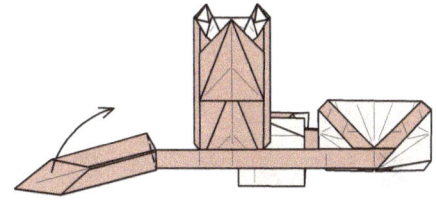

97. Valley fold the flap over.

67

prehistoric car

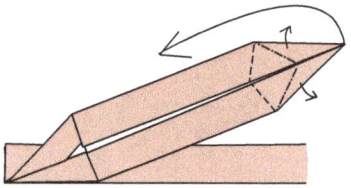

98. Spread apart the flap and squash.

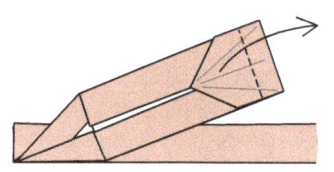

99. Valley fold over, noting that this fold will truncate a corner of the white square to be revealed.

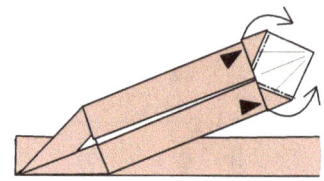

100. Reverse fold the corners.

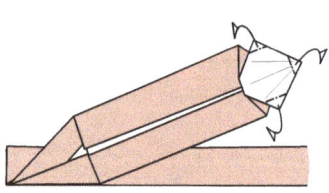

101. Mountain fold the three corners.

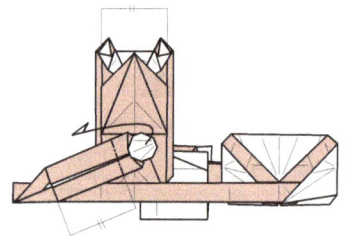

102. Mountain fold to make the flap about the same width as the center flap.

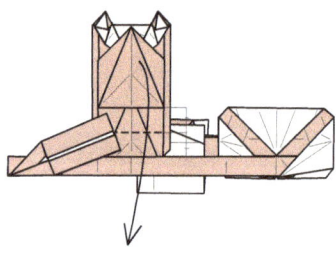

103. Valley fold the center flap down.

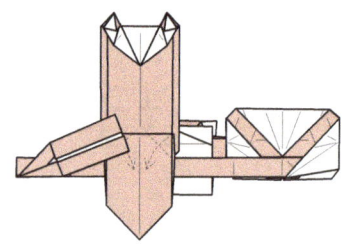

104. Valley fold the clusters of hidden layers to help lock the model together.

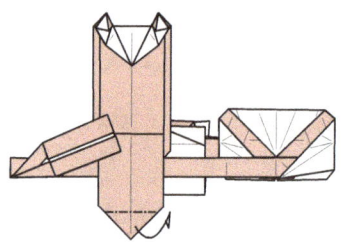

105. Mountain fold the tip.

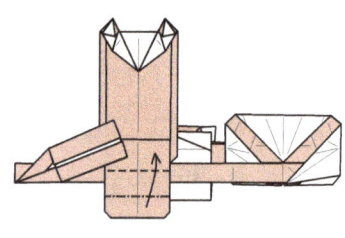

106. Pleat the flap upwards.

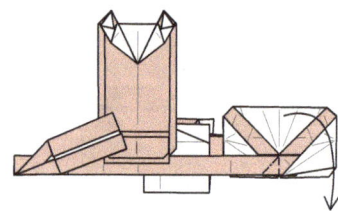

107. Pleat the tip of the flap, allowing the rectangular section to rotate.

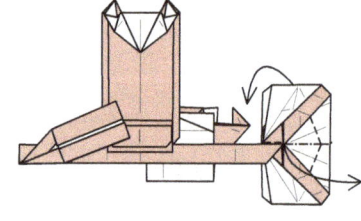

108. Lightly fold the flap in half while incorporating a reverse fold.

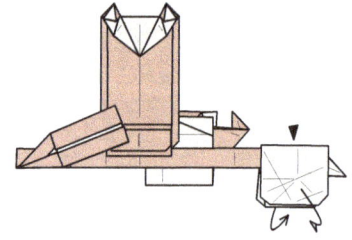

109. Round the flap into a tube shape, allowing the edges to overlap slightly.

prehistoric car

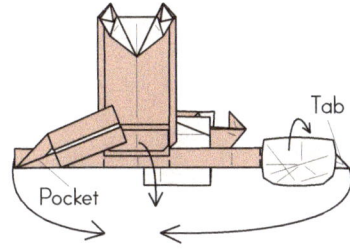

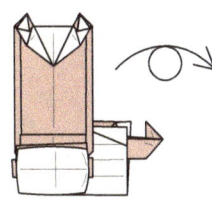

110. Twist the tube section, open out the seat section and tuck the indicated tab into the pocket section.

111. For a stronger lock you can fold over hidden layers at the left axle. Turn over.

112. Tuck the layers into each other and round the flap into a tube shape.

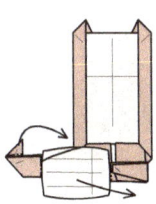

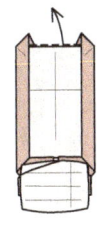

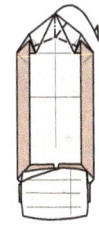

113. Shift the tube section over. Tuck the tip of the left flap into the top edge of the chassis.

114. Swing a flap up from behind.

115. Rabbit ear the flap.

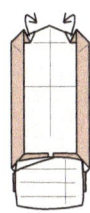

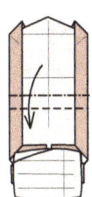

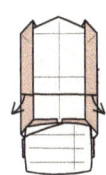

116. Swivel the edges behind.

117. Pleat the top flap.

118. Pull out two edges.

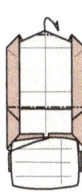

119. Mountain fold the tip and fold the flap down. Round out the flaps to taste.

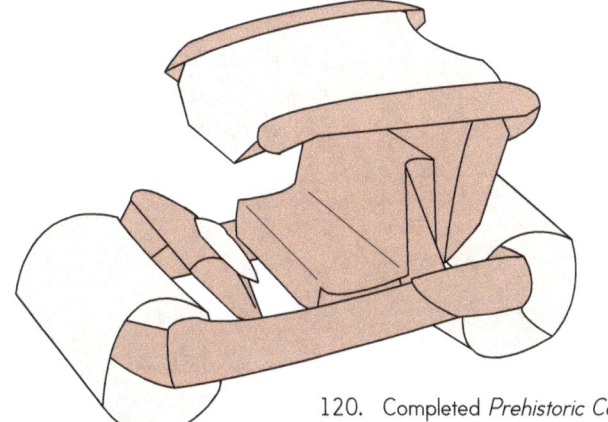

120. Completed *Prehistoric Car*.

Classic Car

The form of this *Classic Car* is loosely based on old childhood drawings of automobiles with large fenders. Neal Elias style box pleating is a major design element to generate the squared-off flaps. There are quite a few unusual sequences to generate the complex color pattern. For extra efficiency, the driver's seat is only suggested.

classic car

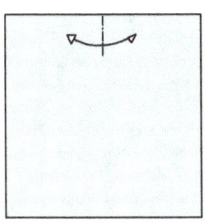
1. Precrease the top edge in half with a mountain fold.

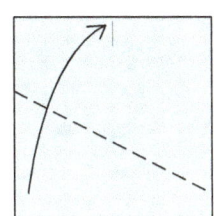
2. Valley fold the corner to meet the crease.

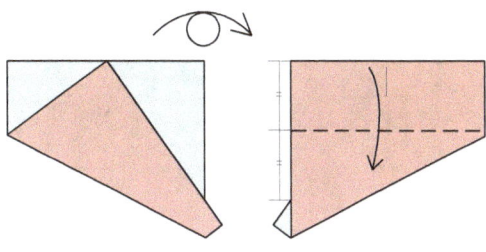
3. Turn over.

4. Valley fold the indicated section in half.

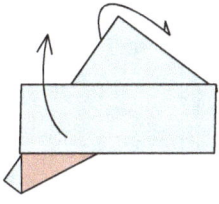

5. Unfold completely to the colored side.

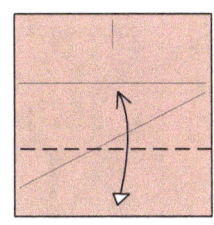
6. Precrease the lower section in half.

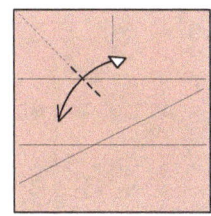
7. Form a pinch through the crease along the angle bisector.

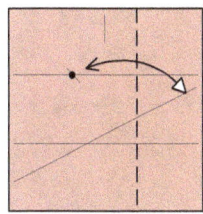
8. Precrease to the indicated intersection.

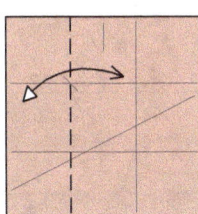
9. Precrease the left section in half.

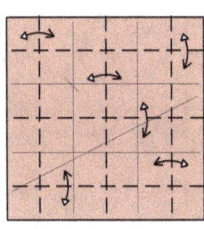
10. Precrease each section in half, both horizontally and vertically.

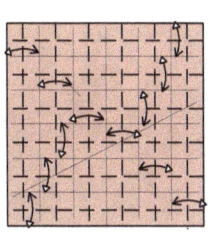
11. Precrease the resulting sections in half.

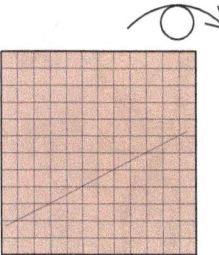
12. Turn over.

71

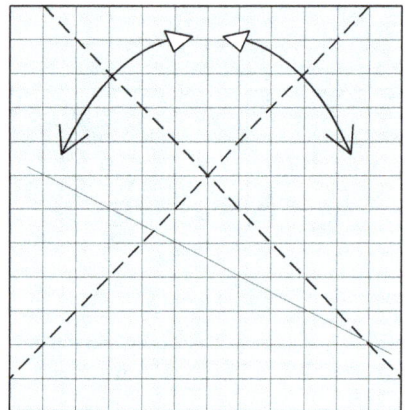

13. Precrease.

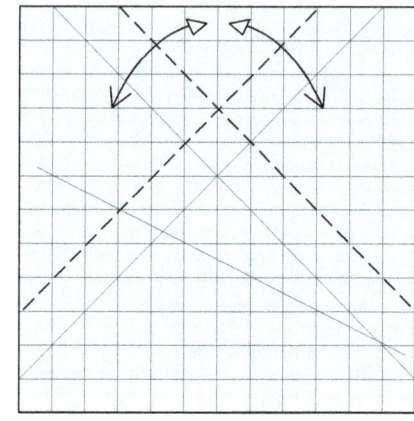

14. Precrease again.

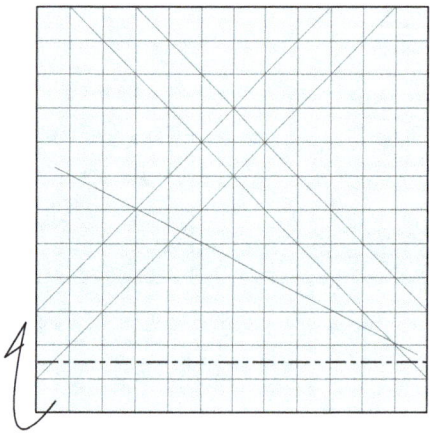

15. Mountain fold, dividing the second row in half.

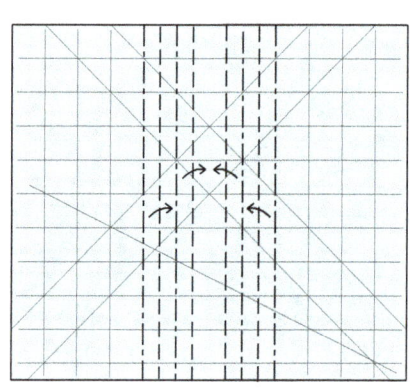

16. Pleat the sides inwards.

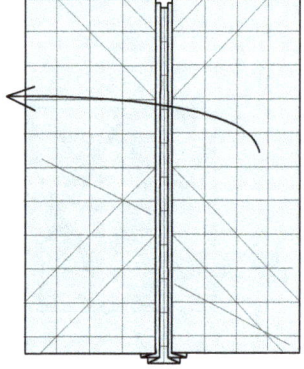

17. Swing over one side.

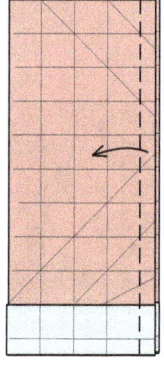

18. Valley fold over one layer.

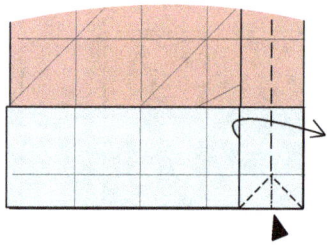

19. Valley fold the layer back over, incorporating a reverse fold at the bottom.

classic car

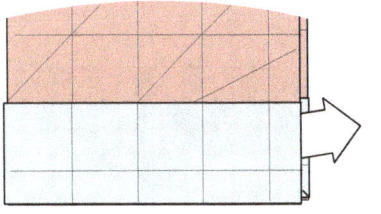

20. Unsink the single layer.

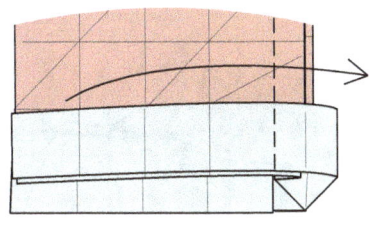

21. Open sink the edge.

22. Valley fold the flap over along the existing crease.

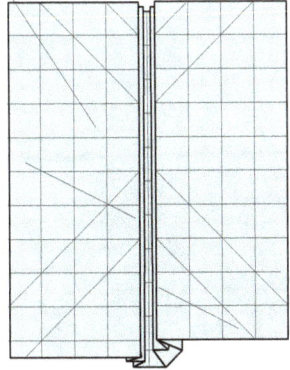

23. Repeat steps 17-22 in mirror image.

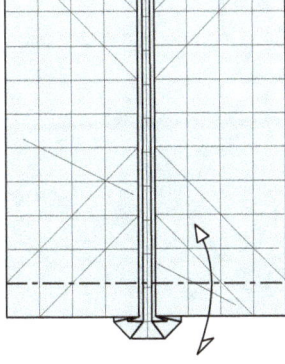

24. Precrease through all layers with a mountain fold.

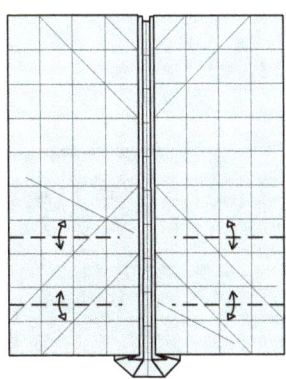

25. Precrease with valley folds on the top layer.

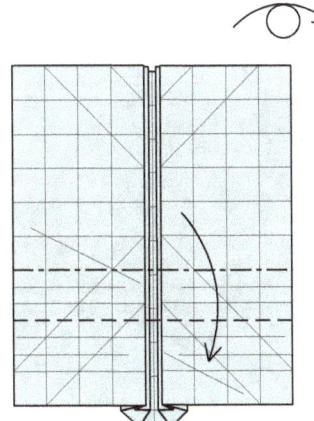

26. Form a pleat and turn over.

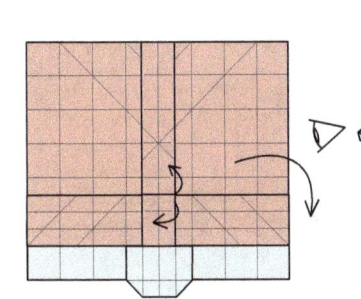

27. Pull apart the cluster of pleats.

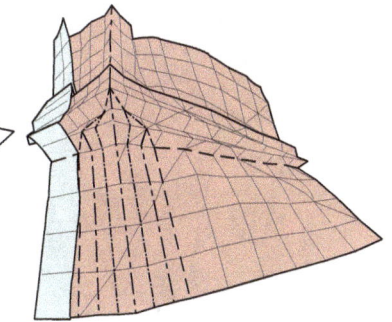

28. View from previous step. Reform the pleated area with additional pleats.

73

classic car

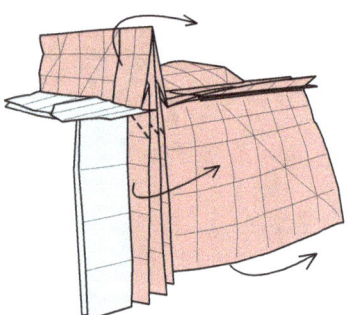

29. Flatten the model by swinging over the indicated sections.

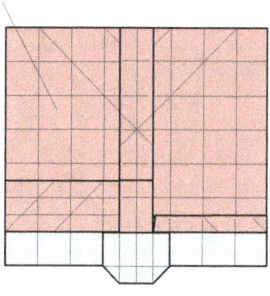

30. Repeat steps 27-29 in mirror image.

31. Swing the flap down.

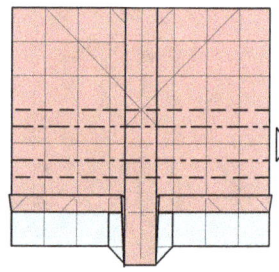

32. Pleat through all layers.

33. Pull out the bottom sets of pleats.

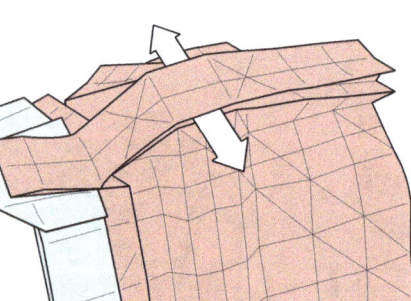

34. Unsink the paper between the pleats. The center will start to buckle inwards.

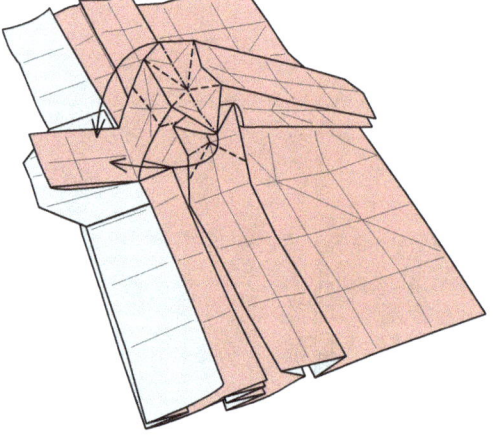

35. Collapse the points flat, allowing the rest of the model to flatten.

classic car

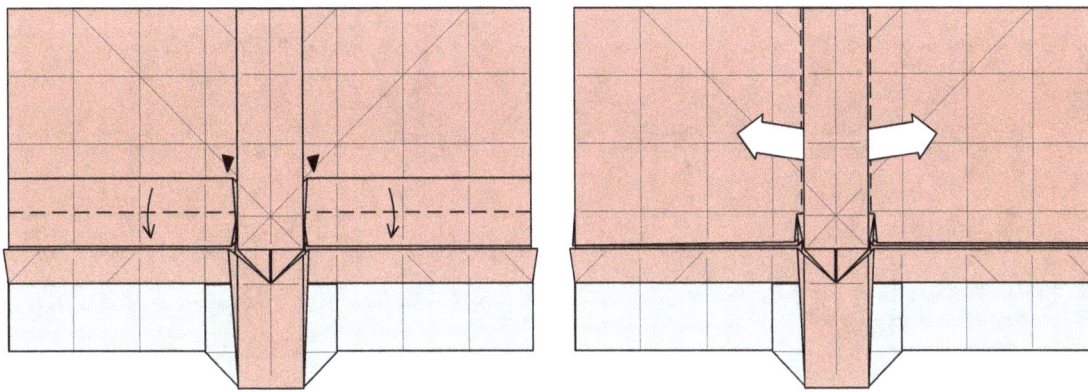

36. Swivel the edges down.

37. Unsink a set of pleats at each side.

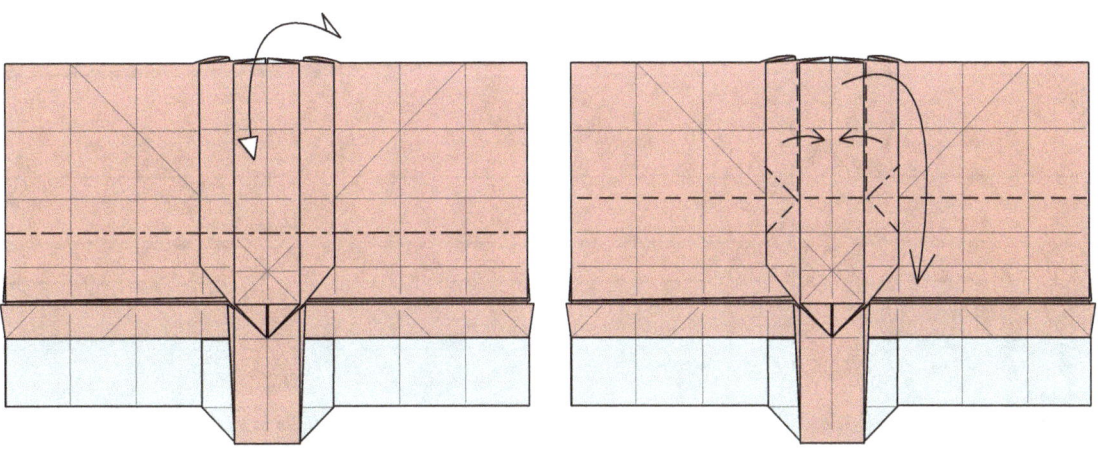

38. Precrease with a mountain fold.

39. Valley fold down while swiveling in the sides.

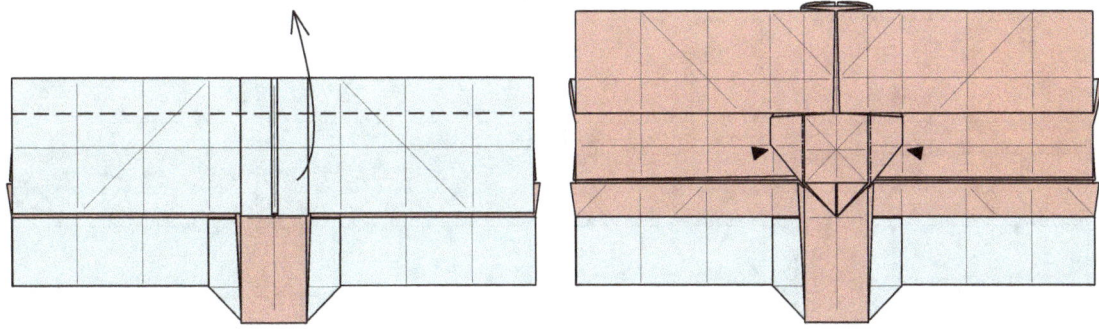

40. Lightly valley fold up.

41. Sink the side flaps triangularly (closed at the top and open at the bottom).

classic car

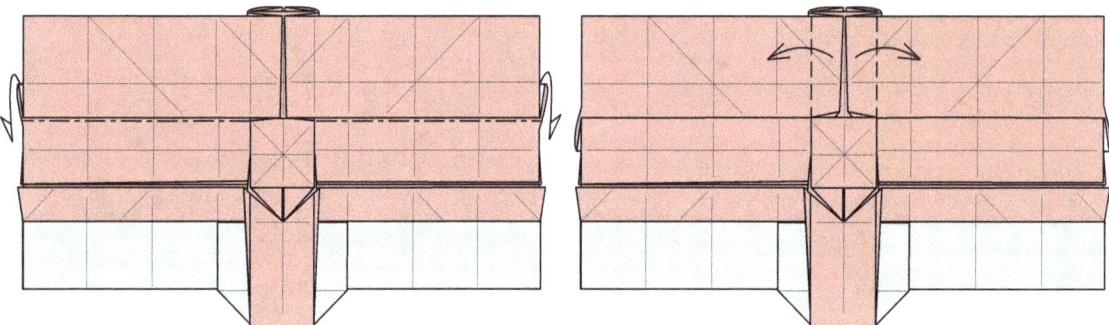

42. Flip the back edge down.

43. Swivel the flaps outwards.

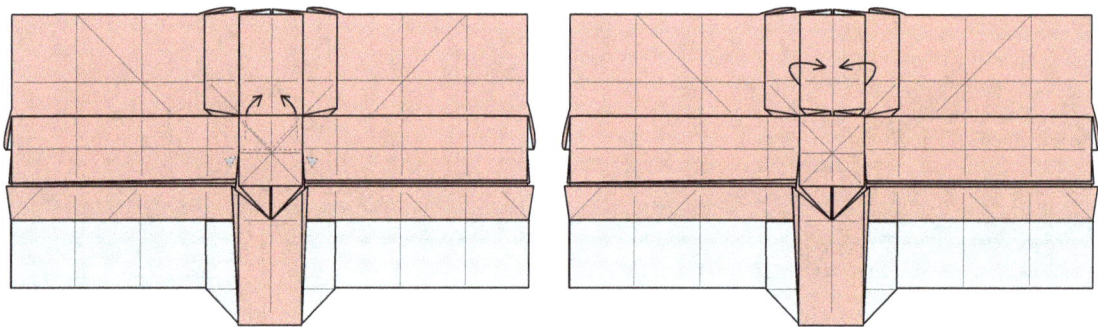

44. Reverse fold the hidden corners.

45. Wrap around a single layer at each side (closed sink).

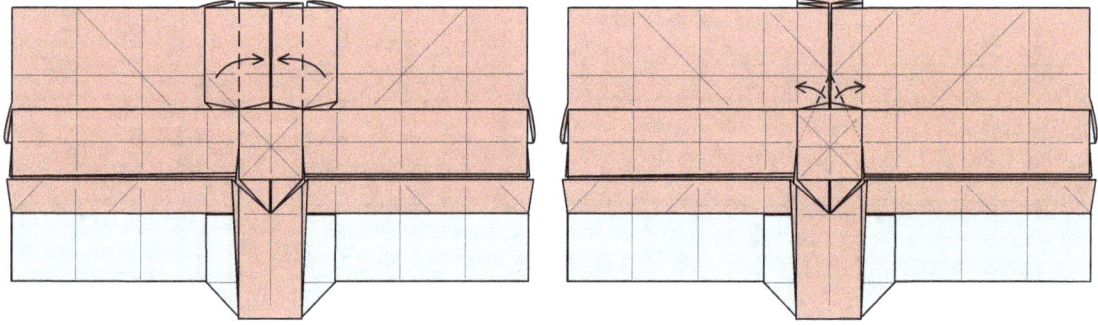

46. Swivel the flaps in.

47. Swivel one layer out at each side.

classic car

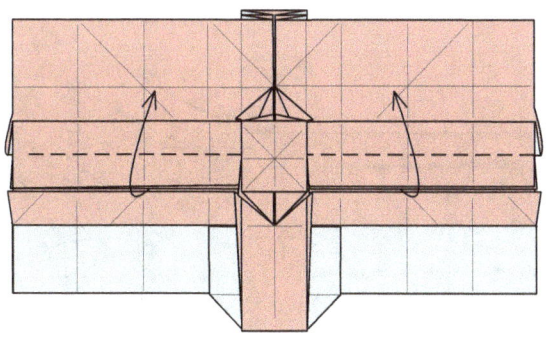

48. Swivel the cluster of flaps up at each side.

49. Valley fold the top edges down, allowing the center pleated section to stretch and squash flat.

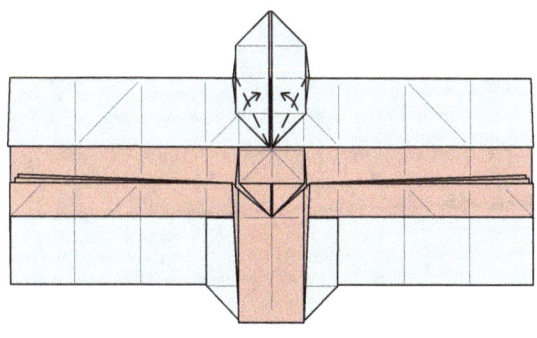
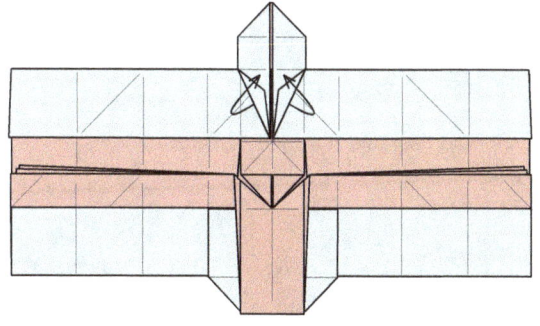

50. Valley fold the top layers.

51. Wrap around a single layer to the surface at each side.

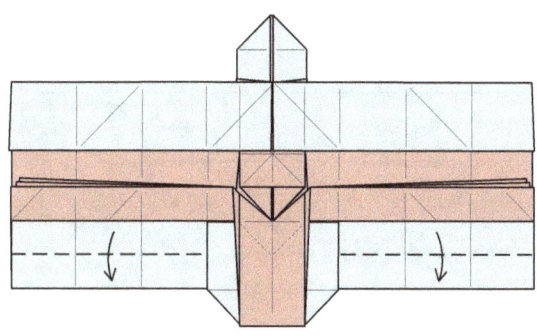
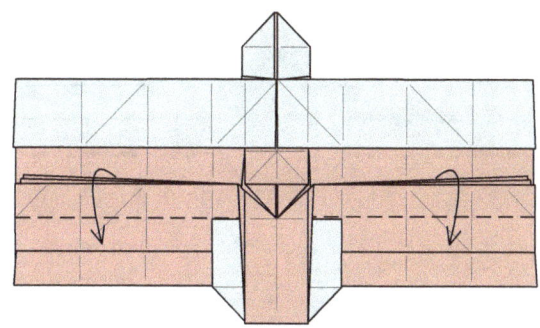

52. Swivel down a single layer at each side.

53. Swivel the cluster of flaps down at each side.

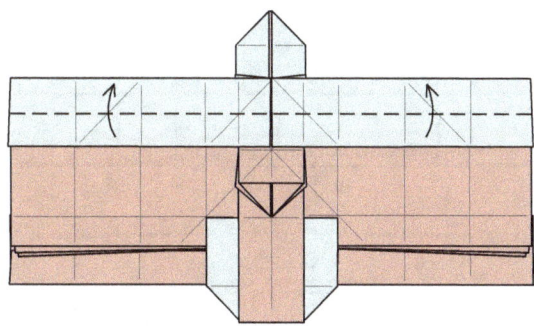
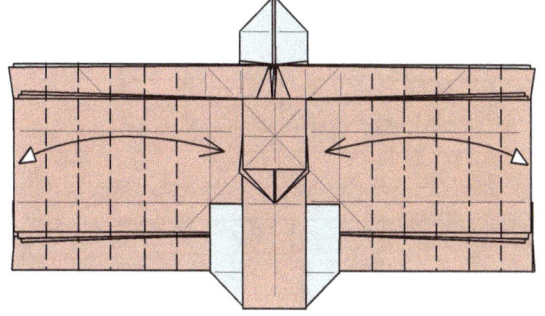

54. Lightly (especially towards the center) valley fold a layer up at each side.

55. Pleat the sides inwards and open out.

classic car

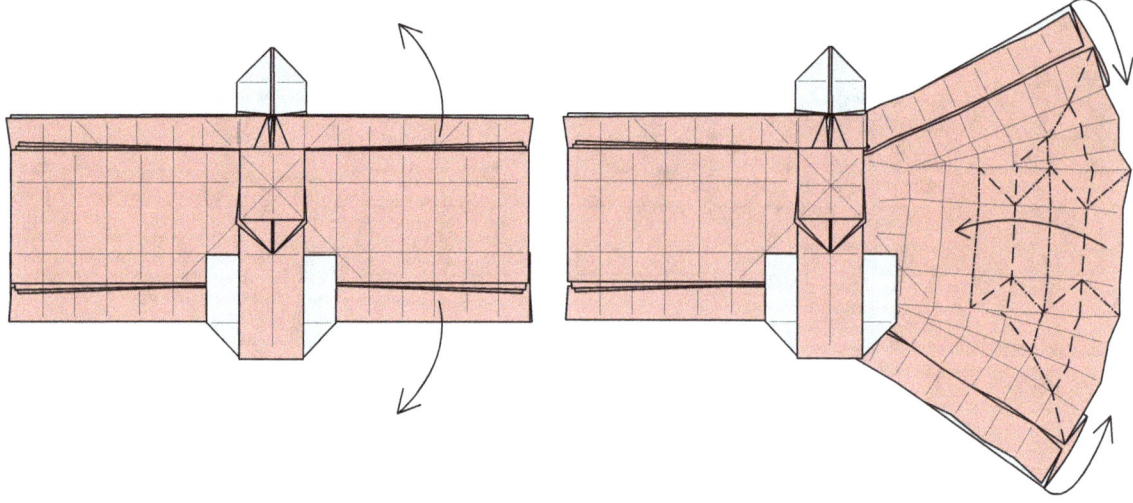

56. Spread apart the inner sets of pleats.

57. Pleat the side inwards while bringing the top and bottom sections towards each other.

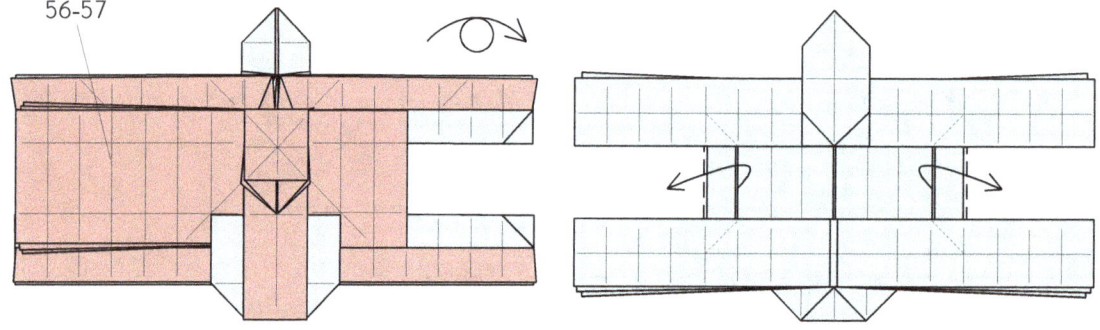

58. Repeat steps 56-57 on the other side. Turn over.

59. Swivel a set of edges outwards at each side.

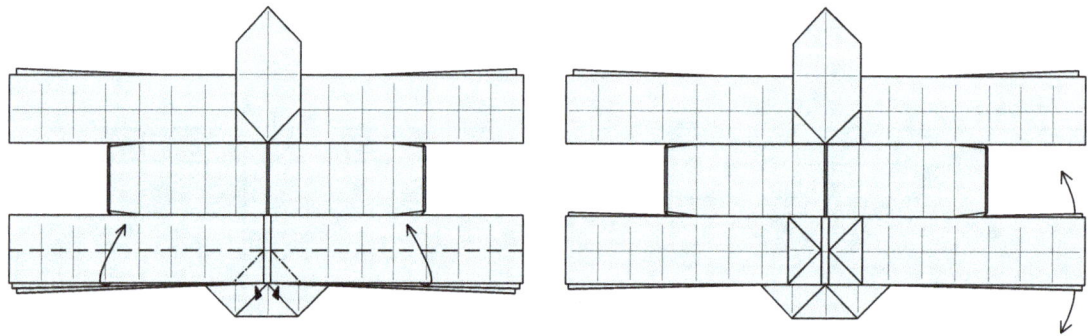

60. Valley fold one layer up at each side, allowing squash folds to form along the center.

61. Spread apart the pleats.

classic car

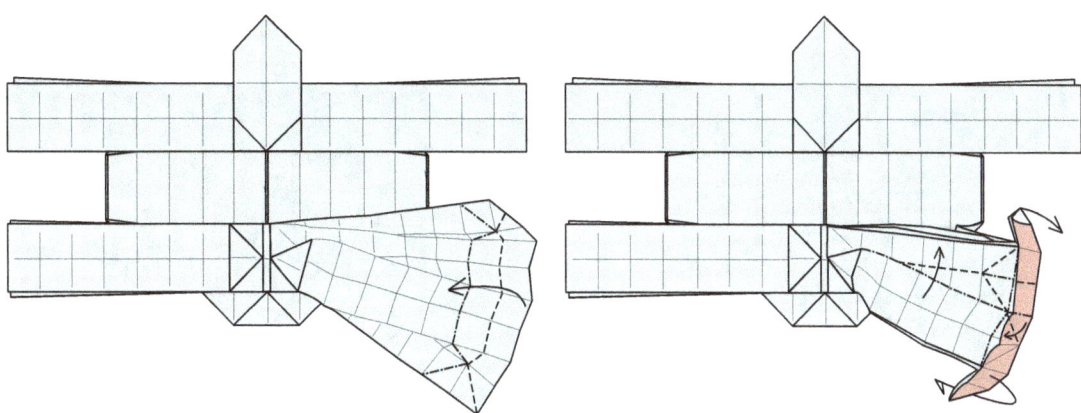

62. Valley fold inwards along the outer crease while swiveling in at the sides.

63. Flatten the pleated structure by collapsing as indicated.

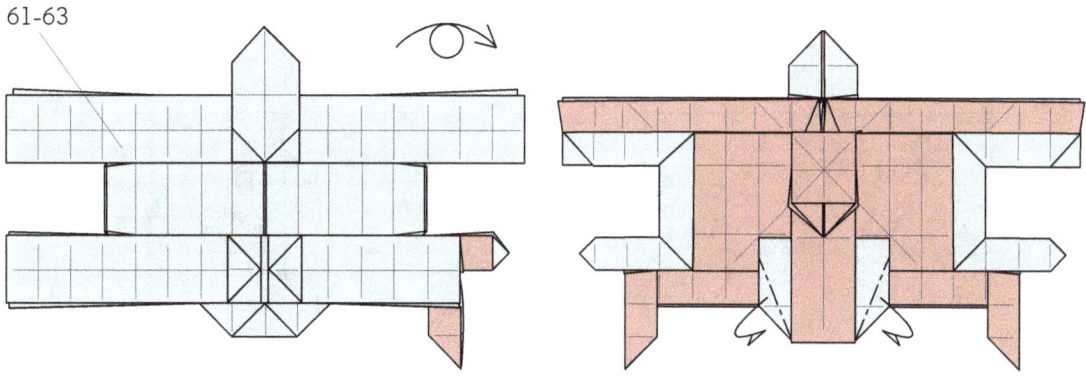

64. Repeat steps 61-63 in mirror image. Turn over.

65. Mountain fold the sides along the angle bisectors.

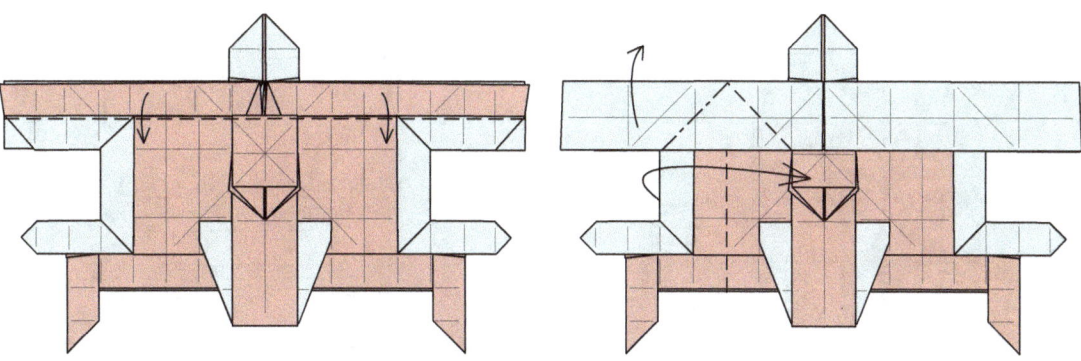

66. Valley fold one layer down at each side.

67. Valley fold over while swiveling out the top single layer.

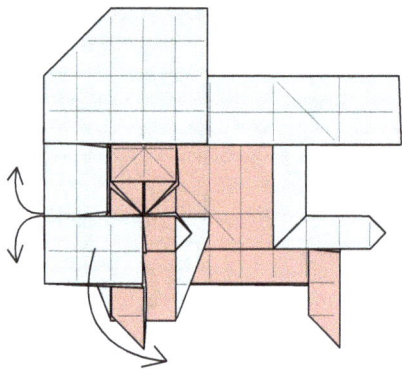

68. Pull apart the outermost pleat.

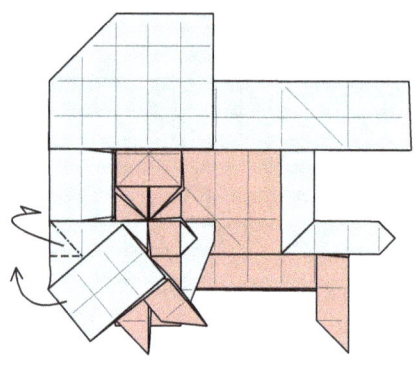

69. Swivel the thick section behind, pulling the model flat again.

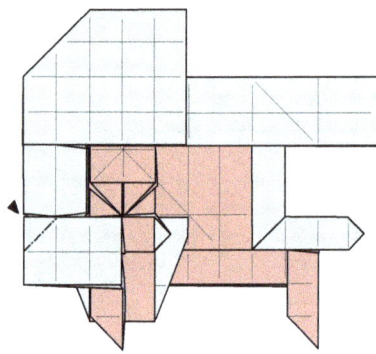

70. Sink the trapped corner.

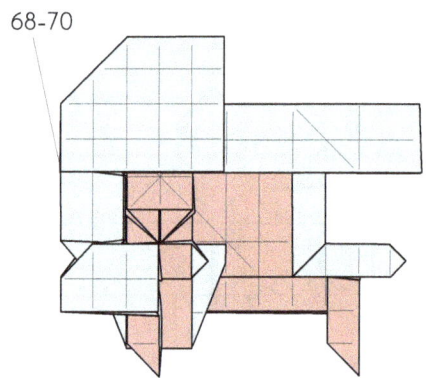

71. Repeat steps 68-70 on the section above.

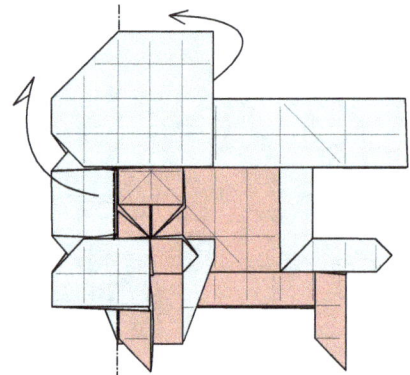

72. Mountain fold the side section down at a 90 degree angle.

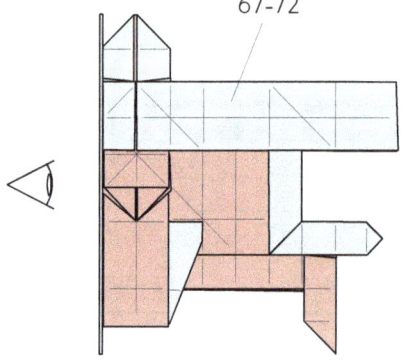

73. Repeat steps 67-72 in mirror image.

classic car

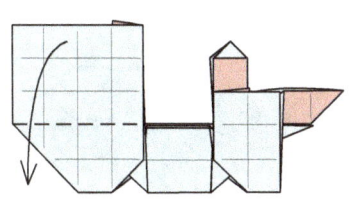

74. Valley fold down.

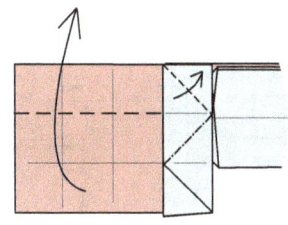

75. Valley fold up while swiveling out the side.

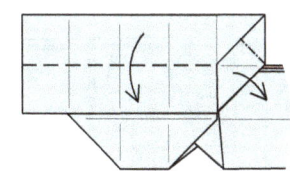

76. Valley fold down while swiveling out the side.

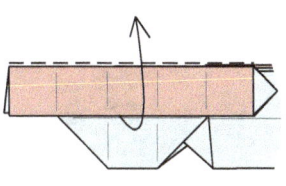

77. Swing the flap up.

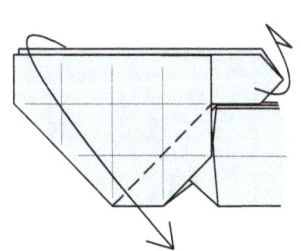

78. Lightly valley fold over.

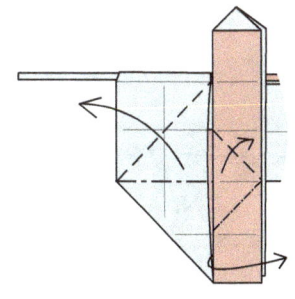

79. Swivel fold at each side.

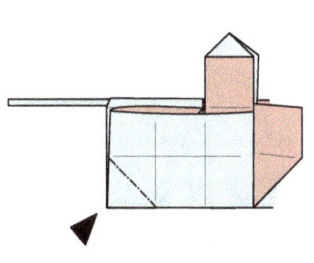

80. Sink the corner.

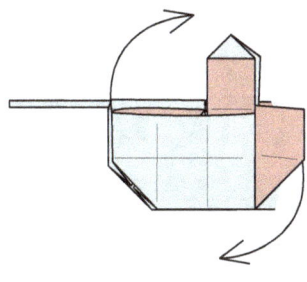

81. Rotate the cluster of flaps.

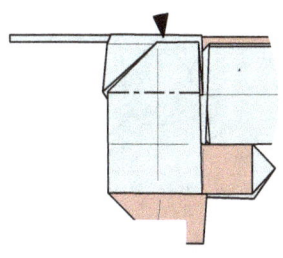

82. Closed reverse fold the flap.

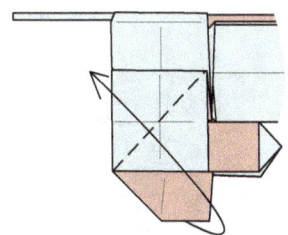

83. Valley fold up.

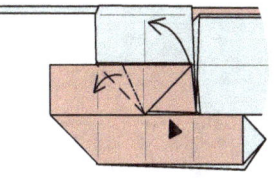

84. Form a pleat on the side, allowing the corner to pull up.

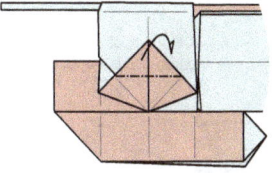

85. Mountain fold halfway.

classic car

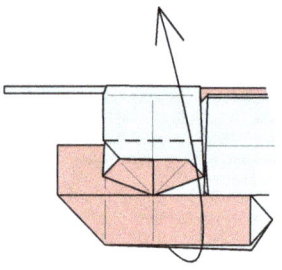
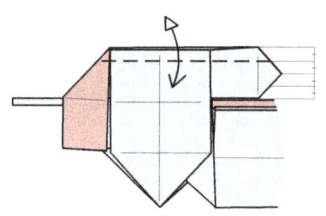
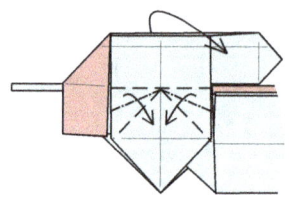

86. Swing the cluster of flaps up.

87. Precrease along the top edge.

88. Pleat through the cluster of layers, allowing the top edge to be pulled down.

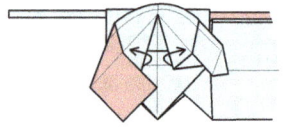
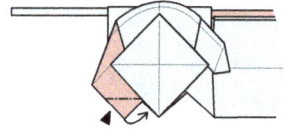
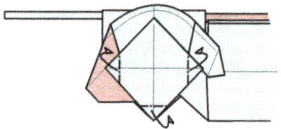

89. Pull around the top layer at each side.

90. Reverse fold the corner.

91. Mountain fold the three corners behind.

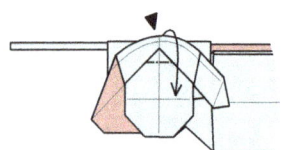
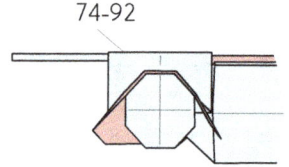
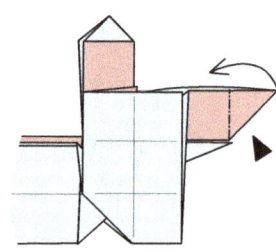

92. Flatten the top corner with a mountain fold, allowing the spoiler to flatten and get rounder.

93. Repeat steps 74-92 on the other side.

94. Reverse fold the corner.

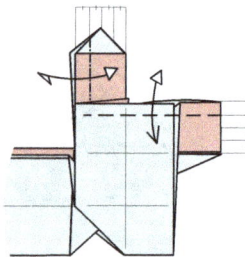
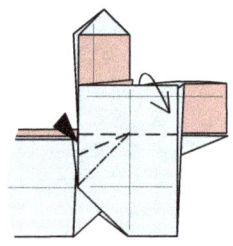
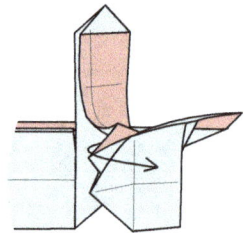

95. Precrease along the side and top edges.

96. Crimp the top layer, allowing the top edge to come down.

97. Swing the ridge over to reveal the layers underneath.

classic car

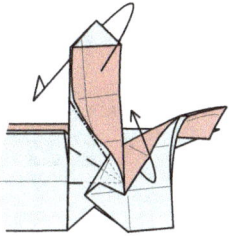

98. Pleat the top flap down, allowing it to open out.

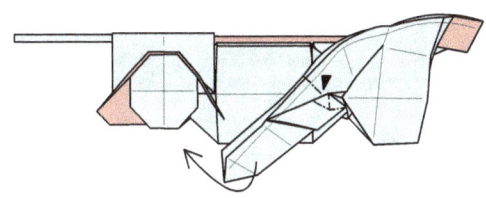

99. Squash the ridge, allowing the flap to rotate into position.

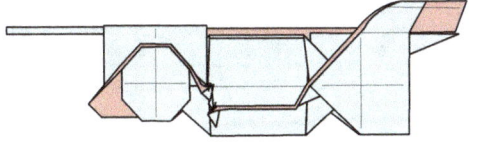

100. Tuck the corner into the pocket of the adjacent flap.

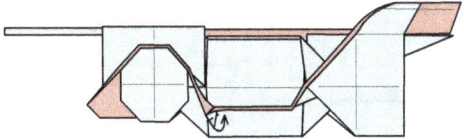

101. Fold the corner over and over to lock the flaps together.

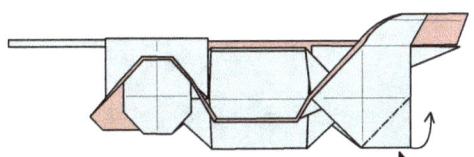

102. Reverse fold the corner.

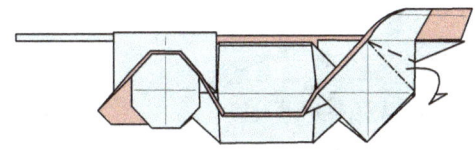

103. Pleat the flap down.

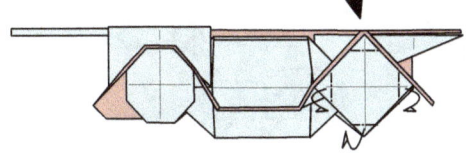

104. Shape the corners of the tire.

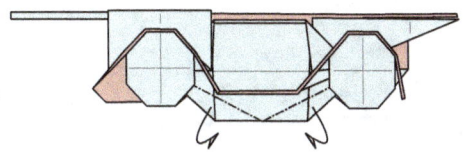

105. Mountain fold the corners behind.

classic car

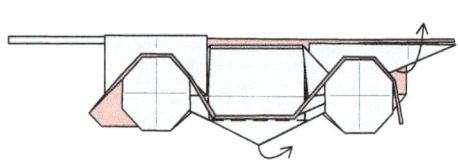
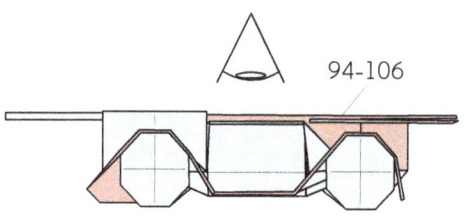

106. Fold the bottom flap up. Lift up the side flap.

107. Repeat steps 94-106 behind.

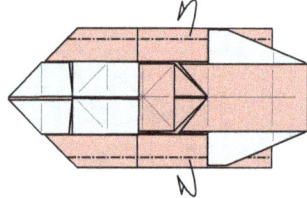
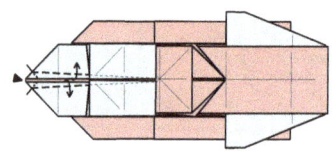
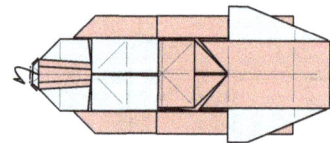

108. Top view. Mountain fold the edges along the existing creases.

109. Valley fold the edges outwards, squashing at the tip.

110. Wrap around a single layer.

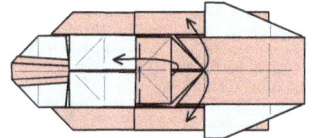
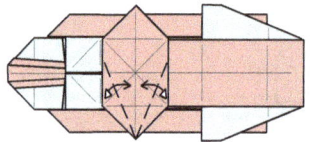
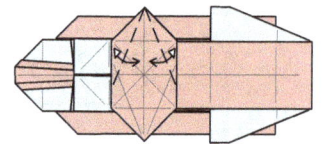

111. Open out the flap.

112. Precrease along the angle bisectors.

113. Precrease along the other set of angle bisectors.

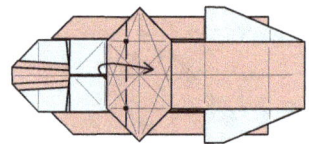
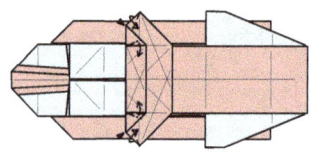
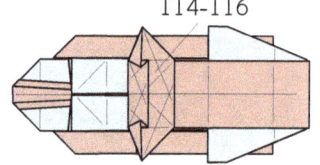

114. Valley fold through the dotted intersection of creases.

115. Swivel fold the sides.

116. Repeat steps 114-116 on the other side.

classic car

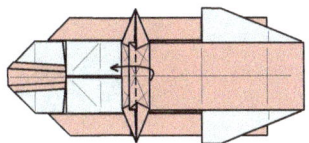

117. Fold the flap in half.

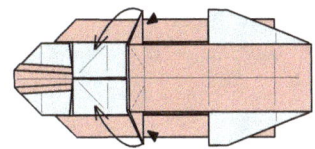

118. Reverse fold the side points.

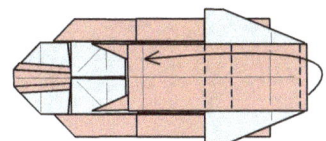

119. Fold the roof flap over, using folds at about 90 degrees.

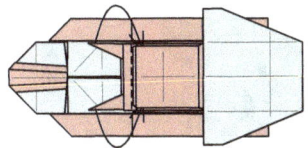

120. Fold the windshield flap up, tucking the tips into the pockets in the roof flap.

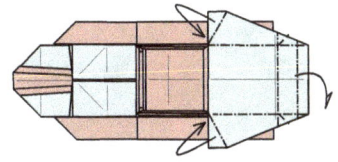

121. Tuck the corners into the pockets at the doors, forming the rear into a box shape.

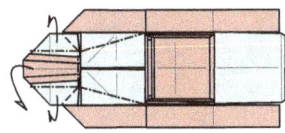

122. Fold the sides down, forming the front into a box shape.

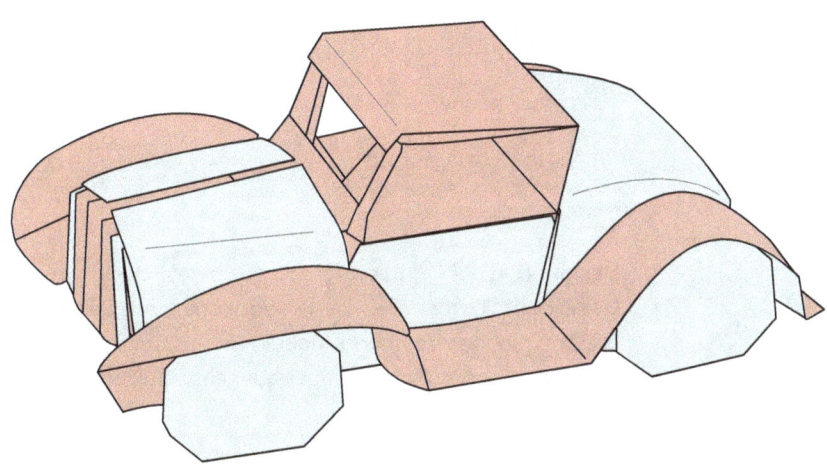

123. Completed *Classic Car*.

85

Dune Buggy

Designed in 1979, this is easily the oldest design in this collection. Coincidentally, it shares some sequences independently devised by origami pioneer Raymond McLain many years prior. This *Dune Buggy* features a handful of locking sequences, making it a fun model to fold.

dune buggy

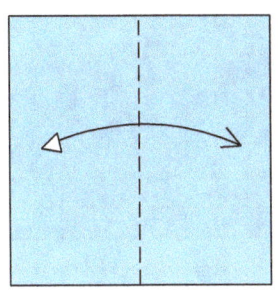

1. Precrease in half.

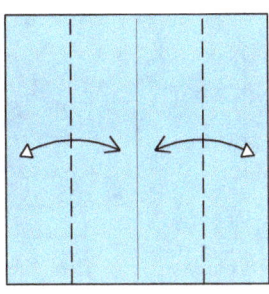

2. Precrease the sides in half.

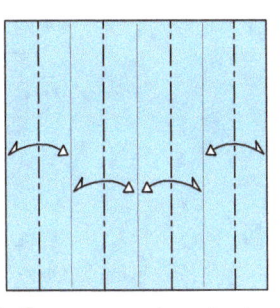

3. Precrease each section in half with a mountain fold.

4. Turn over.

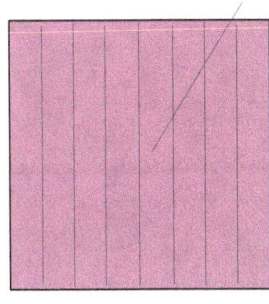

5. Repeat steps 1-3 horizontally.

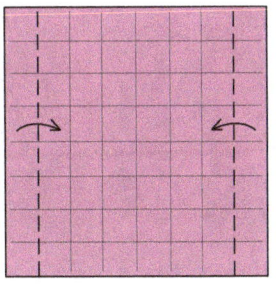

6. Valley fold the sides inwards.

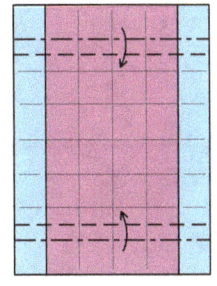

7. Pleat inwards to meet the existing creases.

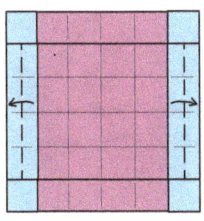

8. Valley fold the edges outwards, allowing swivels to form.

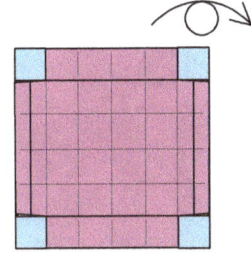

9. Turn over.

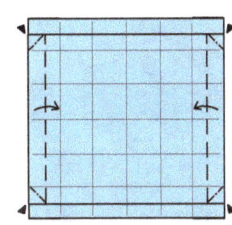

10. Valley fold the sides inwards, allowing the corners to squash.

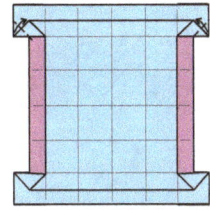

11. Valley fold the corners inwards.

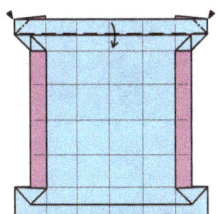

12. Valley fold the edge down, allowing the corners to squash.

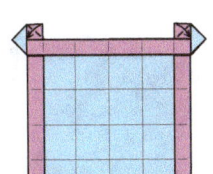

13. Valley fold the corners inwards.

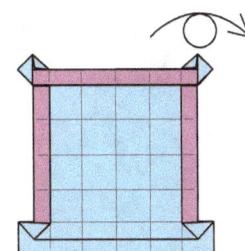

14. Turn over.

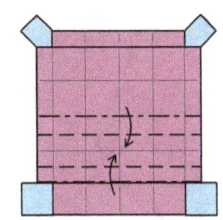

15. Pleat inwards towards the crease.

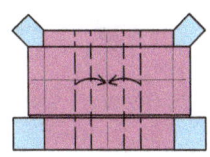

16. Pleat the sides towards the center.

d u n e b u g g y

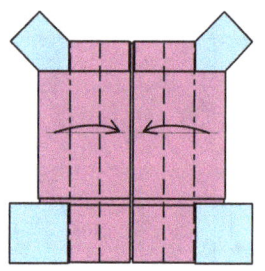

17. Pleat the sides towards the center.

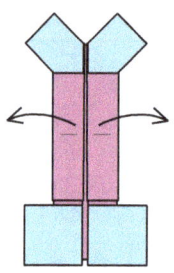

18. Unfold the two sets of pleats.

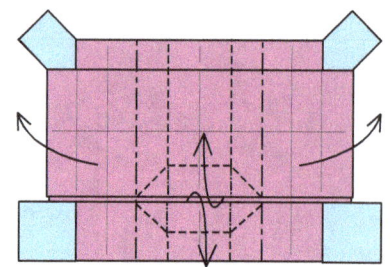

19. Bring the sides down while bringing all of the center layers up. The model will be 3-D.

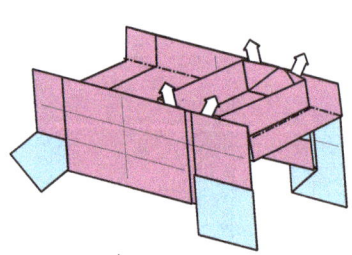

20. Invert the front and back sections up.

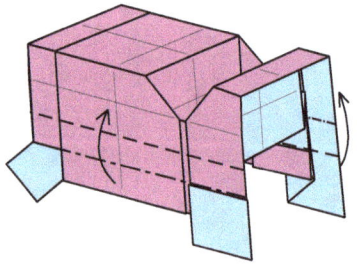

21. Pleat the sides up along the exiting creases.

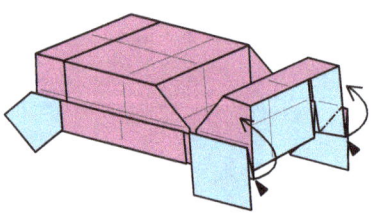

22. Reverse fold the corners.

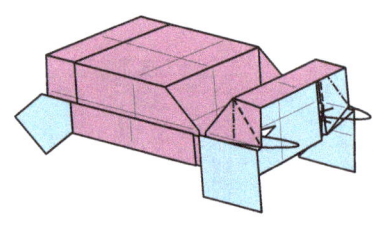

23. Reverse fold the flaps into the pockets.

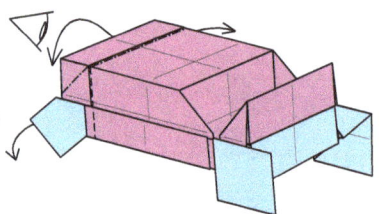

24. Reverse fold the edge down while swinging the sides outwards.

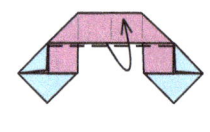

25. View from previous step. Wrap around a single layer.

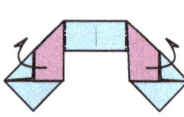

26. Swing the sides back.

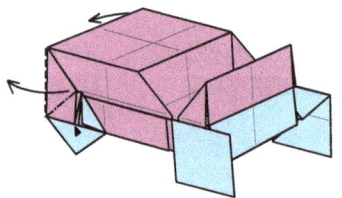

27. Valley fold the flaps forward, allowing squashes to form.

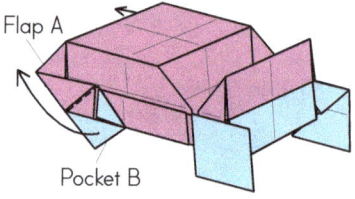

28. Valley fold the flaps forward, tucking flaps A into pockets B.

dune buggy

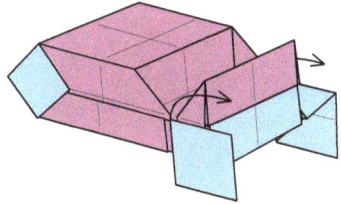

29. Rotate the square flaps.

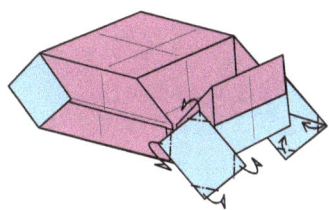

30. Mountain fold the corners.

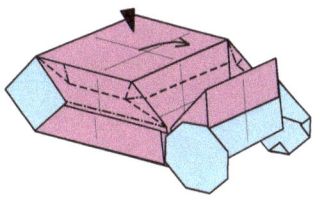

31. Collapse the top section down by inserting a rabbit ear along the sides.

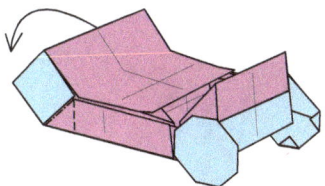

32. Crimp the sides, allowing the front to rotate down.

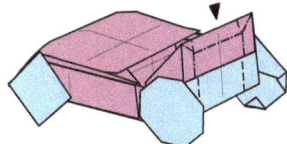

33. Open out the back and pinch the upper corners. You will have to push the sides in slightly to accomplish this.

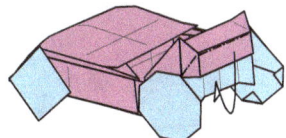

34. Reverse fold the edge.

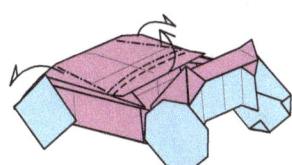

35. Crimp the windshield up, round the sides down, and crimp the grill down to taste (not shown).

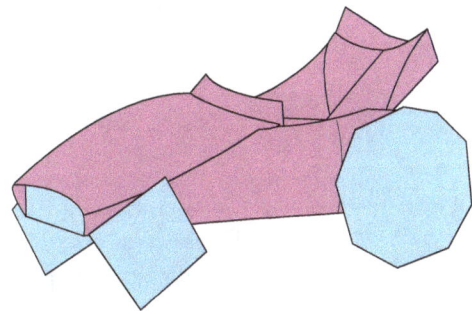

36. Completed *Dune Buggy*.

Biplane

Devising an origami biplane is not a trivial task and adding an alternating color pattern certainly adds to the complexity. One of the surprising elements is the pair of flaps that rest along the fuselage solely to add to this pattern. Also interesting is how the longest set of flaps (for the top wings) come from the middle portion of the paper.

biplane

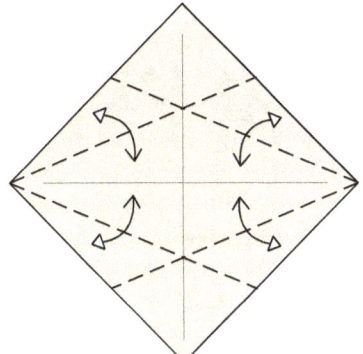
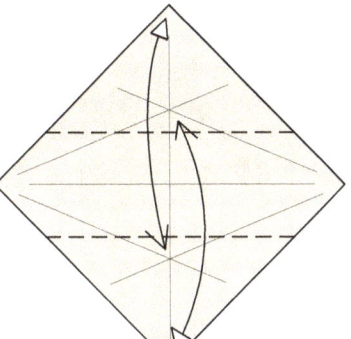
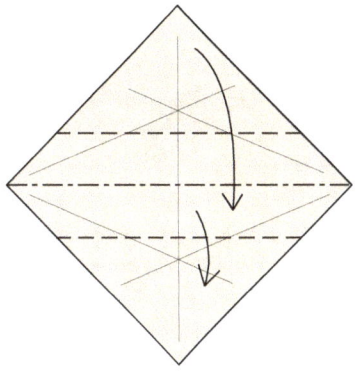

1. This will be the color of the body. Precrease along the angle bisectors.

2. Valley fold the corners to the intersections of creases and unfold.

3. Pleat along the existing creases.

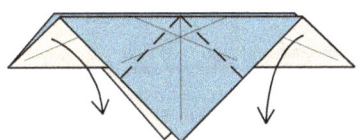
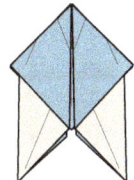
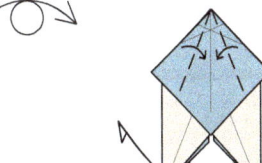

4. Valley fold to the center.

5. Turn over.

6. Fold the sides to the center, allowing the flaps to swing outwards.

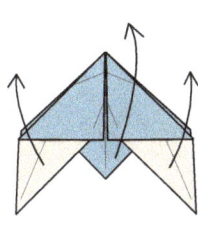
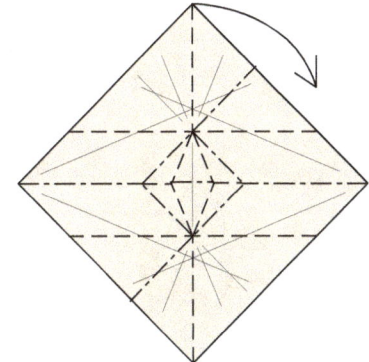
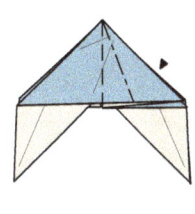

7. Unfold entirely.

8. Collapse.

9. Squash the center flap.

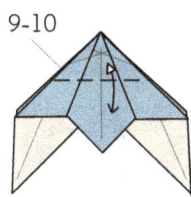
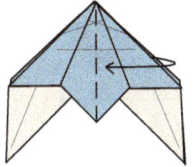
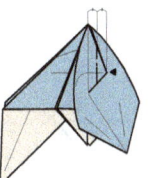

10. Valley fold down as far as possible and unfold. Repeat steps 9-10 behind.

11. Spread open to reveal a small flap.

12. Sink triangularly halfway.

biplane

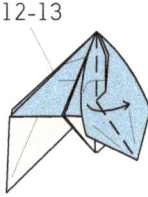

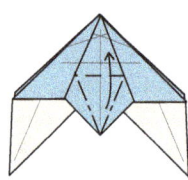

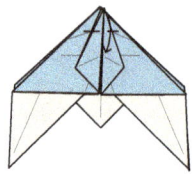

13. Close the flap back up. Repeat steps 12-13 on the other side.

14. Petal fold.

15. Valley fold to the intersection of creases.

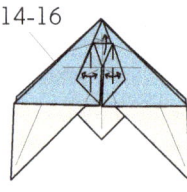

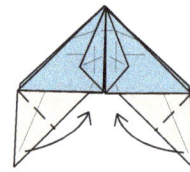

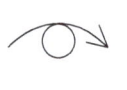

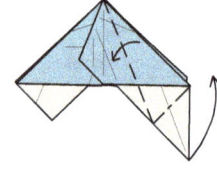

16. Precrease the sides of the flap and then open up. Repeat steps 14-16 behind.

17. Valley fold the corners. Turn over.

18. Swing a flap over, front and back.

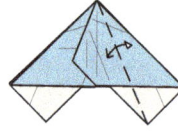

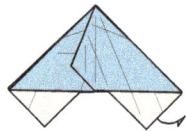

19. Precrease through all layers.

20. Unfold the bottom flap.

21. Squash fold. Do not flatten completely.

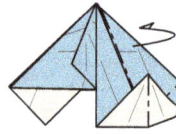

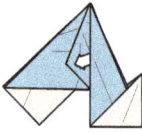

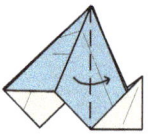

22. Wrap around and flatten.

23. Pull out a single layer.

24. Valley fold over.

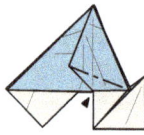

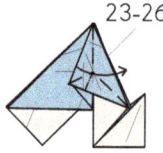

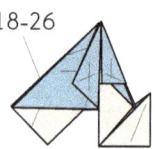

25. Reverse fold.

26. Swing over the flap while incorporating a reverse fold. Repeat steps 23-26 behind.

27. Repeat steps 18-26 in mirror image.

biplane

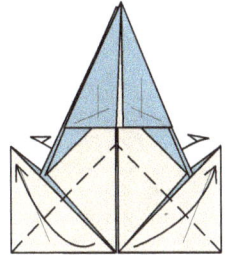

28. Valley fold the corners up.

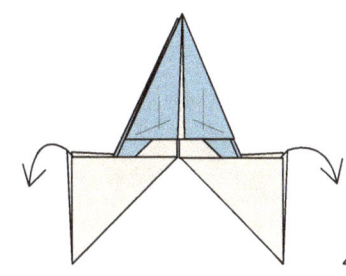

29. Pull out the hidden corners.

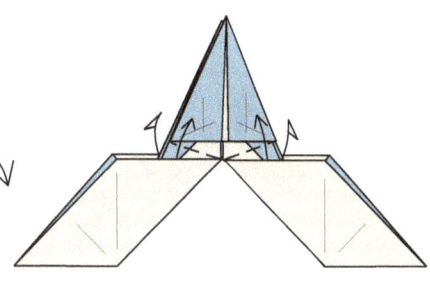

30. Pull out the hidden points.

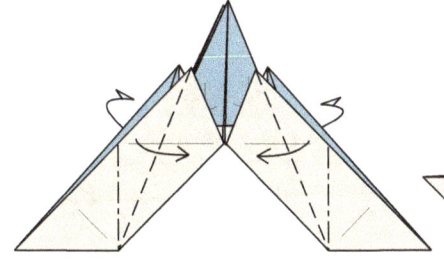

31. Crimp the sides.

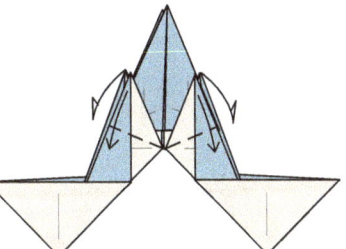

32. Valley fold down four points.

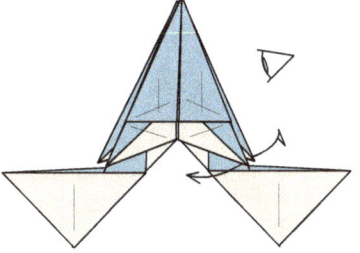

33. Stretch apart the sides.

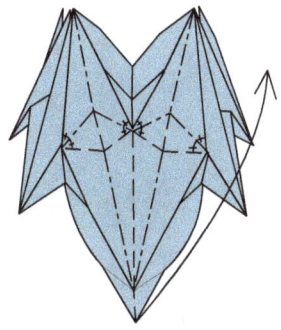

34. View from step 33. Double-crimp upwards and flatten.

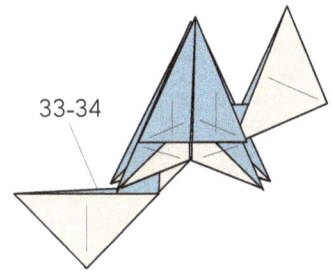

35. Repeat steps 33-34 on the other side.

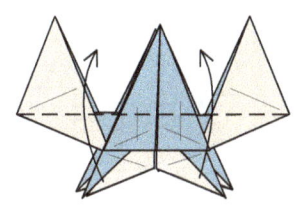

36. Lightly swing up the top section.

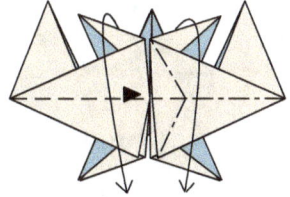

37. Swing back down while collapsing the top single layer outwards.

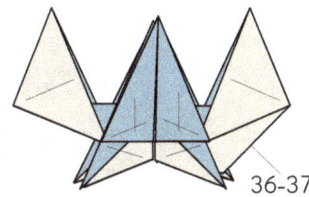

38. Repeat steps 36-37 behind.

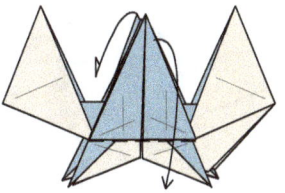

39. Swing down the flaps.

biplane

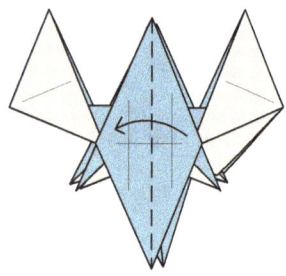

40. Swing over a layer, undoing a reverse fold. Repeat behind.

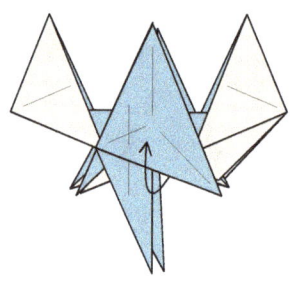

41. Wrap around a single layer. Repeat behind.

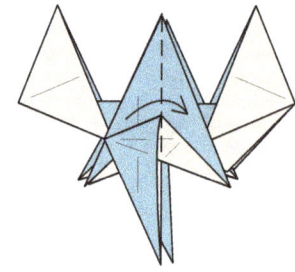

42. Swing back. Repeat behind.

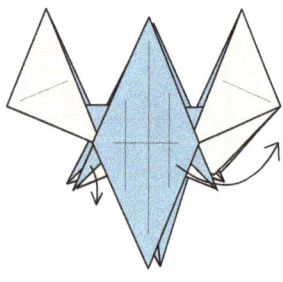

43. Pull the flap out, releasing layers at the left. Repeat behind.

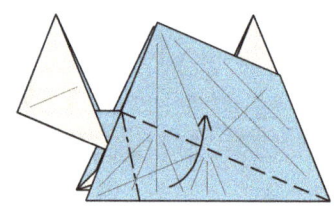

44. Form an asymmetrical squash. Repeat behind.

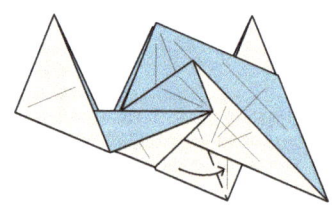

45. Valley fold a layer through. Repeat behind.

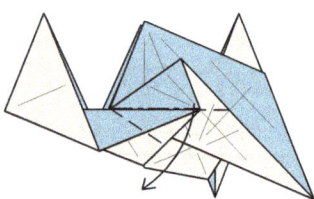

46. Swivel fold down. Repeat behind.

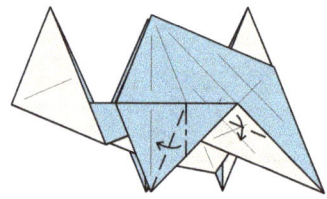

47. Swivel fold over. Repeat behind.

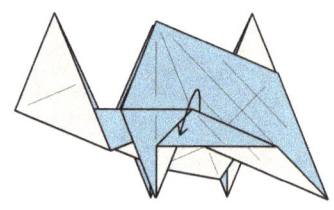

48. Bring a single layer to the surface (closed sink). Repeat behind.

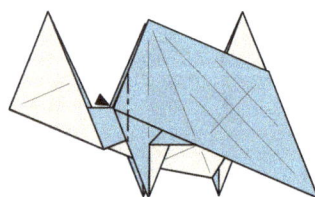

49. Sink triangularly, so as to match up with the folded edge in the middle. Repeat behind.

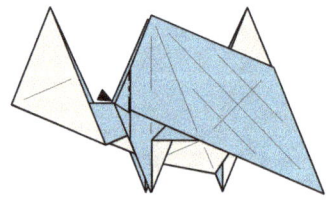

50. Sink triangularly again. Repeat behind.

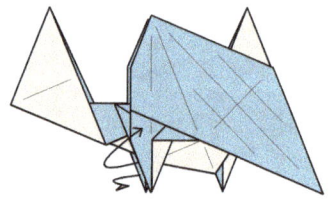

51. Wrap around a single layer. Repeat behind.

biplane

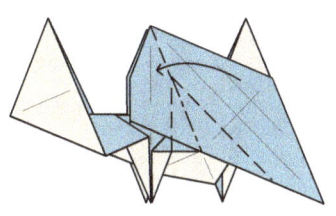
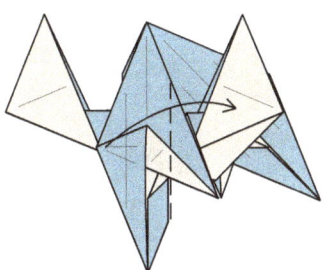
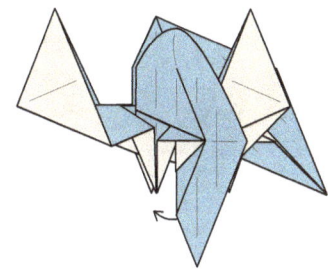

52. Swing the flap over while incorporating a reverse fold along existing creases.

53. Swing over two layers. The model will not lie flat.

54. Pull out a single layer from behind.

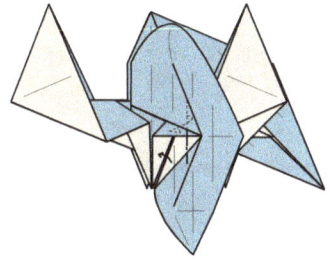
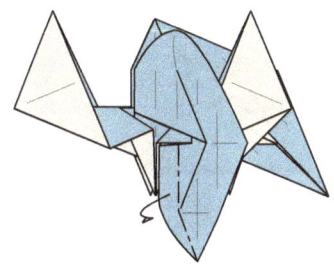
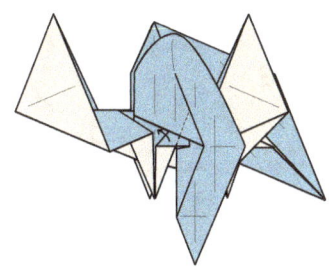

55. Swivel under.

56. Swing a single layer back.

57. Swivel up.

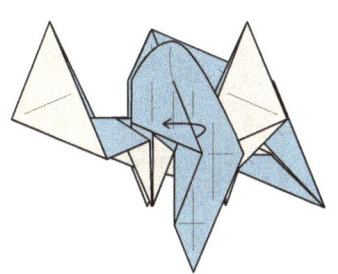
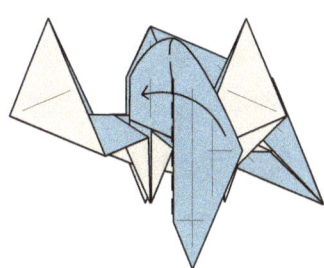
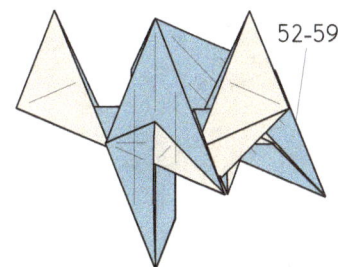

58. Wrap a single layer around (closed sink).

59. Close the model back up.

60. Repeat steps 52-59 behind.

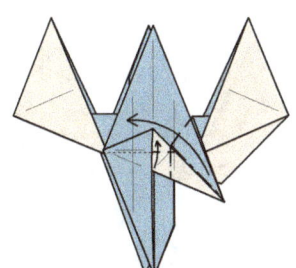
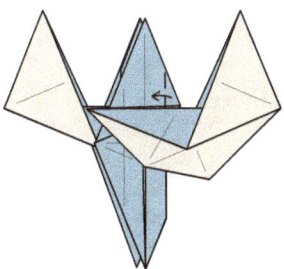
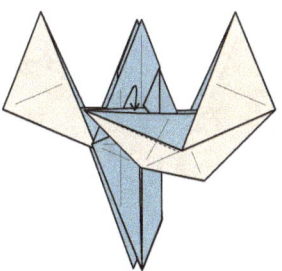

61. Swing over the flap while pulling up a layer through the pocket. Repeat behind.

62. Valley fold along the existing crease. Repeat behind.

63. Swivel down the hidden middle layer into the pocket. Repeat behind.

biplane

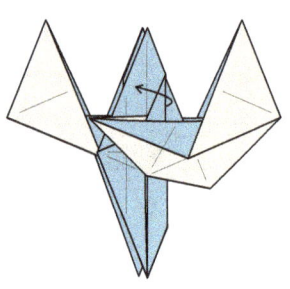

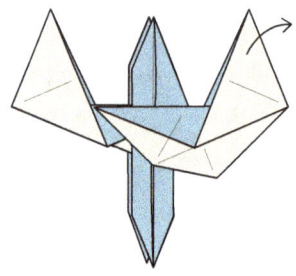

64. Bring a single layer to the surface (closed sink). Repeat behind.

65. Closed sink along the existing crease. Repeat behind.

66. Pull the point outwards.

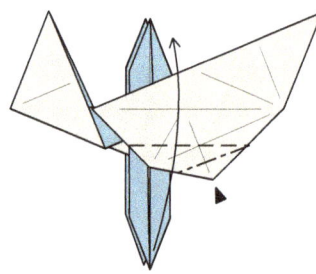
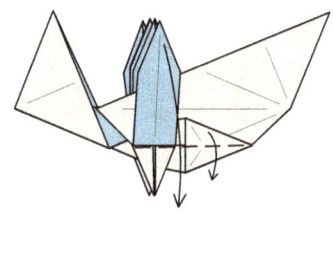
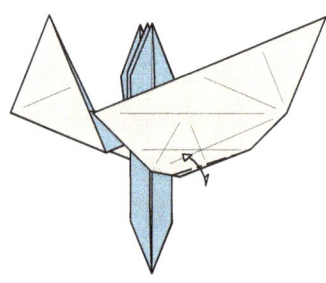

67. Bring the bottom points to the top, allowing the corners to spread sink.

68. Swing down.

69. Precrease. Repeat with the adjacent flap.

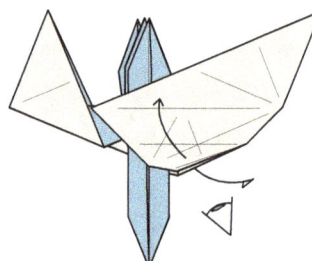
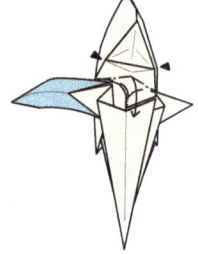
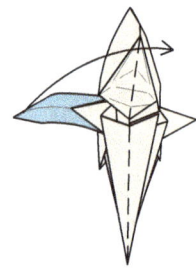

70. Spread apart.

71. View from step 71. Sink a single layer through from behind, using the creases from step 69.

72. The edges of the wing should now be flush. Close the model up.

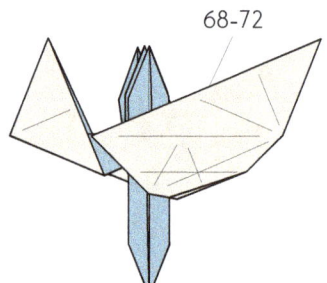
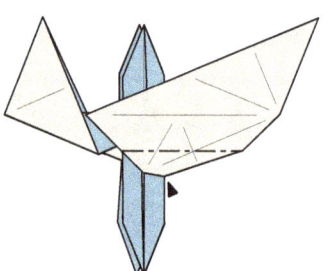
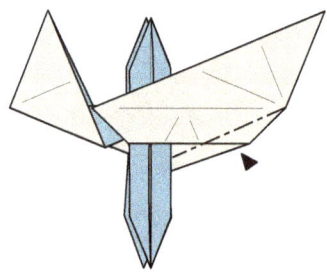

73. Repeat steps 68-72 behind.

74. Sink triangularly along the existing crease. Repeat behind.

75. Closed sink along the existing crease. Repeat behind.

biplane

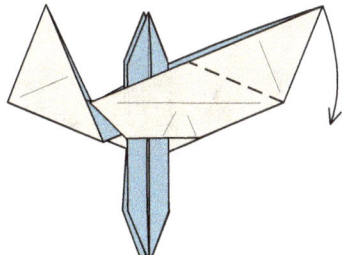
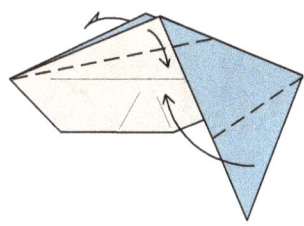
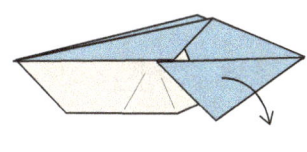

76. Outside reverse fold along the existing crease.

77. Detail of the tail. Valley fold along the angle bisectors.

78. Unfold.

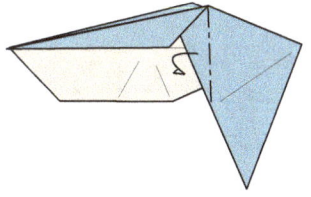
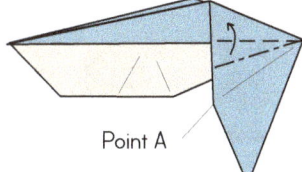
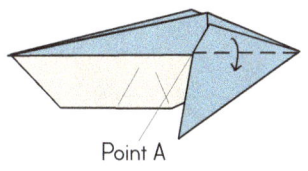

Point A

Point A

79. Swivel fold. Repeat behind.

80. Crimp upwards, so point A meets the colored raw edge.

81. Valley fold down. Repeat behind.

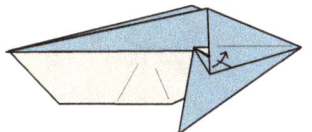
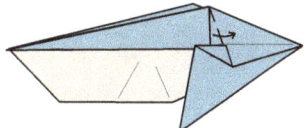
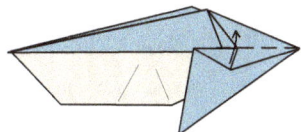

82. Valley fold along the angle bisector. Repeat behind.

83. Swivel fold over. Repeat behind.

84. Valley fold up. Repeat behind.

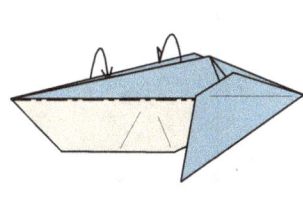
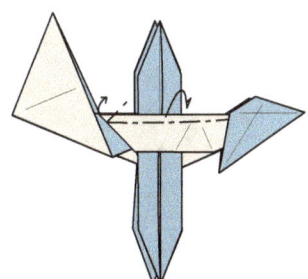
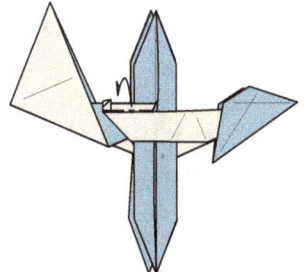

85. Mountain fold the top flaps into the pocket.

86. Mountain the double layer about 1/4th the width. Towards the tail, the fold will terminate at an angle, and at the other end, a swivel will form. Repeat behind.

87. Reverse fold back. Repeat behind.

biplane

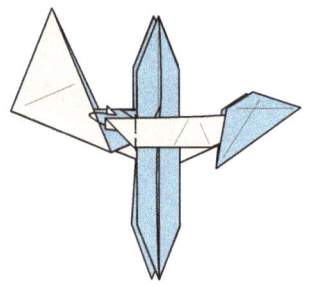

88. Mountain fold behind the wing. Repeat behind.

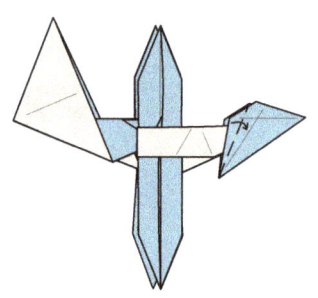

89. Valley fold to the existing crease. Repeat behind.

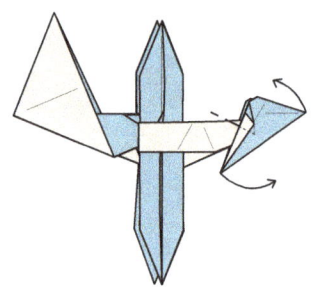

90. Crimp the tail section. See step 91 for positioning.

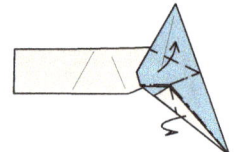

91. Collapse upwards.

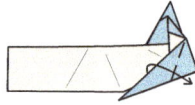

92. Outside reverse fold.

93. Sink the indicated regions.

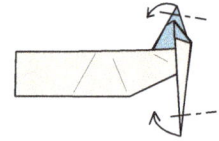

94. Reverse fold the indicated areas.

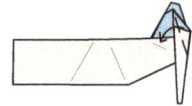

95. Valley fold over a single layer. Repeat behind.

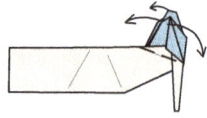

96. Pull the center flap foward while pulling the side flaps outwards.

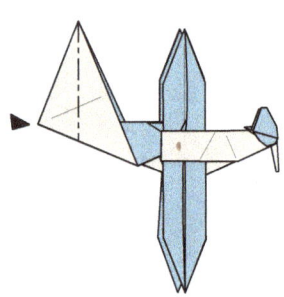

97. Open sink.

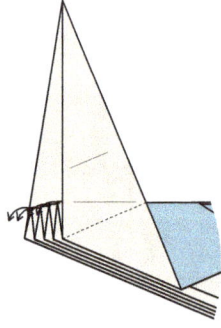

98. Reverse the four hidden corners down.

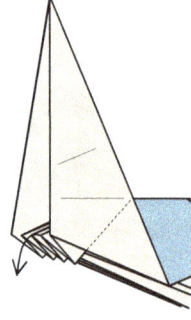

99. Reverse the first of the three points down. Note how the bottom five layers are distributed.

biplane

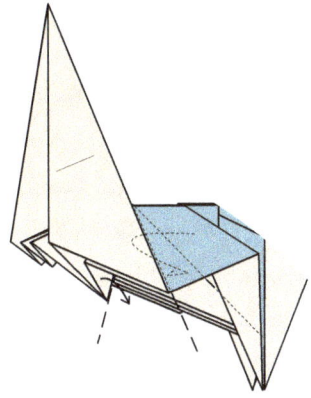

100. Swivel fold.

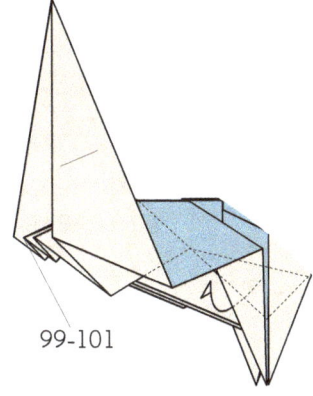

101. Reverse fold into the pocket. Repeat steps 99-101 behind.

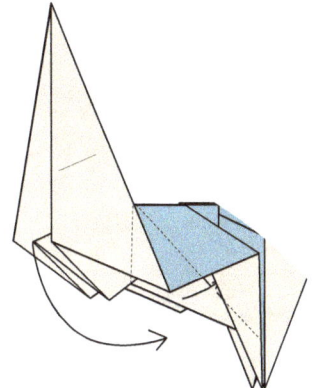

102. Swivel fold.

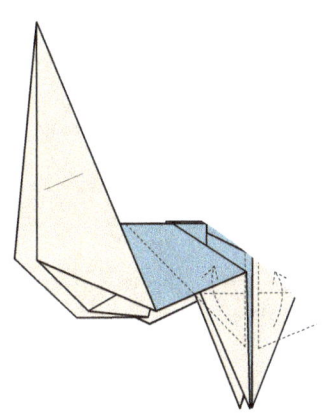

103. Tuck the bottom hidden points into the center of the model.

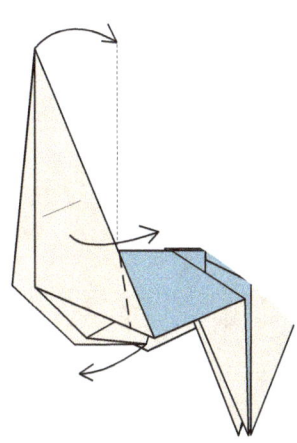

104. Spread apart the flap flat, while pulling it into an upright position.

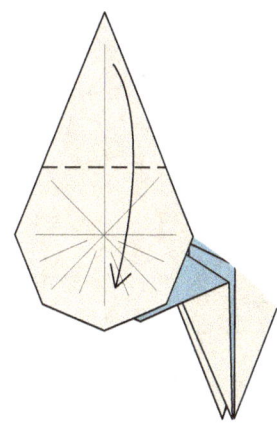

105. Valley fold down.

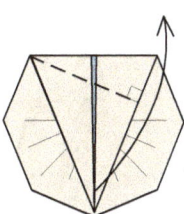

106. Valley fold up.

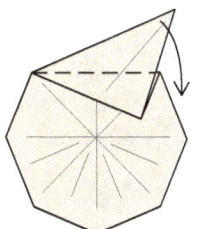

107. Valley fold down.

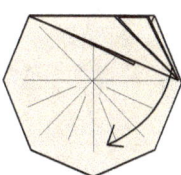

108. Undo the pleat.

biplane

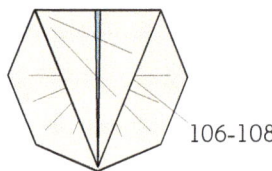

109. Repeat steps 106-108 in mirror image.

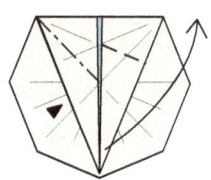

110. Form an asymmetrical squash.

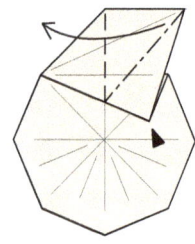

111. Squash fold.

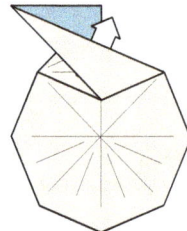

112. Pull out a single layer.

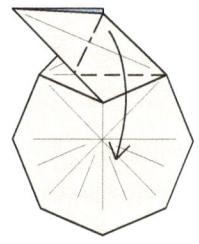

113. Squash fold.

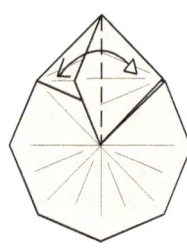

114. Precrease.

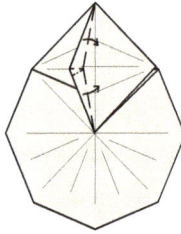

115. Rabbit ear.

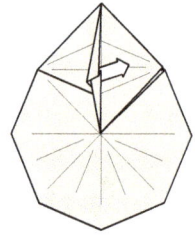

116. Unsink.

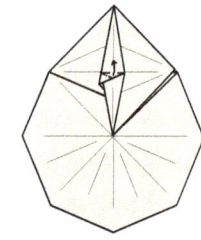

117. Swivel fold up.

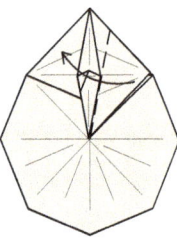

118. Valley fold over.

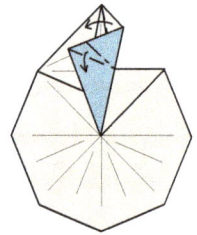

119. Swivel fold.

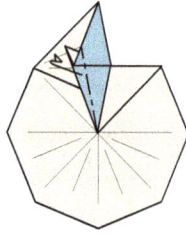

120. Mountain fold behind.

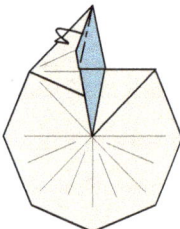

121. Mountain fold behind.

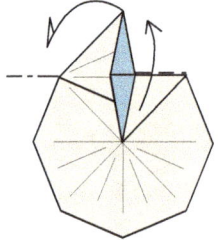

122. Flip the points.

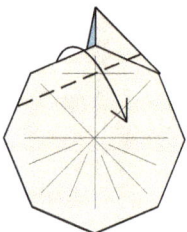

123. Valley fold through the intersection of creases. See step 124 for positioning.

biplane

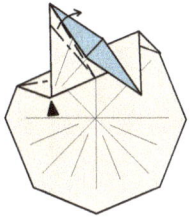

124. Spread squash.

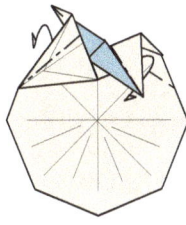

125. Swivel fold at each side.

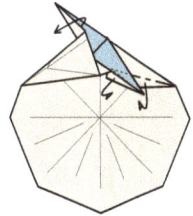

126. Swivel fold at the right. Bring the colored layer to the surface.

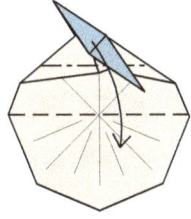

127. Pleat downwards.

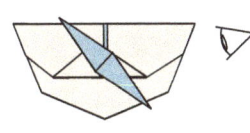

128. Completed propeller.

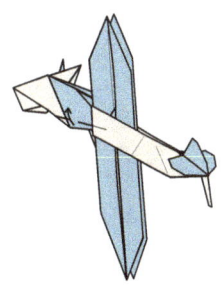

129. Valley fold up (there are no reference points).

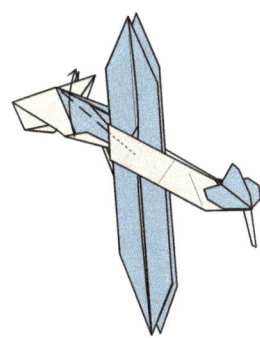

130. Pull the single layer up as far as possible.

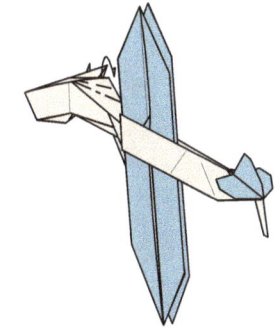

131. Pleat the excess into the center pocket.

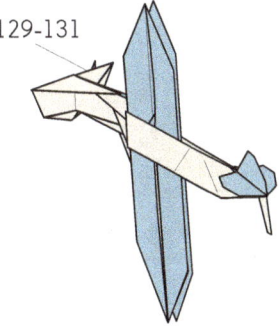

132. Repeat steps 129-131 behind.

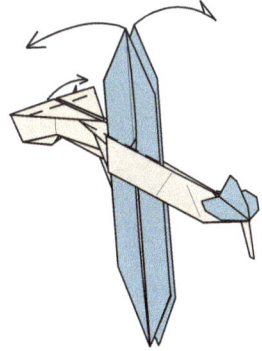

133. Spread the wings apart, allowing the front to spread apart too. To flatten, fold the top of the cowl over.

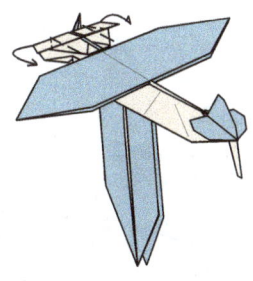

134. Collapse the sides inwards at 90º. You can trim the sides to taste with mountain folds.

135. Completed cowl.

biplane

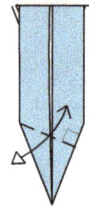 136. View of the lower wing. Precrease.

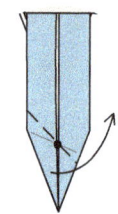 137. Valley fold at 45° through the dotted intersection.

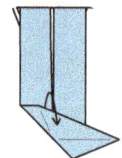 138. Wrap a single layer around.

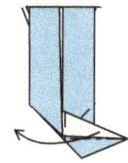 139. Squash fold over.

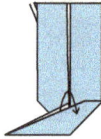 140. Wrap a single layer around.

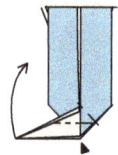 141. Spread squash.

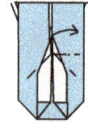 142. Rabbit ear the tip of the strut.

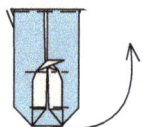 143. Raise the wing and strut, tucking its tip into the pocket on the upper wing. Repeat steps 136–143 on other wing.

 144. Detail of the landing gear. Precrease.

 145. Valley fold up.

 146. Pull out a single layer from each side.

 147. Valley fold down while incorporating reverse folds.

 148. Shape with mountain folds.

 149. Round off with mountain folds.

 150. Completed wheel. Repeat steps 144–149 behind.

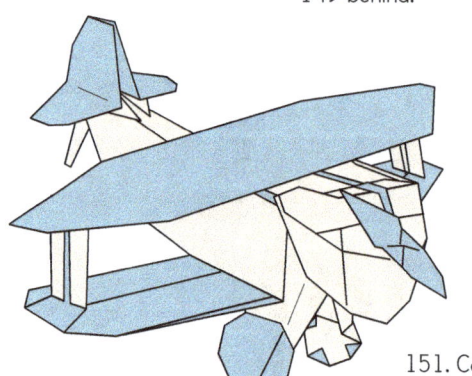

151. Completed *Biplane*.

Catching a Plane

This model continues the biplane theme with a few other elements thrown in. The primate portion is of course the focal point and provides an excellent vehicle to exercise some interesting shaping folds (the dip around the eyes adds for a lot of expression. Much of the paper and folding is devoted towards the plane section, making this composition an unusual part of this collection.

catching a plane

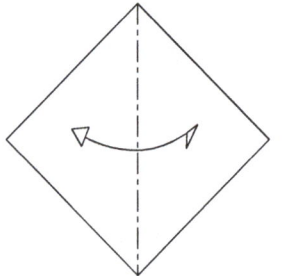
1. Precrease in half.

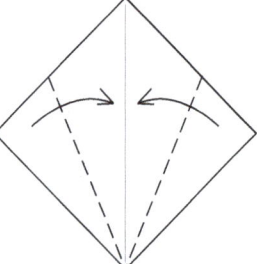
2. Valley fold to the center.

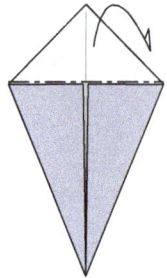
3. Mountain fold the corner.

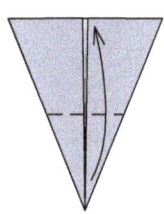
4. Valley fold to the top.

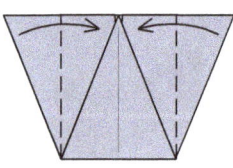
5. Valley fold the sides to the center.

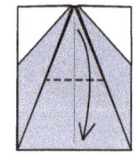
6. Valley fold to the bottom edge.

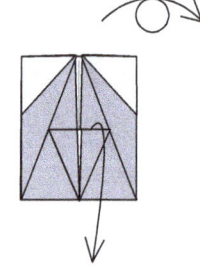
7. Swing down the bottom flap and turn over.

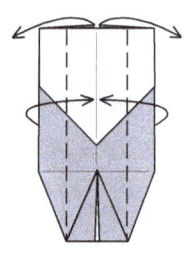
8. Valley fold the sides to the center, allowing the flaps from behind to flip forward.

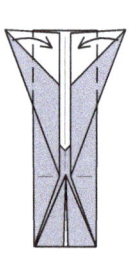
9. Valley fold the corners to the center.

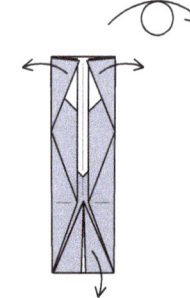
10. Unfold the sides and bottom.

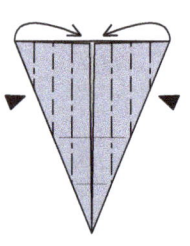
11. Reverse fold the sides in and out along the existing creases.

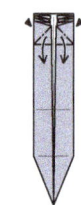
12. Squash fold the top corners down.

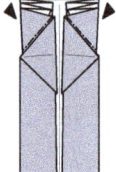
13. Reverse fold the next set of corners.

14. Pull the corners down, stretching the set of center flaps flat.

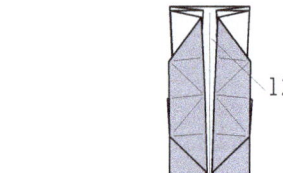
15. Repeat steps 12-14 on the remaining sets of pleats.

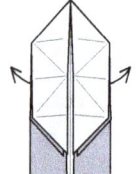
16. Pull out the trapped single layers.

catching a plane

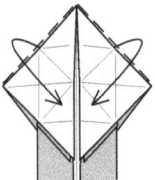 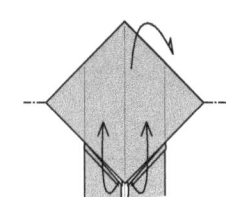 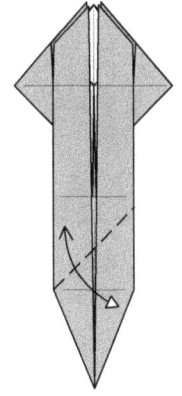 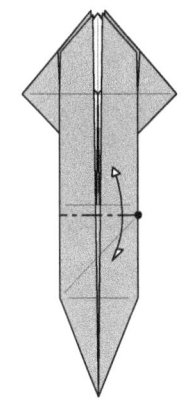

17. Wrap around the flap from behind.

18. Flip the flap back.

19. Precrease.

20. Precrease again.

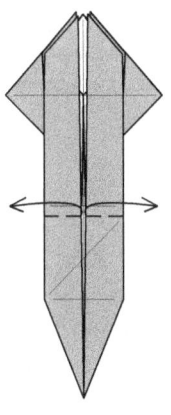 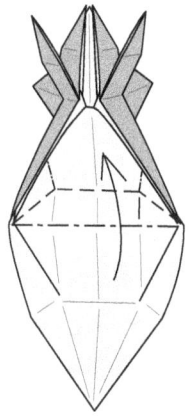 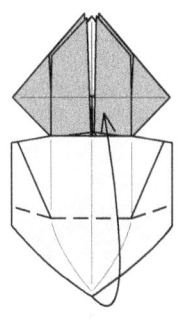 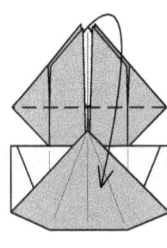

21. Open out the side layers, allowing a ridge to form at the last crease.

22. Collapse upwards.

23. Fold the flap up to flatten.

24. Flip the flaps back down.

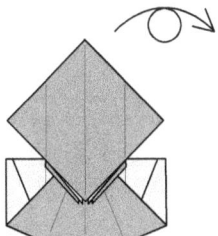 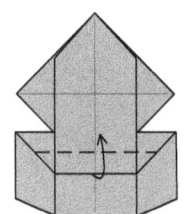 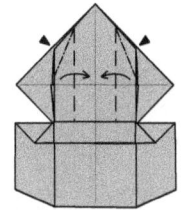 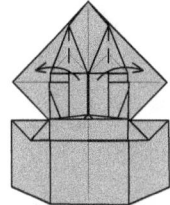

25. Turn over.

26. Valley fold the edge up.

27. Swivel in the sides, allowing the corners to squash flat.

28. Fold the sides back out.

105

catching a plane

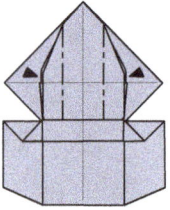
29. Closed sink the sides.

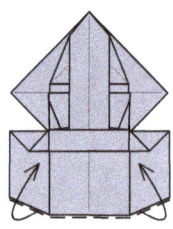
30. Wrap around the single layer from behind.

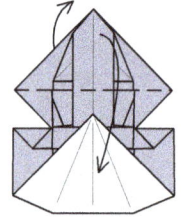
31. Flip the flap down.

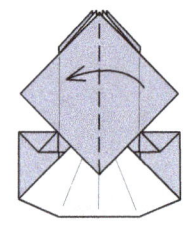
32. Swing over one layer.

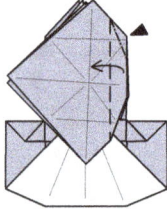
33. Valley fold in the side, allowing the corner to squash flat.

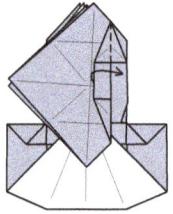
34. Swing the side back out.

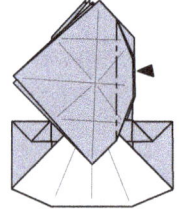
35. Closed sink the side.

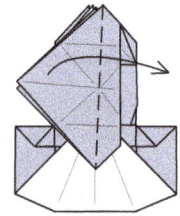
36. Swing the flap back over.

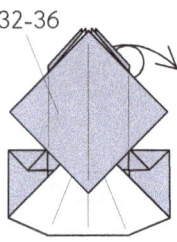
37. Repeat steps 32-36 in mirror image. Turn over.

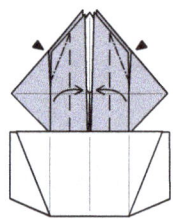
38. Swivel in the sides, allowing the corners to squash flat.

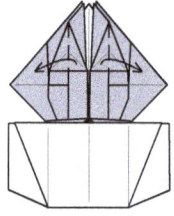
39. Swing the sides back out.

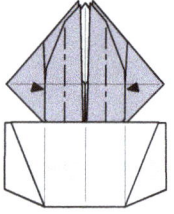
40. Closed sink the sides.

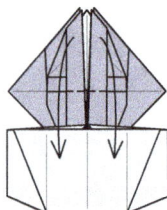
41. Swing the flaps down.

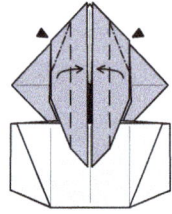
42. Valley fold in the sides, allowing the corners to squash flat.

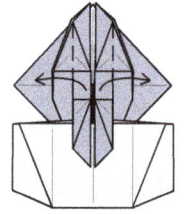
43. Swing the sides back out.

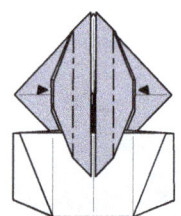
44. Closed sink the sides.

catching a plane

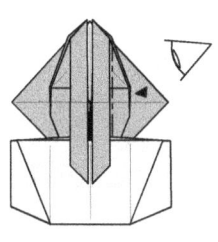

45. Open sink the flap.

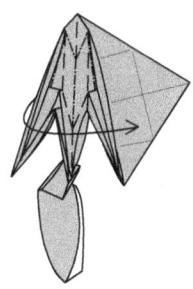

46. View from previous step in progress.

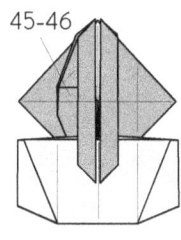

47. Repeat steps 45-46 on the other side.

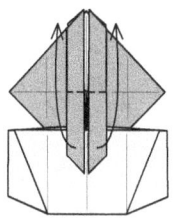

48. Swing the flaps up.

49. Turn over.

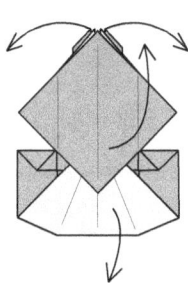

50. Open out the center portion.

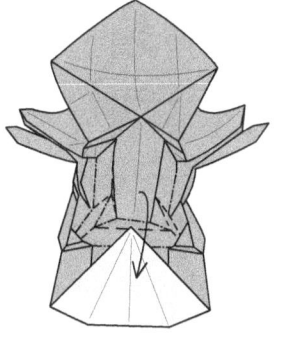

51. Reform the direction of some of the creases and flatten.

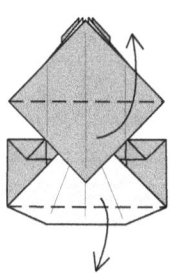

52. Lightly fold the flaps out of the way.

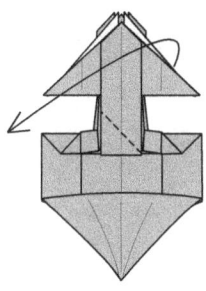

53. Swing over the cluster of flaps.

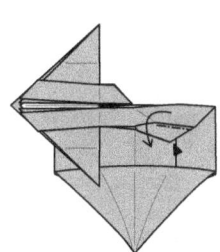

54. Sink the corner in, allowing the layers to flatten.

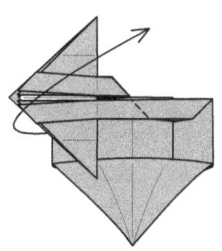

55. Swing the flaps back up.

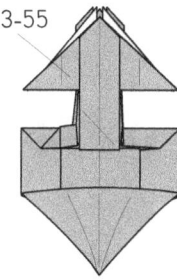

56. Repeat steps 53-55 in mirror image.

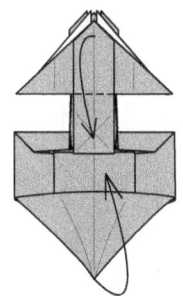

57. Bring the flaps back towards the middle.

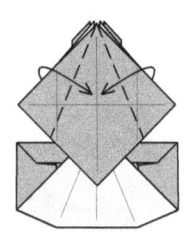

58. Valley fold to the center.

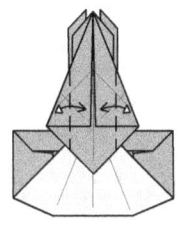

59. Precrease to the center.

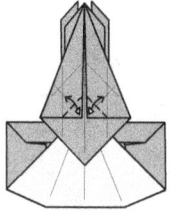

60. Precrease the corner flaps.

catching a plane

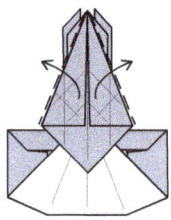 61. Open out the flaps.

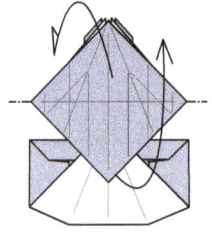 62. Flip the flaps behind.

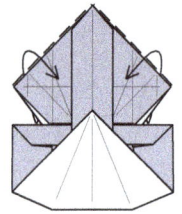 63. Wrap around a single layer from behind.

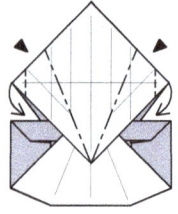 64. Reverse fold the sides in and out.

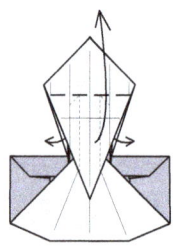 65. Valley fold up, allowing the inner layers to squash outwards.

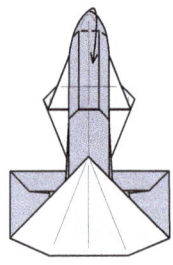 66. Squash the tip down to flatten it.

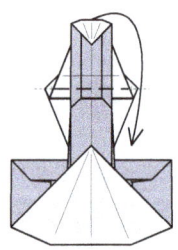 67. Valley fold down, alliging with the outer corners.

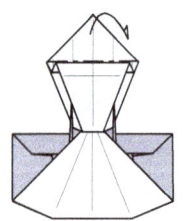 68. Mountain fold to align with the front edges.

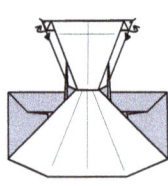 69. Reverse fold the corners.

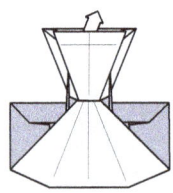 70. Unsink the single layer.

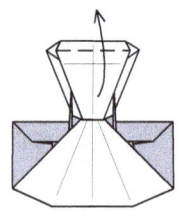 71. Swing the top flap up.

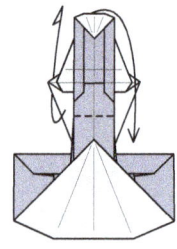 72. Flip the top section down.

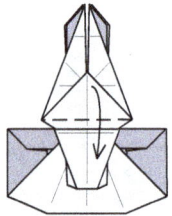 73. Swing the top flap down.

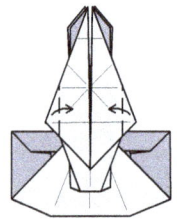 74. Valley fold the sides in.

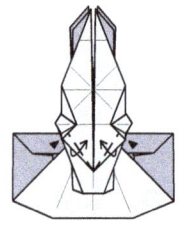 75. Swivel the edges in.

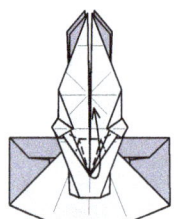 76. Valley fold the flap up while swiveling in the sides.

catching a plane

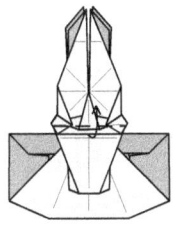
77. Valley fold the edges up.

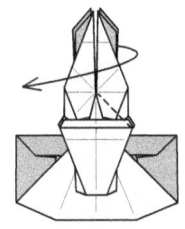
78. Valley fold the flaps over.

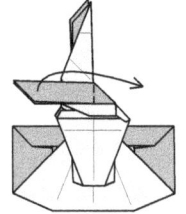
79. Swing over one flap.

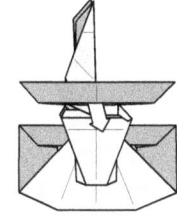
80. Unsink.

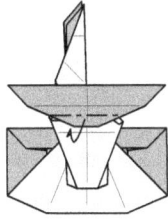
81. Mountain fold about 1/4 of the width.

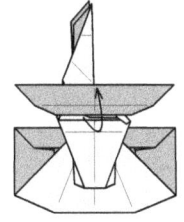
82. Pull around the flap to the surface.

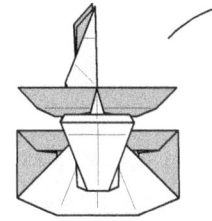
83. Turn over.

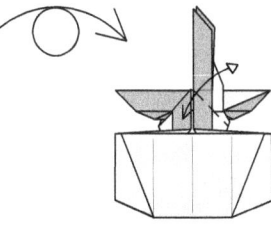
84. Precrease the top flaps.

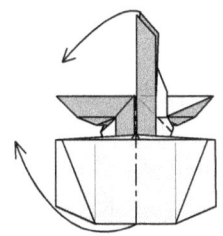
85. Lightly fold the bottom flap in half while pulling it over with the top flaps.

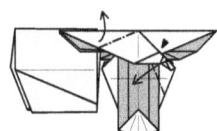
86. Swivel the flap over.

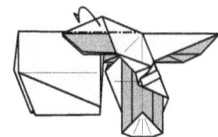
87. Mountain fold into the pocket.

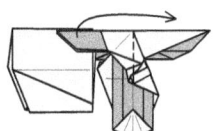
88. Swing over the top flap.

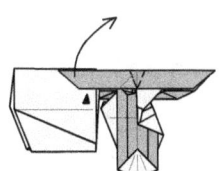
89. Squash fold up as symmetrically as possible.

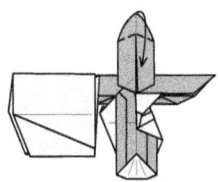
90. Wrap around the top corner to flatten.

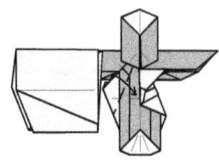
91. Valley fold the cluster of flaps towards the center.

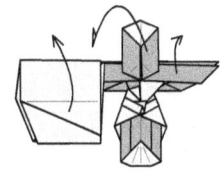
92. Flip the flaps over to open out the left flap. The center will not lie flat.

catching a plane

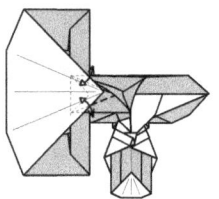

93. Precrease along the hidden angle bisectors.

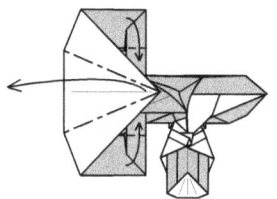

94. Petal fold the flap over.

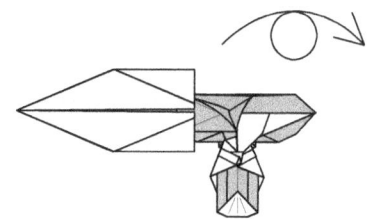

95. Turn over.

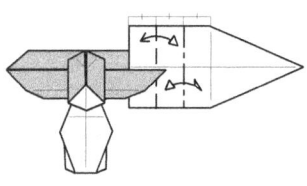

96. Precrease the indicated section into thirds.

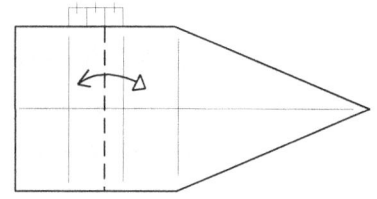

97. Detail of the flap. Precrease along the indicated 1/3rd mark.

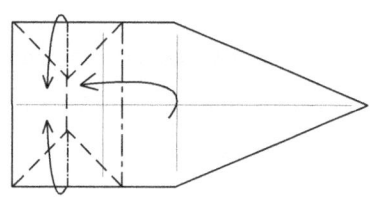

98. Pleat the flap over while reverse folding through all layers.

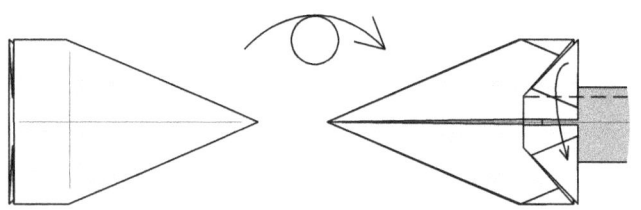

99. Turn over.

100. Swing down the top flap.

101. Pull out a single layer.

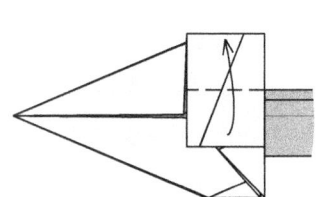

102. Close the flap back up.

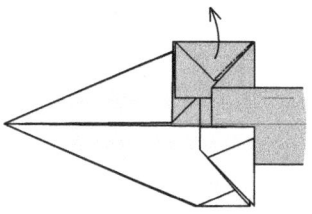

103. Pull out the trapped layers and flatten.

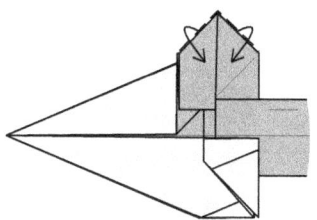

104. Wrap around the layers from behind.

catching a plane

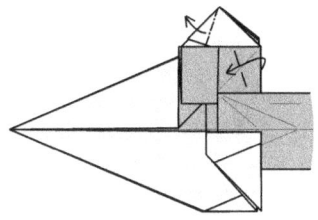
105. Swivel over a single layer.

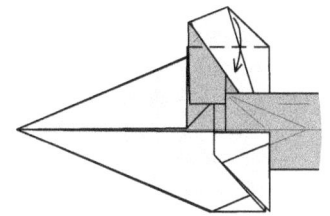
106. Valley fold down.

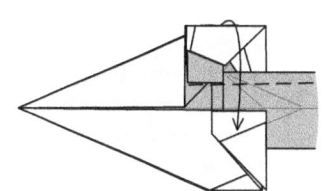
107. Open out the flap.

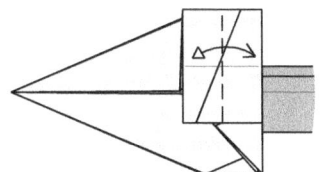
108. Precrease the top layer in half.

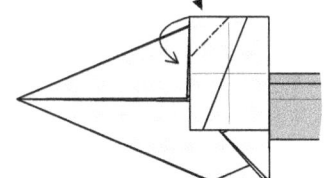
109. Reverse fold the corner.

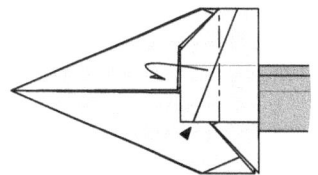
110. Reverse fold the single layer inside.

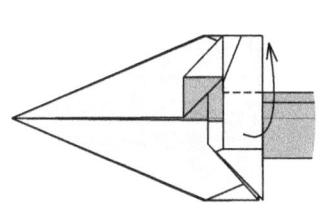
111. Swing the flap back up.

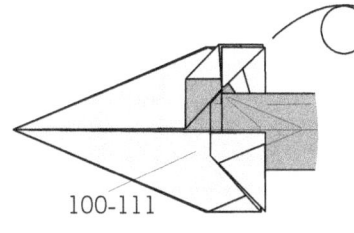
112. Repeat steps 100-111 on the bottom. Turn over.

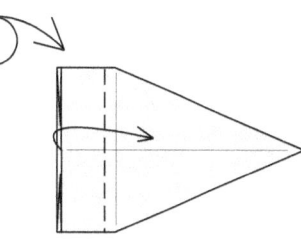
113. Open out the flap.

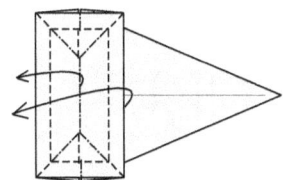
114. Close the flap back up while sinking the top layer outwards.

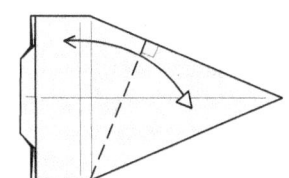
115. Precrease.

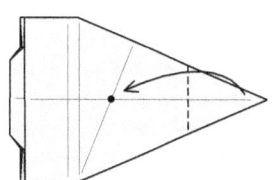
116. Valley fold to the dotted intersection.

111

catching a plane

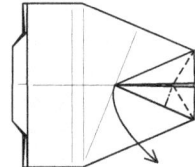

117. Rabbit ear the flap down.

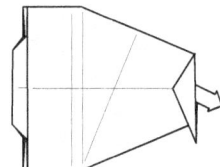

118. Pull out the single layer.

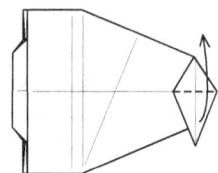

119. Swing the flap up.

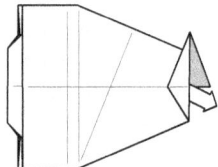

120. Pull out the single layer.

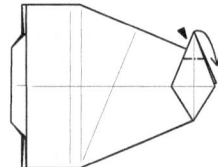

121. Reverse fold the tip.

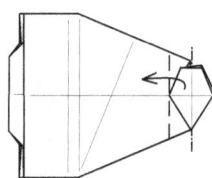

122. Pleat the flap forward.

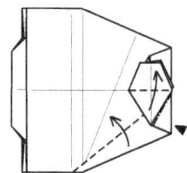

123. Swing the flap up while squash folding.

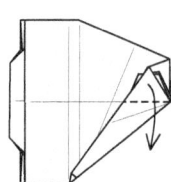

124. Swing the flap back down.

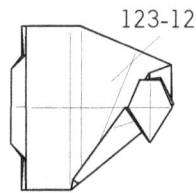

125. Repeat steps 123-124 at the top.

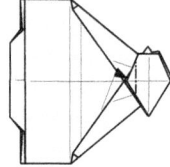

126. Open sink the tip about halfway.

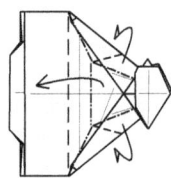

127. Pleat the flap forward while swiveling in the sides.

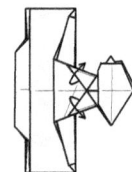

128. Tuck the flaps between the layers.

catching a plane

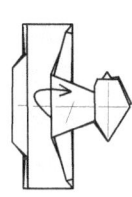

129. Wrap around the single layer to the surface (closed sink).

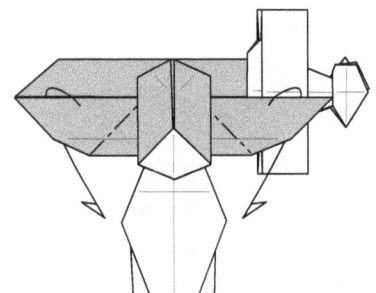

130. Mountain fold the side flaps.

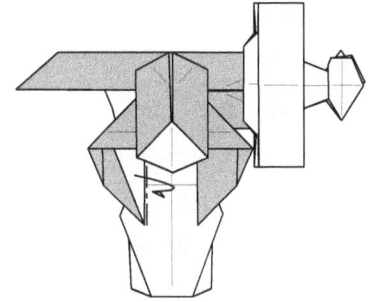

131. Wrap around a layer.

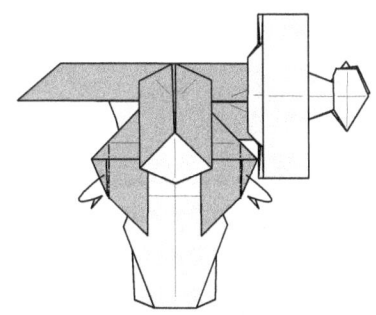

132. Mountain fold the sides.

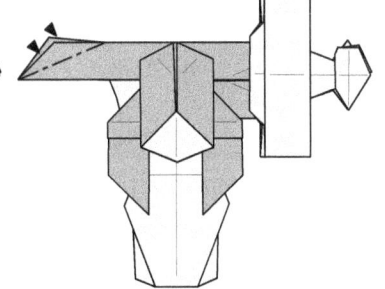

133. Closed sink the corners.

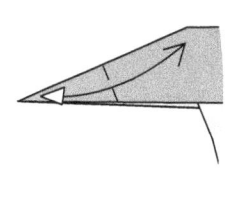

134. Detail of flap. Precrease the top edge in half.

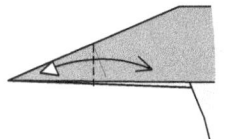

135. Precrease again.

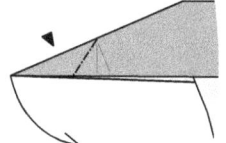

136. Reverse fold down.

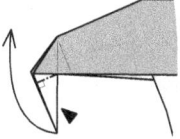

137. Reverse fold up.

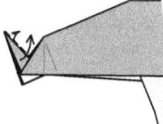

138. Slide the single layers forward.

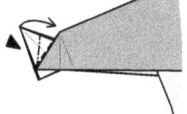

139. Squash fold down.

140. Petal fold the flap.

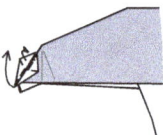
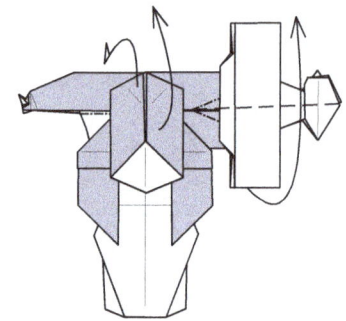

141. Rabbit ear while folding the side behind.

142. Tuck the sides in.

143. Flip the top section behind while reverse folding the plane section.

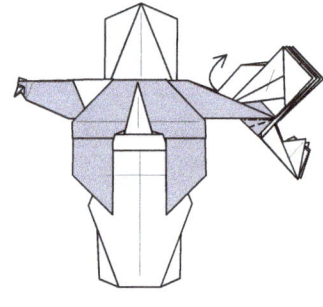
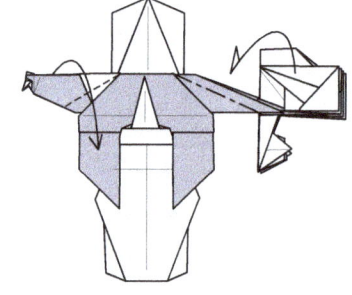
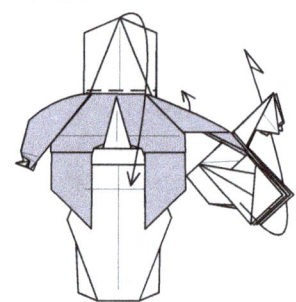

144. Slide the layers to rotate the plane.

145. Lightly fold the arms into position.

146. Swing the head back down while bringing the plane up. The arm will open out.

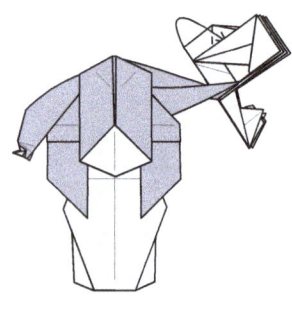
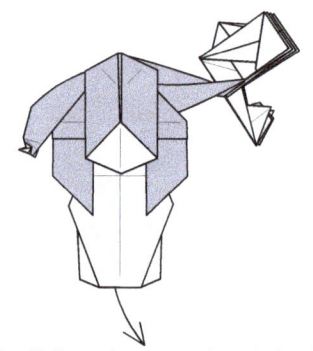
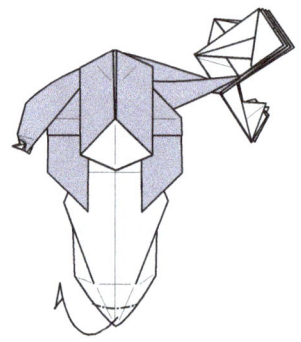

147. Tuck the corner in to lock.

148. Pull out the corner from behind.

149. Mountain fold.

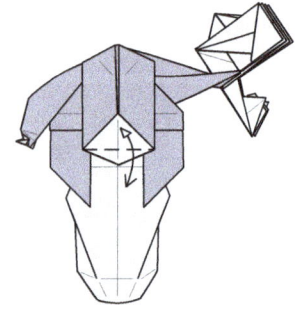
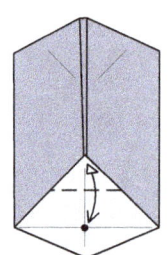
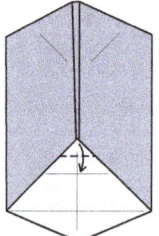

150. Lightly precrease.

151. Precrease the top section in half.

152. Valley fold to the last crease.

catching a plane

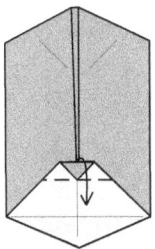

153. Valley fold down along the existing crease.

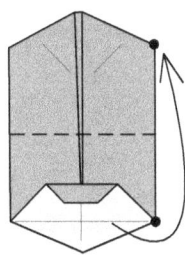

154. Valley fold up so the indicated points meet.

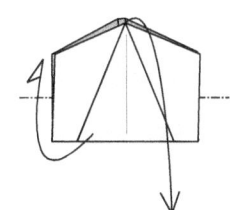

155. Mountain fold, swinging the top section down.

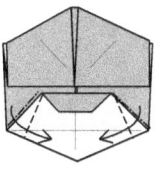

156. Swivel in the sides, causing the face to round out.

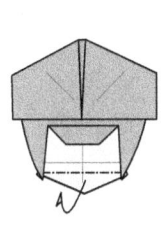

157. Mountain fold.

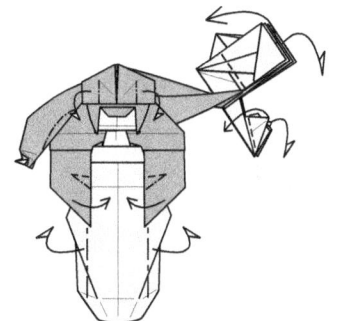

158. Open out the wings on the plane. Shape the model to taste.

159. Completed *Catching a Plane*.

Monoplane

Many years had elapsed since designing the *Biplane*, making this *Monoplane* feel a bit more modern in folding style. A few of the elements were kept consistent to give the two models a similar look and feel. The wings are also from the middle portion of the paper but consuming a larger portion for better efficiency. This was important as this model had one less set of wings and one less set of flaps to cover the fuselage.

monoplane

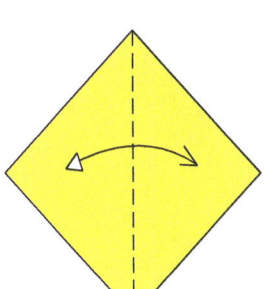 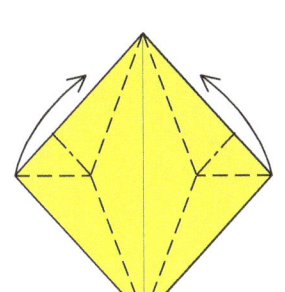 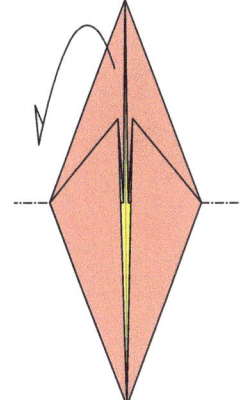 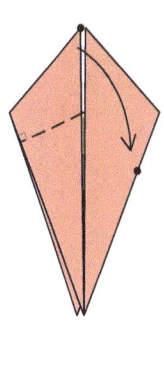

1. Precrease in half.
2. Rabbit ear both sides.
3. Mountain fold the top flap down.
4. Valley fold over, such that the corner hits the edge.

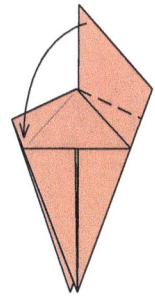 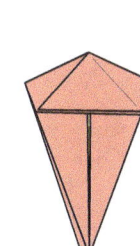 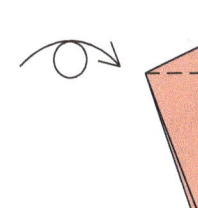 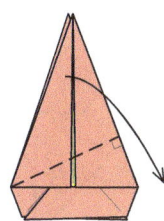

5. Valley fold over the other side.
6. Turn over.
7. Valley fold up two flaps.
8. Valley fold the top flap over.

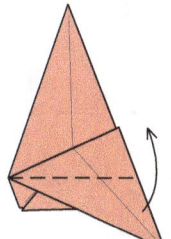 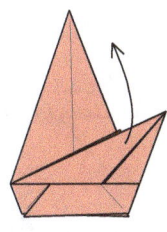 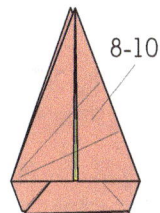 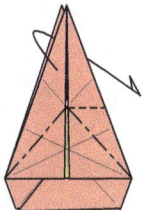

9. Valley fold along the angle bisector.
10. Unfold the pleat.
11. Repeat steps 8-10 in mirror image.
12. Rabbit ear the top flap behind.

117

monoplane

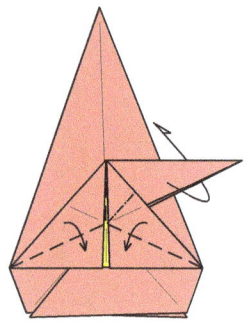

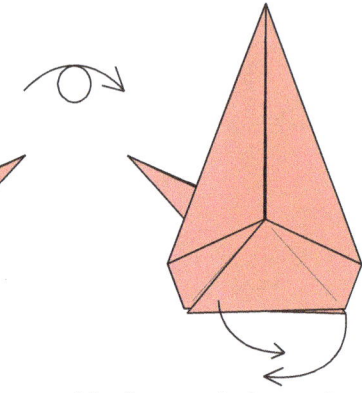

13. Rabbit ear again, allowing the flap to be brought forward.

14. Turn over.

15. Open out the bottom flaps.

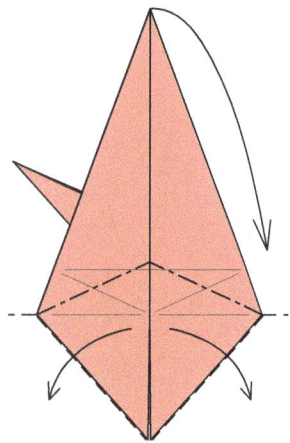
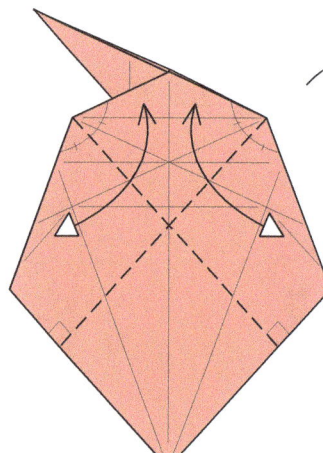
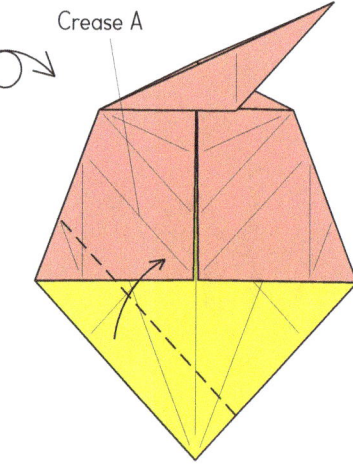

16. Swing the flap down while opening out the sides and squashing flat.

17. Precrease, and then turn over.

18. Valley fold the raw edge to meet crease A.

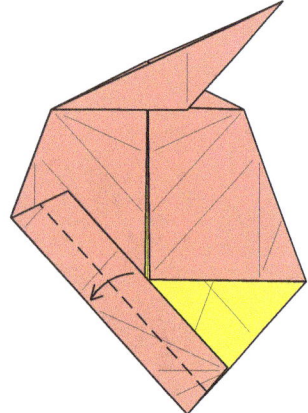
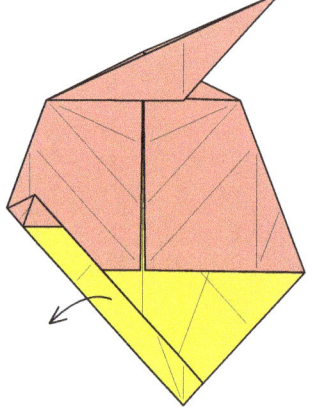
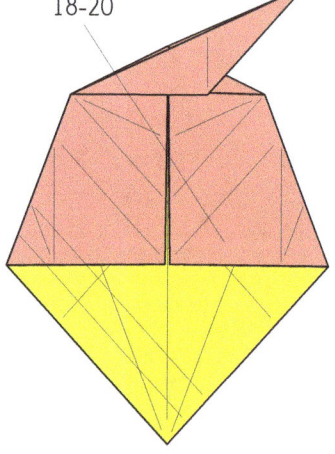

19. Valley fold the raw edge towards the outer edge.

20. Open out the pleat.

21. Repeat steps 18-20 in mirror image.

monoplane

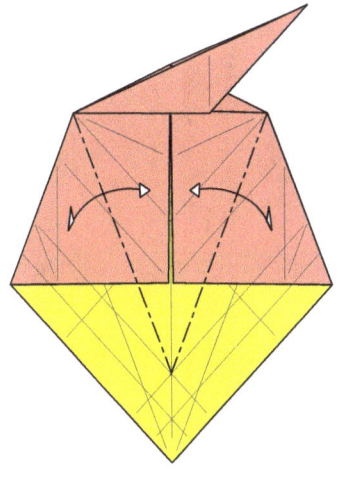

22. Precrease with mountain folds.

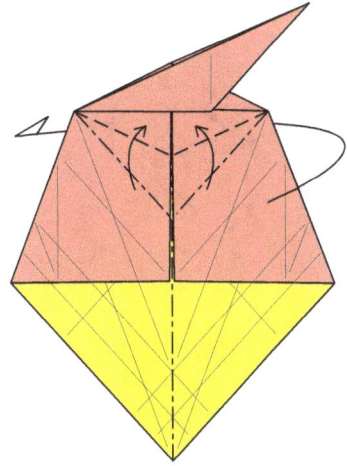

23. Crimp upwards while mountain folding in half.

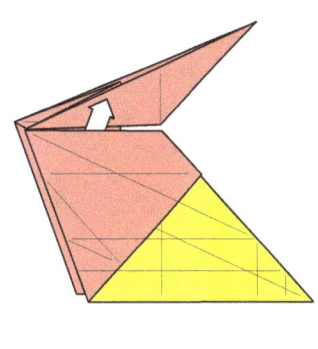

24. Pull out a single layer.

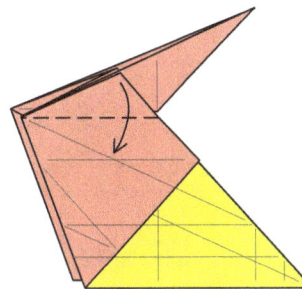

25. Valley fold down.

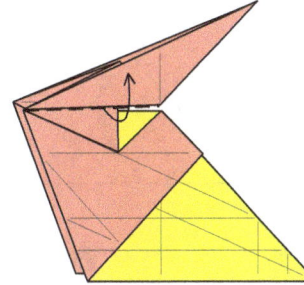

26. Wrap another single layer around, as in steps 24-25.

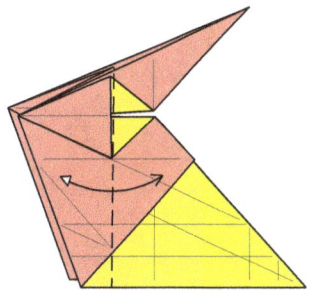

27. Precrease by swinging the top flap over as far as possible, and then back.

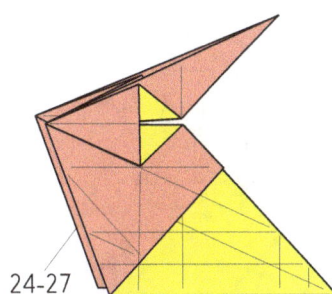

28. Repeat steps 24-27 behind.

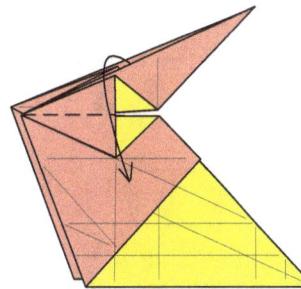

29. Pull down two layers, to reveal the center flap. The top will not lie flat.

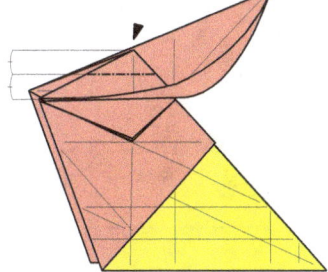

30. Open sink the flap halfway.

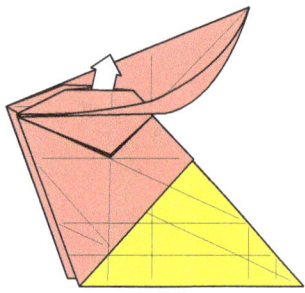

31. Undo the open-sink.

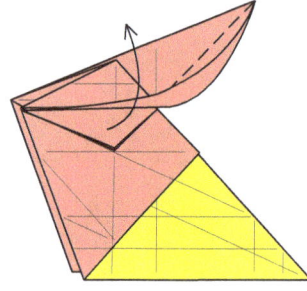

32. Raise the two flaps back up.

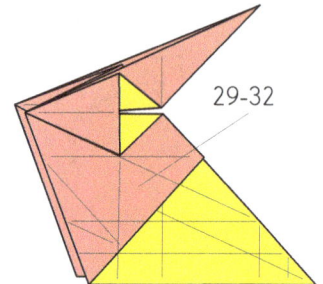

33. Repeat steps 29-32 on the lower hidden flap.

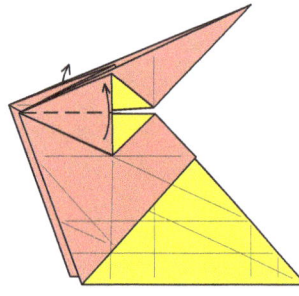

34. Swing the two small outer flaps up.

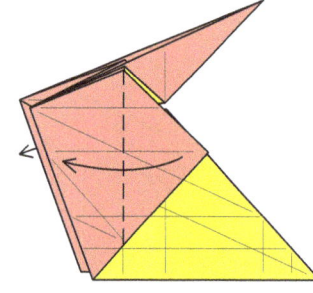

35. Valley fold the raw corners towards the outer edge.

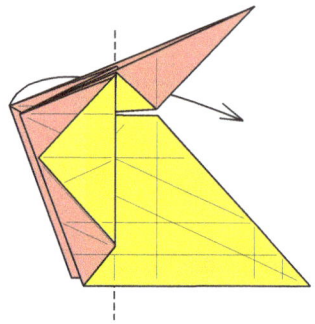

36. Swing over the back flap.

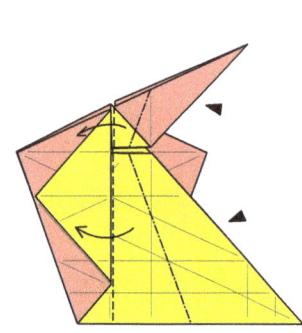

37. Spread squash the two flaps. Each flap's hidden ridge will be squashed as well.

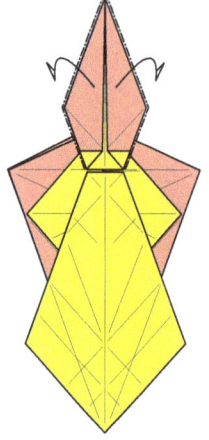

38. Wrap around a single layer at each side.

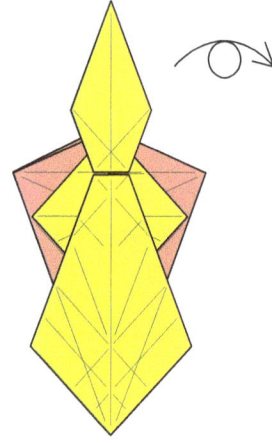

39. Turn over.

monoplane

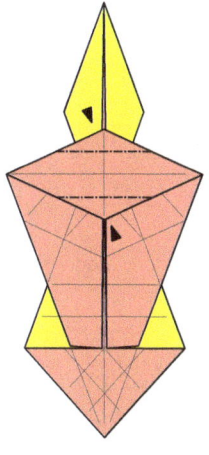
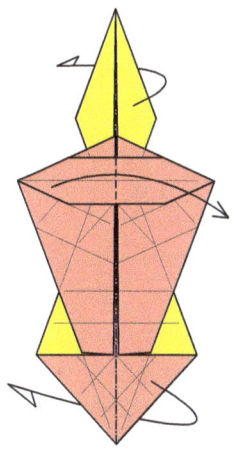
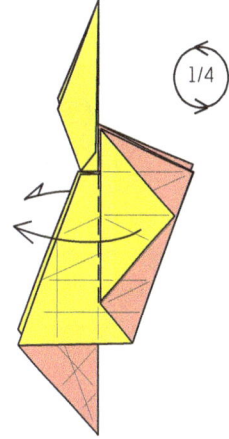

40. Open sink the trapped corners along the existing creases.

41. Swing the top flap to the right, and the lower flaps to the left.

42. Swing over a flap at each side. Rotate 1/4 turn.

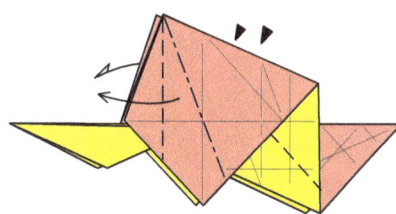
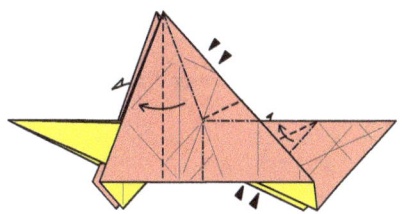

43. Squash fold at each side.

44. Squash fold each side, allowing the right side to crimp upwards.

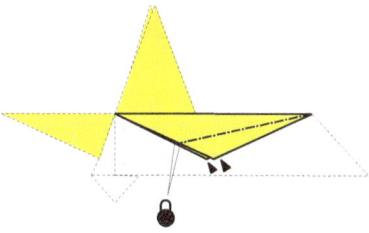
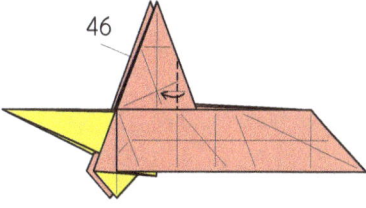

45. Closed sink the hidden flaps along the angle bisector.

46. Valley fold over to match the edge behind. Repeat behind.

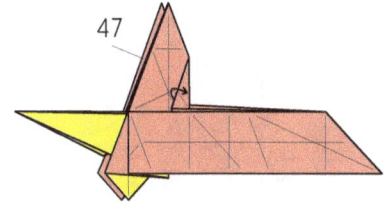
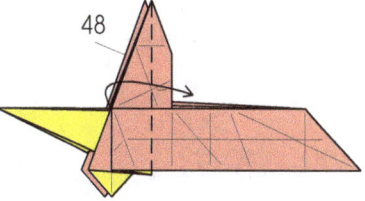

47. Wrap around a single layer to the surface (closed sink). Repeat behind.

48. Swing over three flaps at each side.

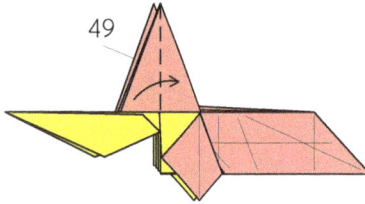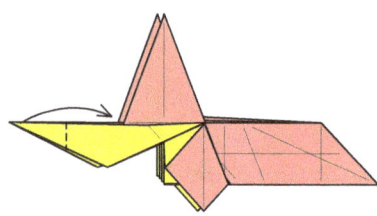

49. Swing over a layer, releasing the trapped paper. Repeat behind.

50. Valley fold over to the intersection of edges.

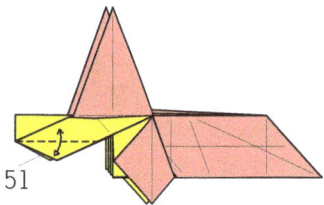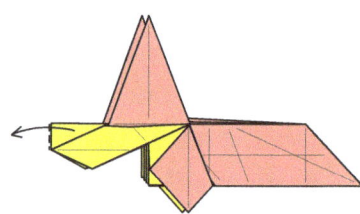

51. Precrease the bottom corner. Repeat behind.

52. Unfold.

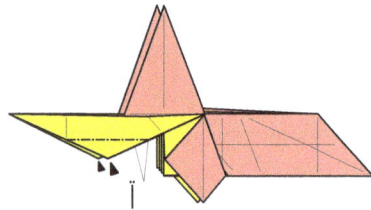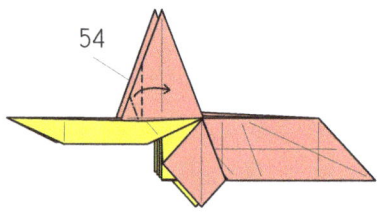

53. Closed sink the bottom corners.

54. Valley fold over to match the edge behind, releasing the hidden trapped paper. Repeat behind.

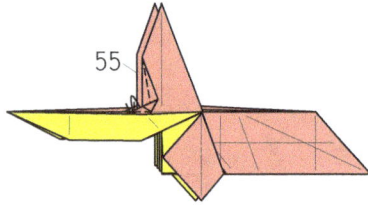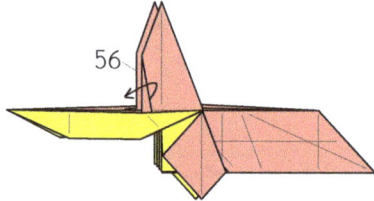

55. Narrow the flap along the angle bisector, swiveling the excess paper underneath the white single layer. Repeat behind.

56. Wrap around a single layer to the surface (closed sink). Repeat behind.

monoplane

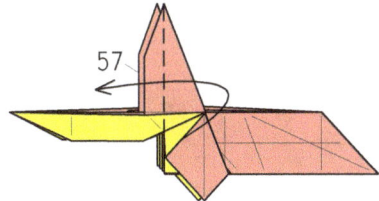

57. Swing over two flaps. Repeat behind.

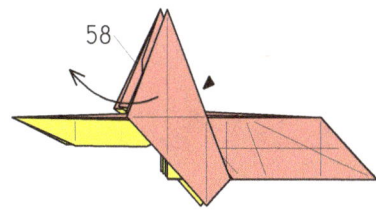

58. Grasp the top flap and pull upwards, allowing a pleat at the right to come undone. Repeat behind.

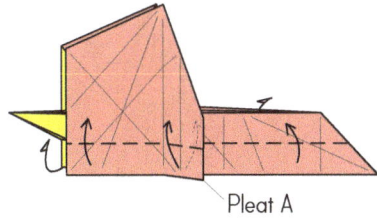

59. Wrap the raw edge upward, using the existing creases as a guide. You will have to undo pleat A slightly to accomplish this.

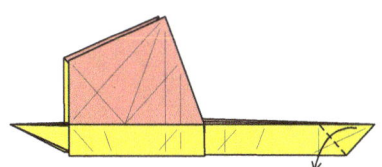

60. Valley fold the tip down.

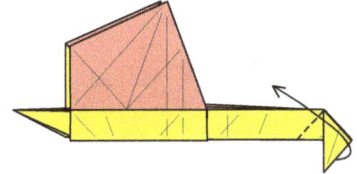

61. Valley fold upwards.

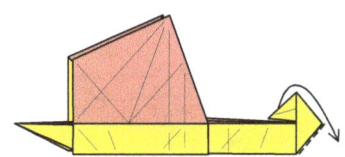

62. Unfold.

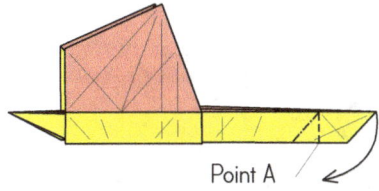

63. Crimp the tip inwards. Point A should fall in-between all of the layers at the center.

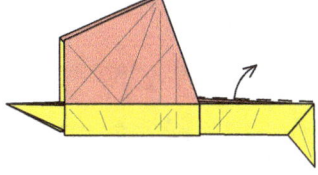

64. Raise the back section upwards.

monoplane

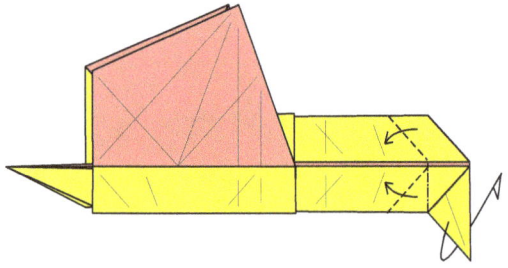

65. Rabbit ear, allowing the back flap to swing to the forefront.

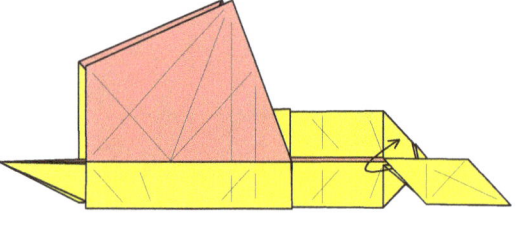

66. Wrap around a single layer to the surface.

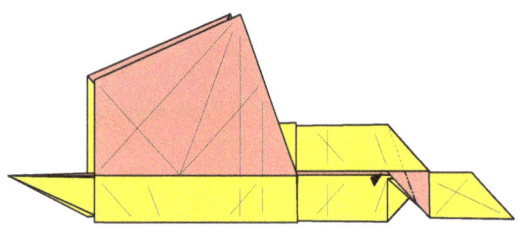

67. Sink along the angle bisector.

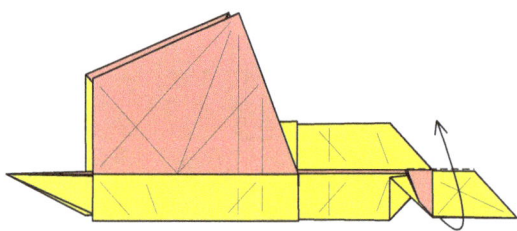

68. Swing the center flap upwards.

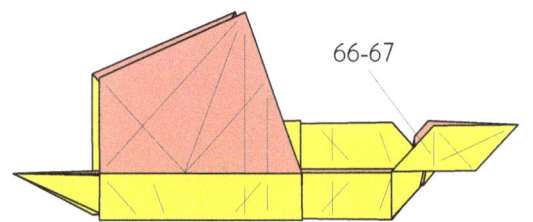

69. Repeat steps 66-67 on the bottom.

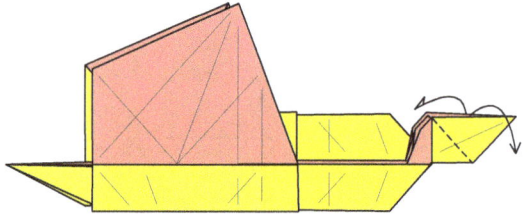

70. Outside reverse fold.

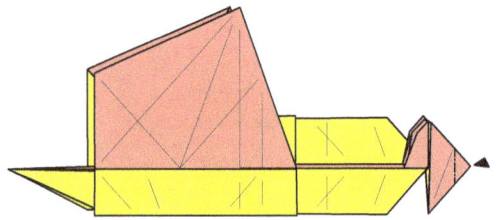

71. Sink the corner, noting how it lies next to the angle bisector precrease.

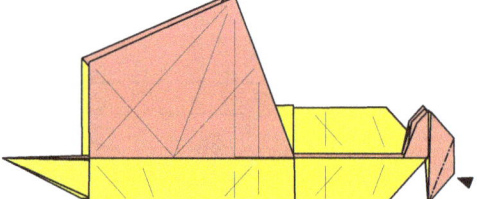

72. Sink again.

monoplane

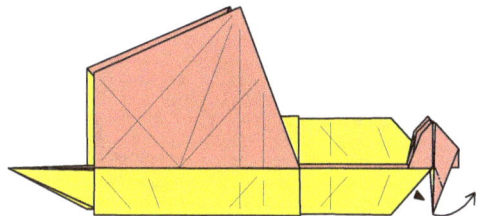

73. Reverse fold the tip.

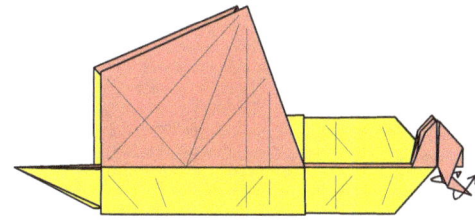

74. Wrap around a single layer at each side.

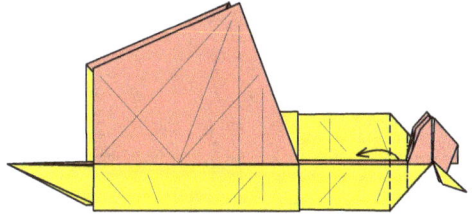

75. Pleat the tail assembly forward.

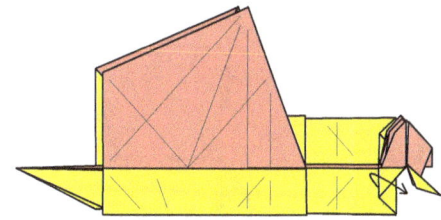

76. Wrap around a single layer to the surface.

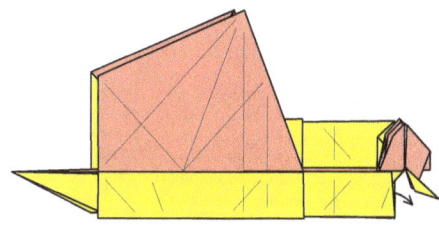

77. Slide out some paper. This will cause the flap to stick out slightly.

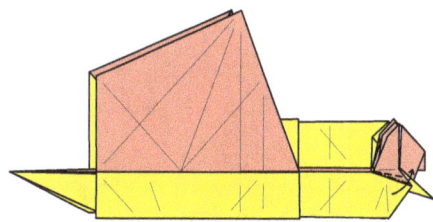

78. Flatten the flap by pleating the colored portion.

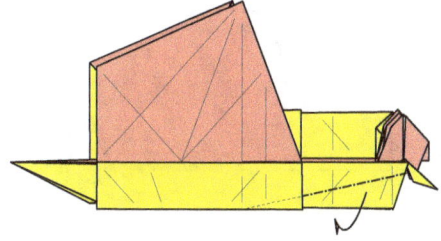

79. Mountain fold, wrapping around the hidden thickness.

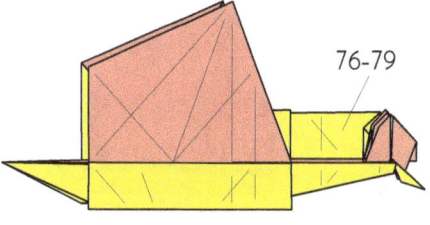

80. Repeat steps 76-79 above.

monoplane

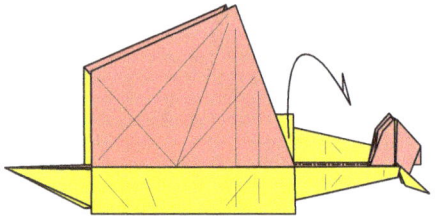

81. Mountain fold the top section.

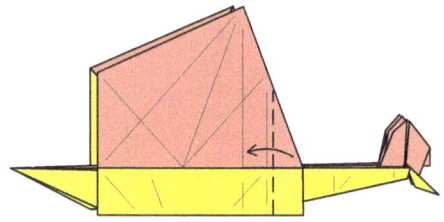

82. Valley fold the top flap to meet the center crease.

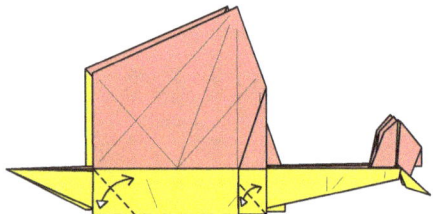

83. Precrease along the angle bisector on the indicated flaps.

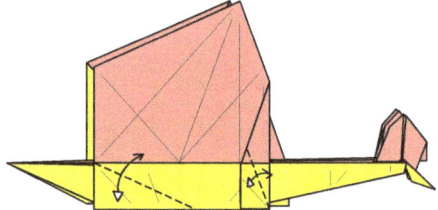

84. Precrease both flaps again along the indicated angle bisectors.

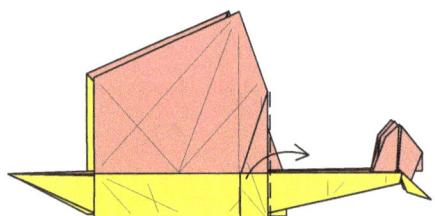

85. Swing the flap back.

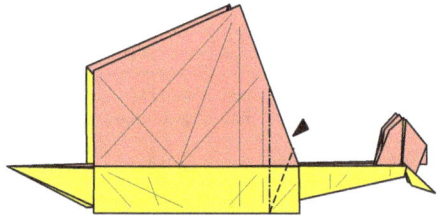

86. Closed reverse fold in and out along the existing creases.

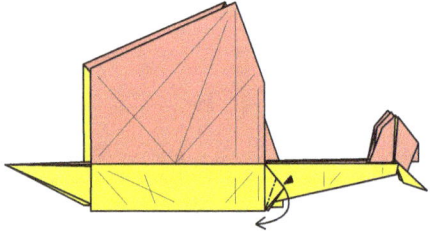

87. Reverse fold the flap. Do not crease too sharply.

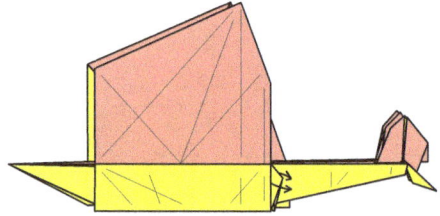

88. Slide a single layer out from each side of the flap and then flatten.

monoplane

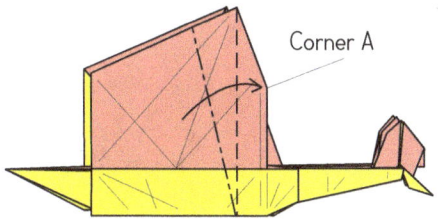

89. Pleat the flap, such that the mountain fold hits corner A.

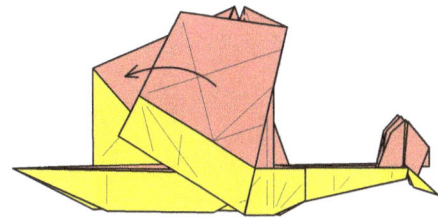

90. Undo the pleat.

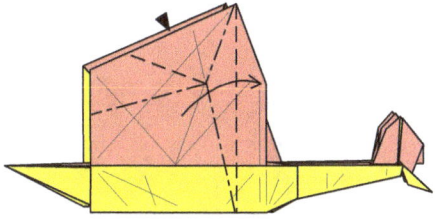

91. Form an asymmetrical petal fold.

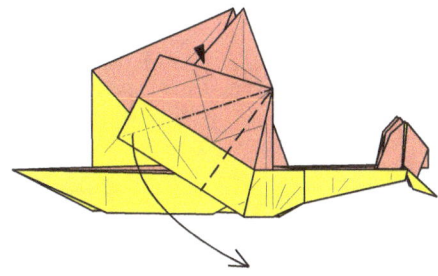

92. Squash the flap.

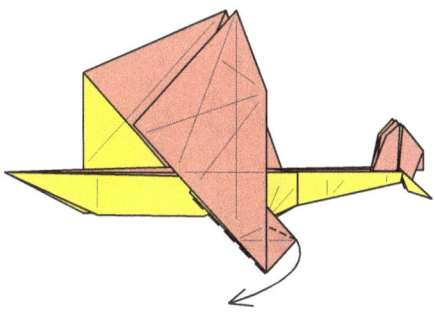

93. Twist the corner down, allowing the side to swivel in.

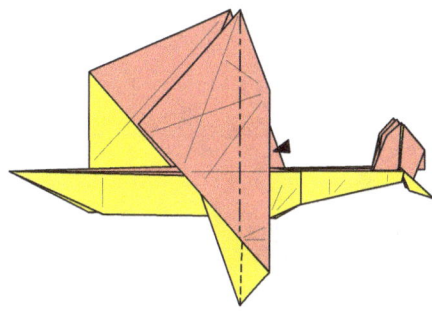

94. Closed sink.

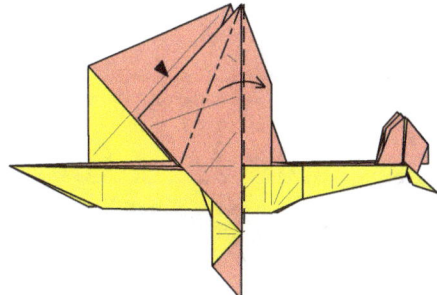

95. Squash fold.

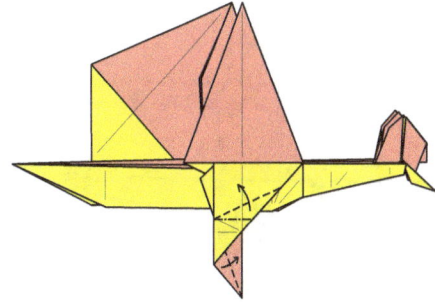

96. Swivel fold.

127

monoplane

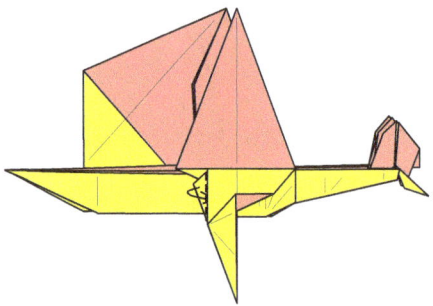

97. Valley fold in, to make it flush with the flap above.

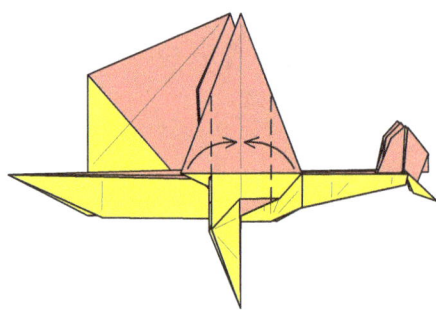

98. Valley fold the corners to the center.

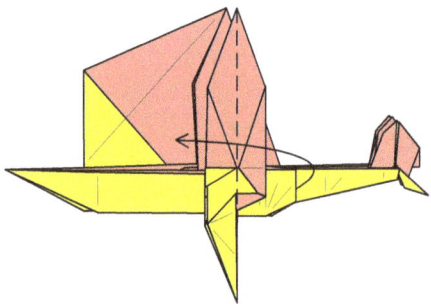

99. Swing over two flaps.

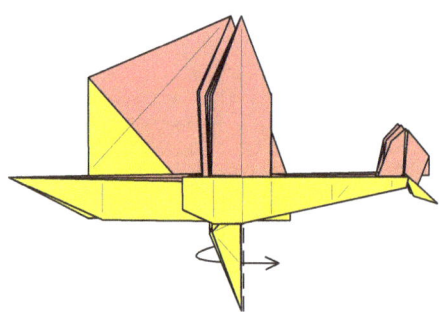

100. Open out the bottom flap.

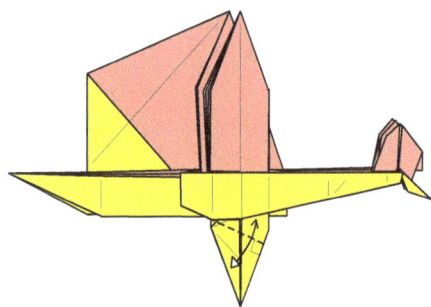

101. Precrease.

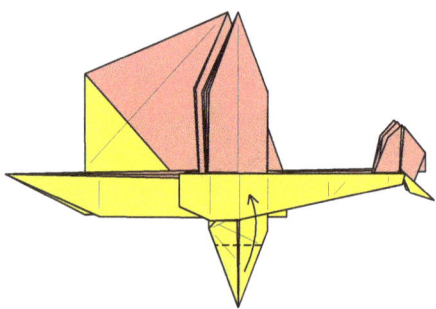

102. Valley fold up.

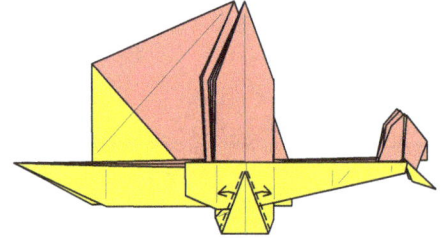

103. Slide out a single layer from each side, until the edges are straight.

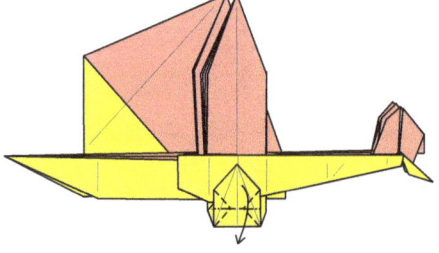

104. Valley fold down while reverse folding the sides.

monoplane

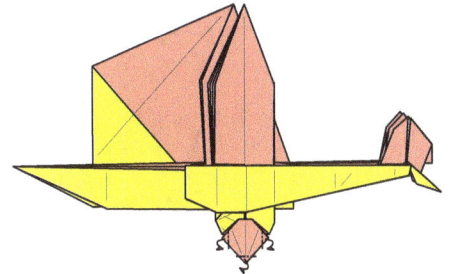

105. Mountain fold the corners.

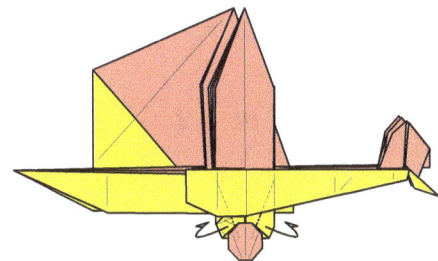

106. Mountain fold the sides.

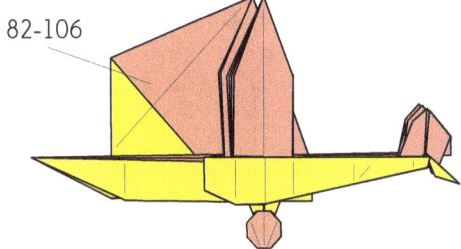

107. Repeat steps 82-106 behind.

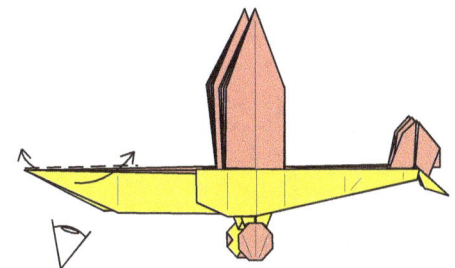

108. Open out the flap, such that it is flat.

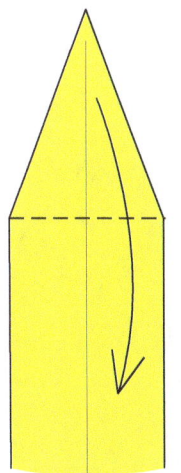

109. View of flap in upright position. Valley fold.

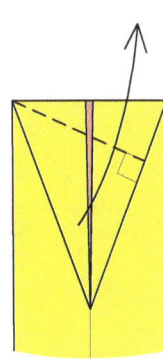

110. Valley fold up.

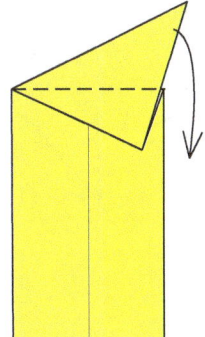

111. Valley fold down.

monoplane

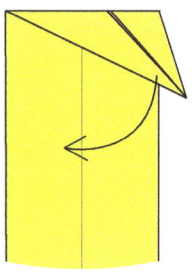

112. Undo the pleat.

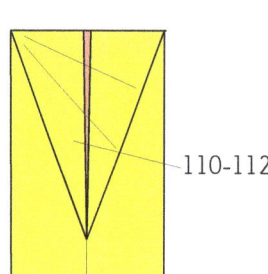

113. Repeat steps 110-112 in mirror image.

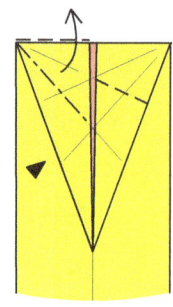

114. Squash asymmetrically.

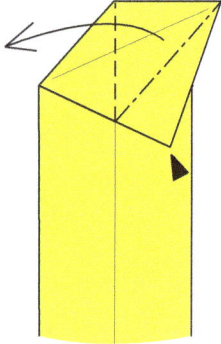

115. Squash fold.

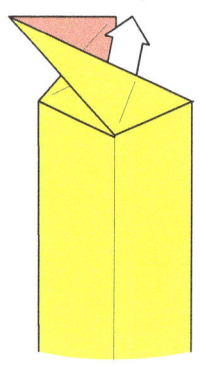

116. Pull out the single layer.

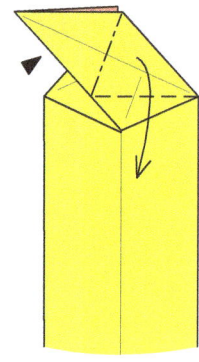

117. Squash fold.

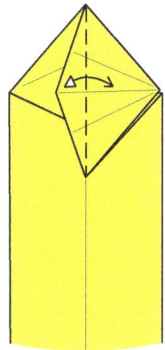

118. Precrease.

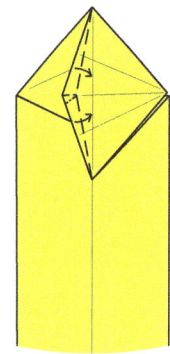

119. Rabbit ear.

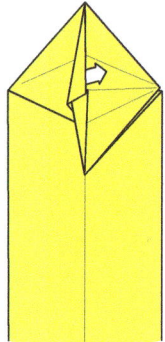

120. Unsink the single layer.

monoplane

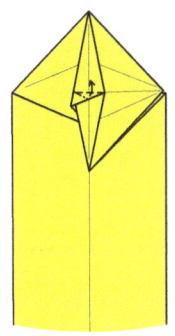

121. Swivel upwards.

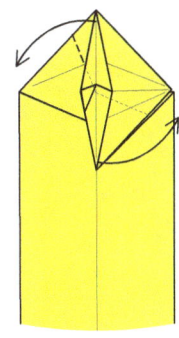

122. Twist the flap.

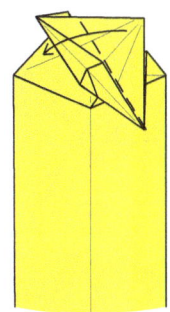

123. Valley fold.

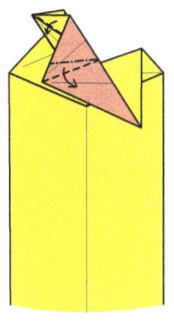

124. Swivel fold.

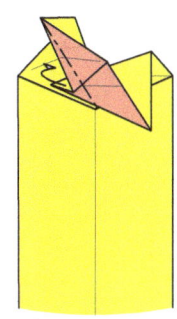

125. Mountain fold.

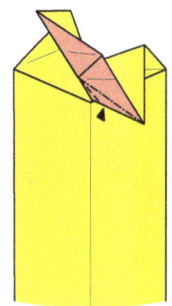

126. Reverse fold.

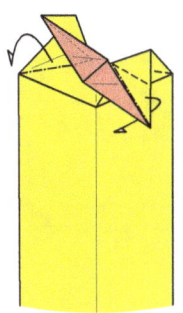

127. Swivel fold.

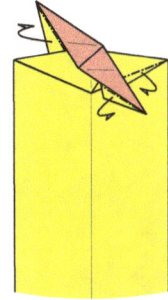

128. Swivel again.

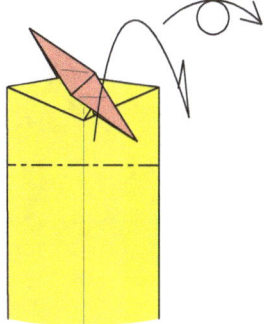

129. Mountain fold. Turn over.

monoplane

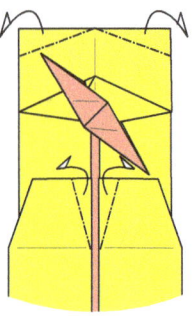 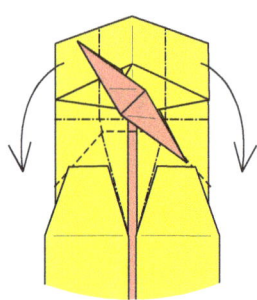 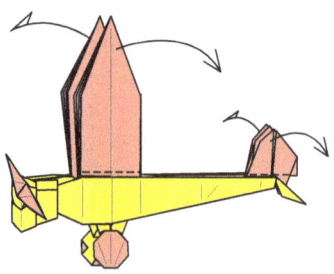

130. Mountain fold the two flaps, and at the top.

131. Form the cowl into a box shape, tucking the side flaps into the pockets created.

132. Swing the wings out at 90 degree angles.

133. Completed *Monoplane*.

Helicopter

Originally a box-pleated design, the flaps in this *Helicopter* were shifted to give it a less boxy look. A bit of luck helped that a simple rabbit ear was able to set the tail rudder on the outer portion of the model. It is easy for the folds to shift out of alignment, so part of the sequence is devoted towards ensuring that everything is straight.

helicopter

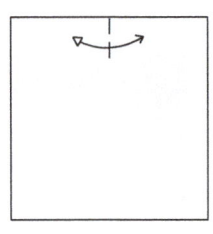

1. Pinch the top edge in half.

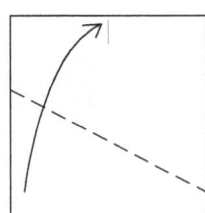

2. Valley fold the corner to the crease.

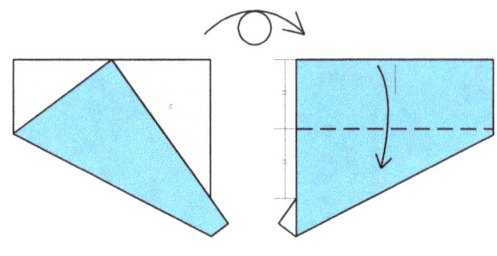

3. Turn over.

4. Valley fold to the intersection of edges.

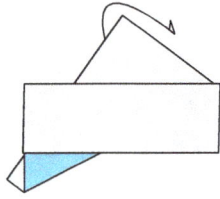

5. Swing down.

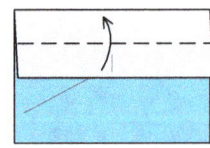

6. Valley fold up.

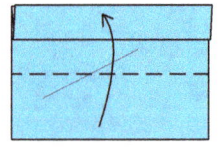

7. Valley fold to the top.

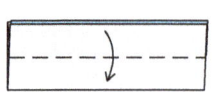

8. Valley fold down.

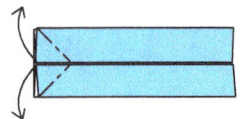

9. Reverse fold.

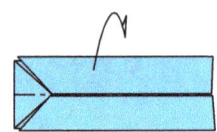

10. Mountain fold in half.

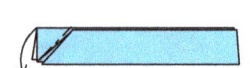

11. Reverse fold.

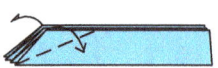

12. Valley fold along the angle bisector. Repeat behind.

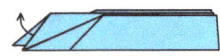

13. Undo the reverse fold.

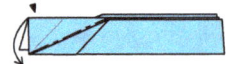

14. Reverse fold.

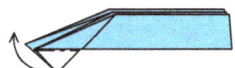

15. Reverse fold again.

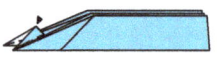

16. Reverse fold again.

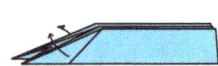

17. Lift the flaps, front and back.

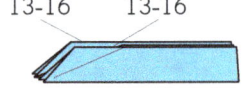

18. Repeat 13-16 on the front and back.

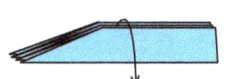

19. Swing the top layer down.

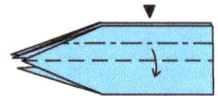

20. Spread squash the center flap.

h e l i c o p t e r

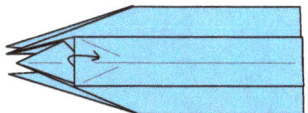

21. Unsink the hidden triangle to the surface.

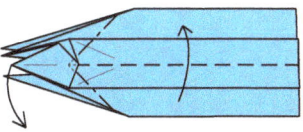

22. Valley fold in half while outside reverse folding.

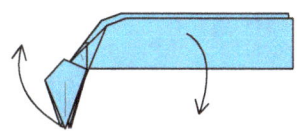

23. Open back up.

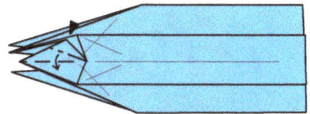

24. Spread squash.

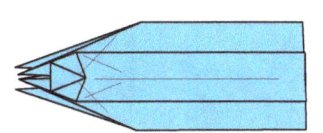

25. Turn over.

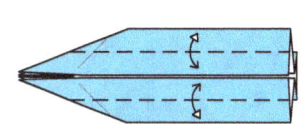

26. Precrease.

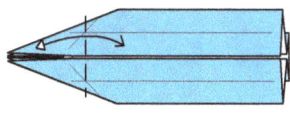

27. Precrease through the intersection of creases.

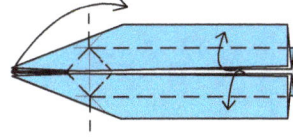

28. Swivel two layers outwards using the existing creases as a guide.

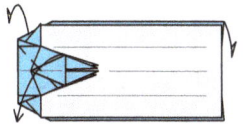

29. Outside reverse fold.

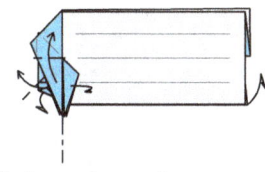

30. Similar to the previous step.

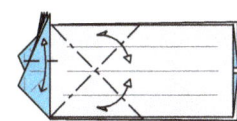

31. Precrease where indicated (note the use of mountain folds).

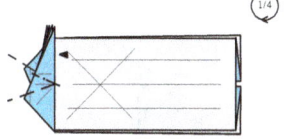

32. Squash fold, distributing the layers evenly. Form the mountain folds first (note how they terminate at the crease). Allow valley folds to form naturally. Rotate the model.

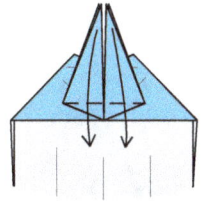

33. Swing down.

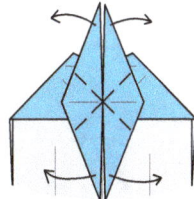

34. Valley fold outwards.

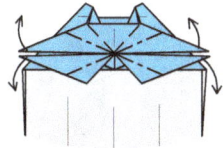

35. Squash fold the four flaps, distributing the layers evenly.

36. Reverse fold the sides along the angle bisectors.

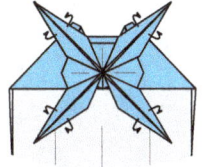

37. Wrap all the layers around to color change.

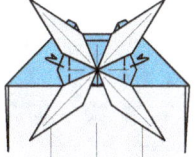

38. Mountain fold the protruding layers as far as possible.

135

helicopter

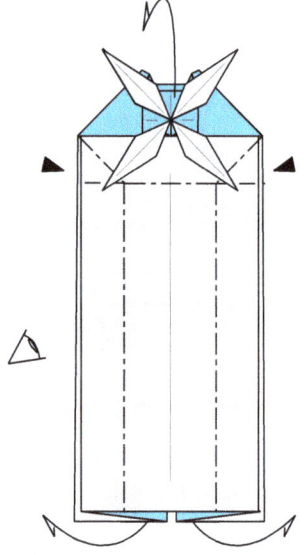

39. Collapse into 3-D.

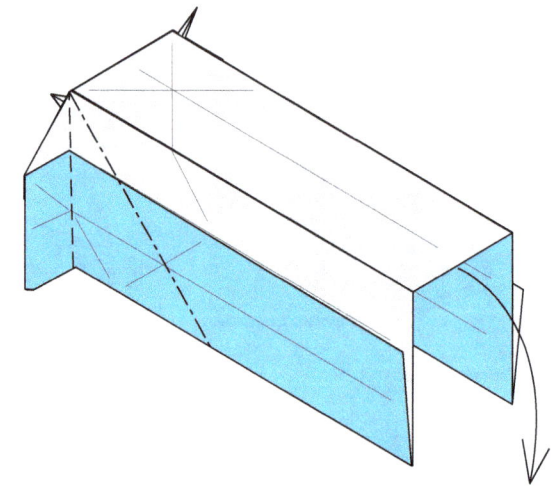

40. View from step 39. Squash fold flat.

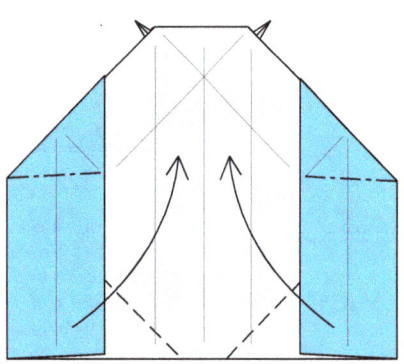

41. Swivel upwards.

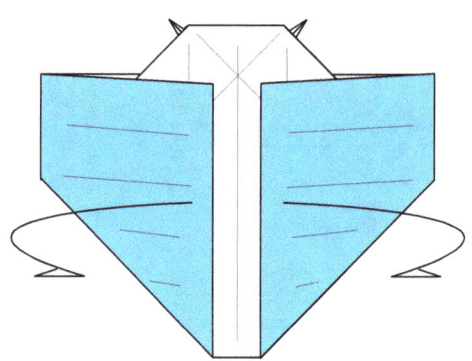

42. Wrap around.

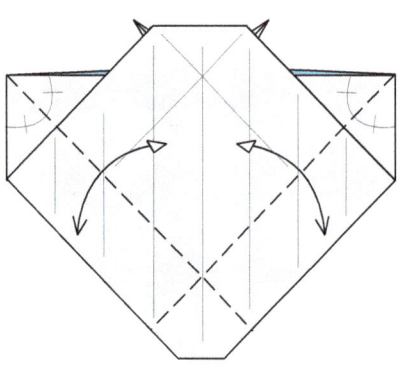

43. Precrease and turn over.

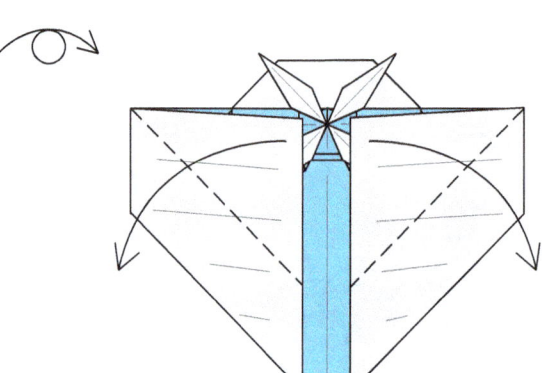

44. Valley fold outwards.

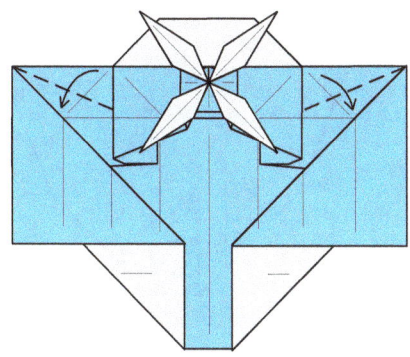

45. Swivel in along the angle bisectors.

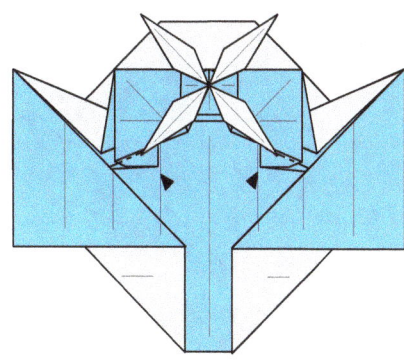

46. Reverse fold.

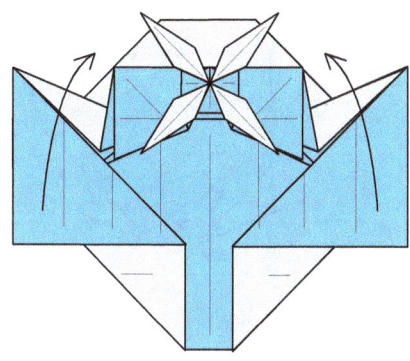

47. Swing up.

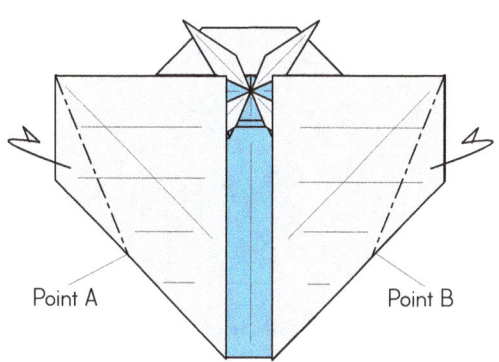

48. Mountain fold, ensuring points A and B are even with each other.

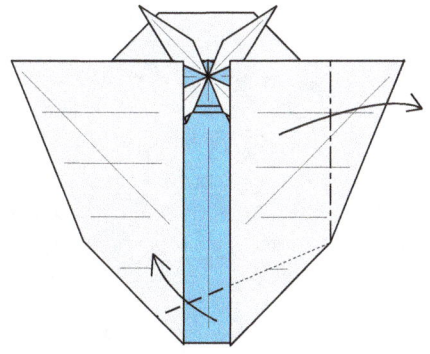

49. Swivel.

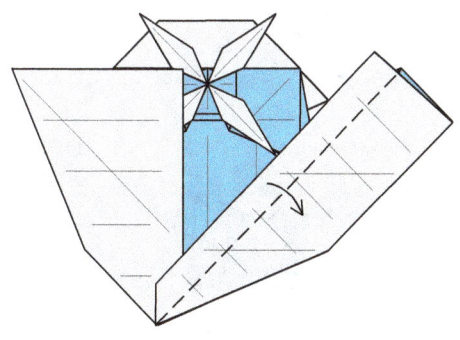

50. Valley fold. Depending on accuracy, the model may not lie flat at the bottom.

helicopter

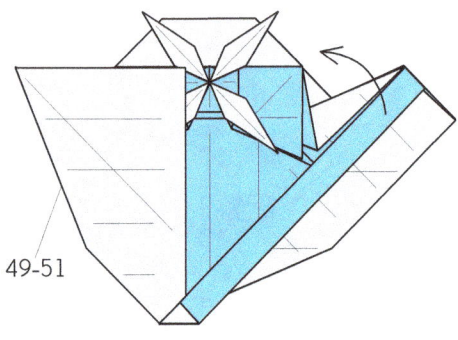

51. Return to the position of step 49. Repeat steps 49-51 on the other side.

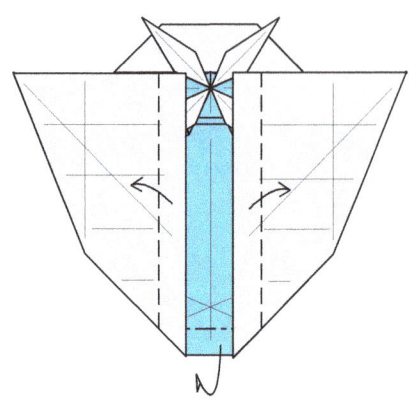

52. Form a hem along the existing creases.

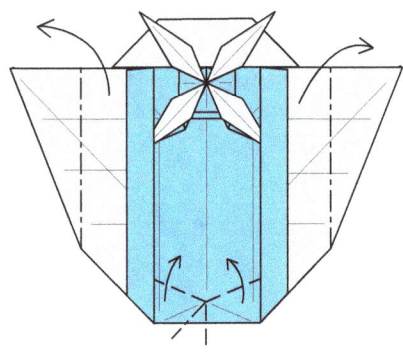

53. Pull the sides outwards; a rabbit ear will form at the bottom.

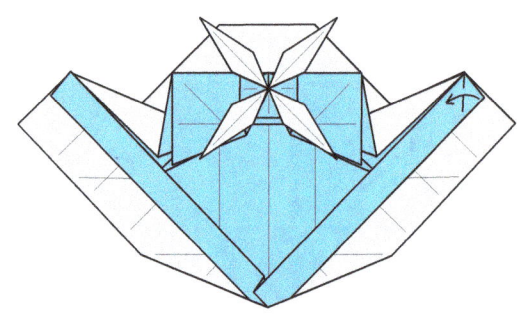

54. Valley fold the corner.

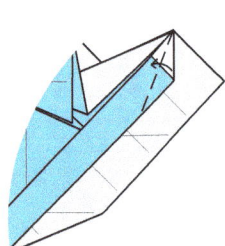

55. Valley fold again.

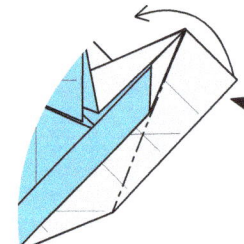

56. Reverse fold.

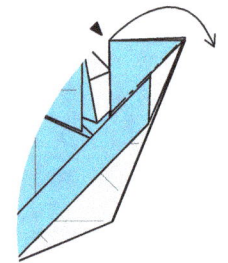

57. Reverse fold.

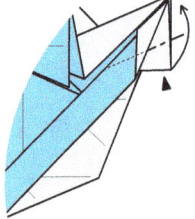

58. Reverse fold again.

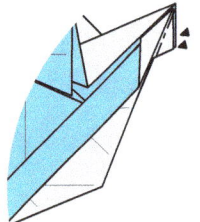

59. Reverse fold twice.

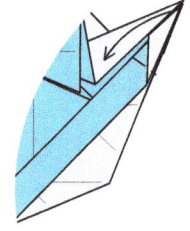

60. Stretch downwards.

helicopter

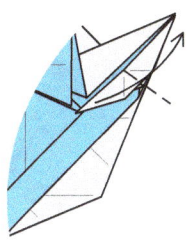
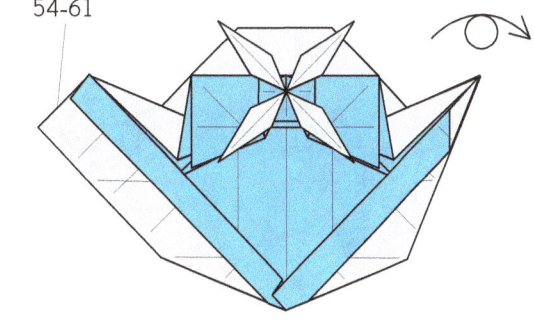

61. Swing back up.

62. Repeat steps 54-61 on the other side. Turn over.

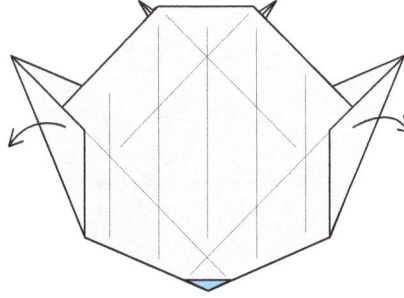
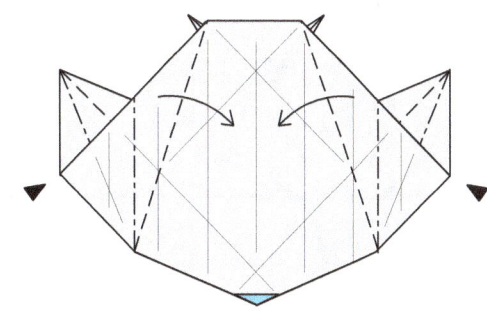

63. Swing outwards.

64. Spread squash.

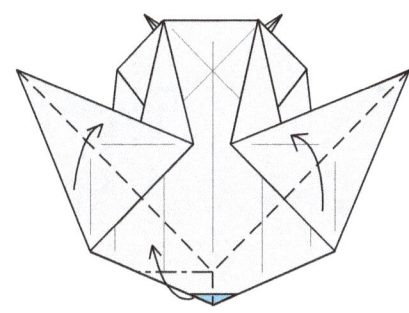
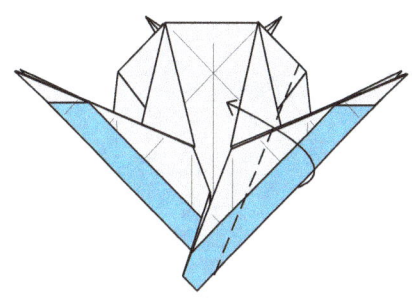

65. Rabbit ear.

66. Valley fold the right edge to the center.

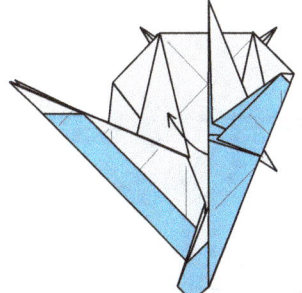
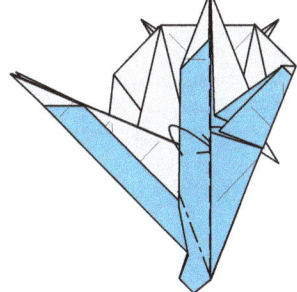
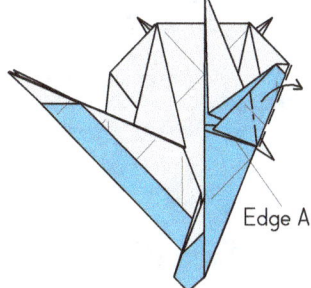

67. Pull out a single layered hem from underneath.

68. Tuck the hem into the bottom pocket.

69. Slide over, so that edge A lies vertically.

helicopter

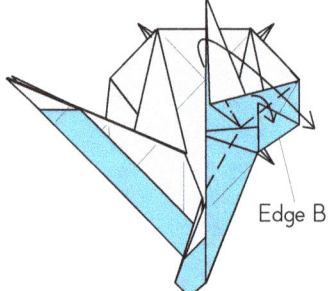
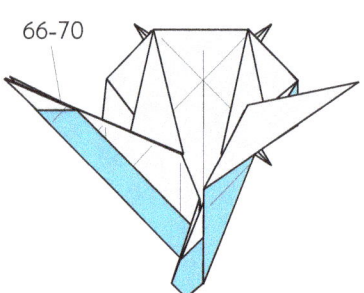
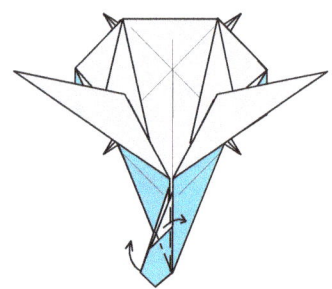

70. Valley fold the long edge along edge B. At the same time reverse fold down a single layer.

71. Repeat steps 66-70 on the other side.

72. Squash fold upwards.

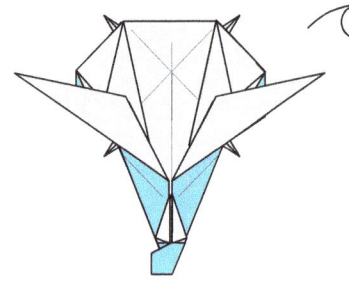
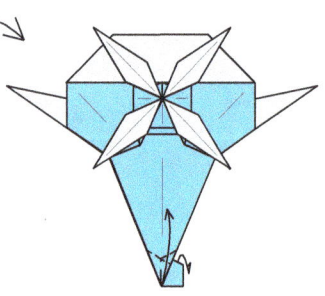
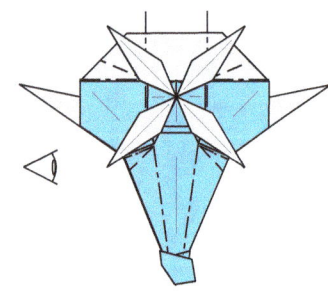

73. Turn over.

74. Rabbit ear.

75. Collapse the body into 3-D, crimping the windshield and tail.

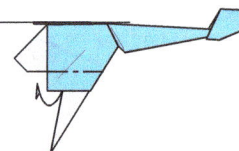
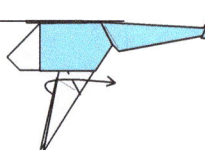
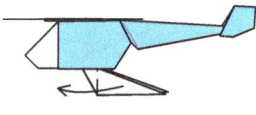

76. View from step 75. Fold in the sides.

77. Valley fold over both points together. Repeat behind.

78. Swing over. Repeat behind.

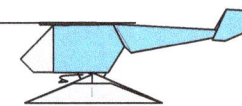
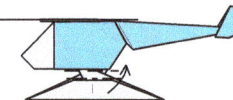

79. Wrap a layer around. Repeat behind.

80. Pleat the struts of the landing gear.

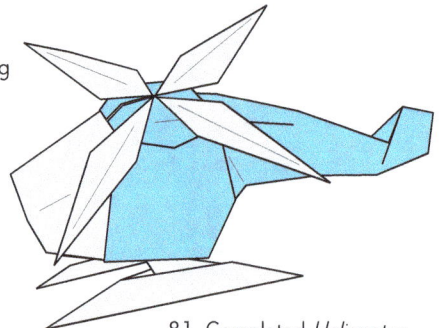

81. Completed *Helicopter*.

Chopper

Notably, this is the easiest model to fold in this collection. Wrapping around layers is still a challenge, so special care must be taken with those steps. The simpler sequence creates a more modern look, hence the name *Chopper*. Notice how the color patterns mimic the more complex *Helicopter* model, despite having a very different structure.

chopper

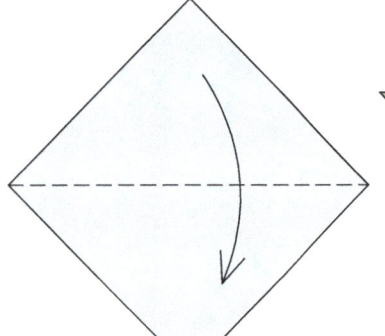

1. Valley fold in half.

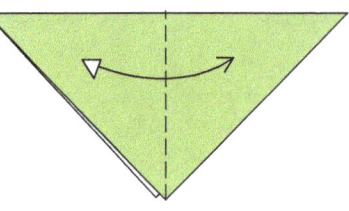

2. Precrease in half.

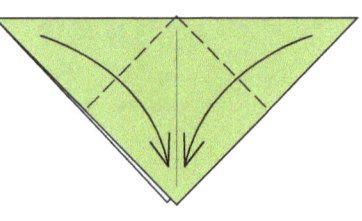

3. Valley fold the corners down.

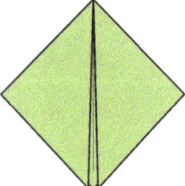

4. Turn over.

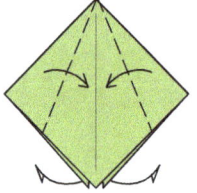

5. Valley fold to the center, allowing the back flaps to swing towards the front.

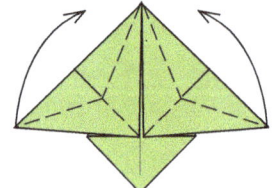

6. Rabbit ear up.

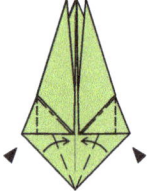

7. Reverse fold at the bottom.

8. Stretch upwards, allowing the small center flaps to flatten.

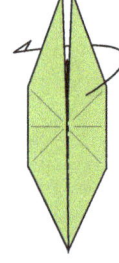

9. Mountain fold in half.

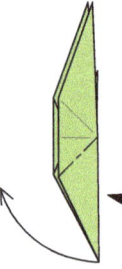

10. Reverse fold.

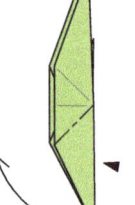

11. Wrap a single layer around at each side.

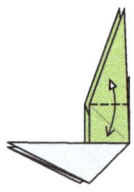

12. Lightly precrease.

chopper

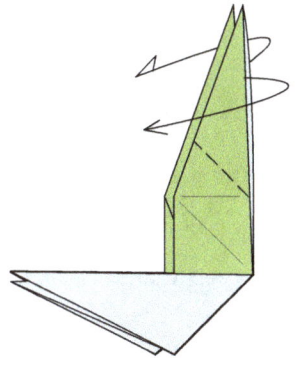

13. Outside reverse fold (1 layer in front, and 2 layers behind).

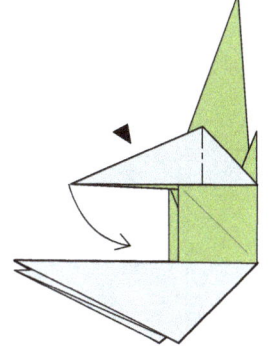

14. Squash fold.

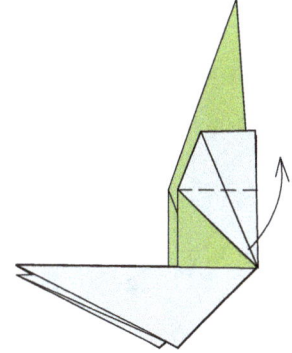

15. Lightly valley fold up.

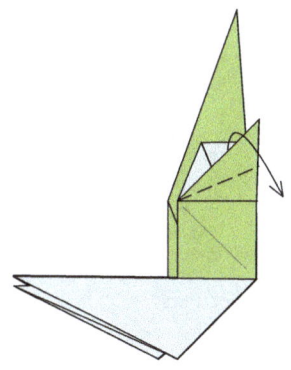

16. Valley fold down.

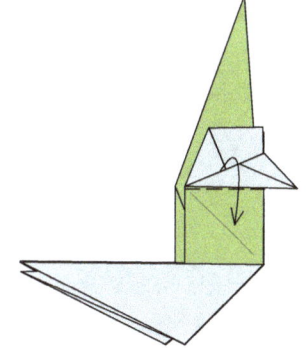

17. Swing down.

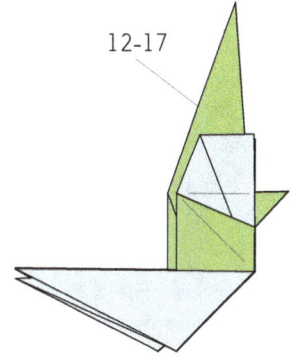

18. Repeat steps 12-17 behind.

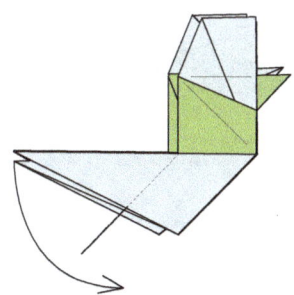

19. Reverse fold the inner flap.

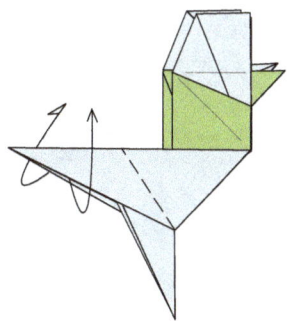

20. Outside reverse fold.

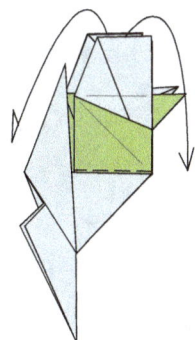

21. Swing down the front and back sections.

143

chopper

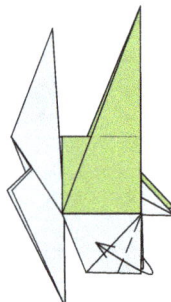

22. Valley fold the flaps together.

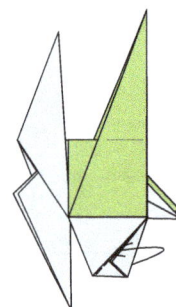

23. Tuck into the pocket.

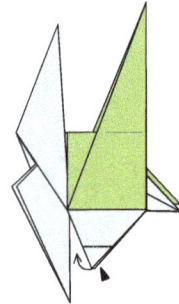

24. Reverse fold.

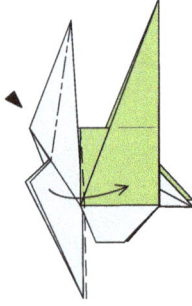

25. Spread apart the sides, allowing a squash fold to form.

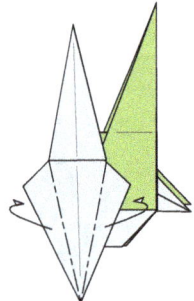

26. Mountain fold the sides.

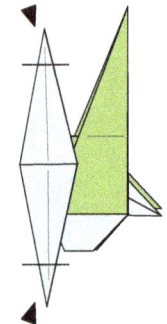

27. Sink the corners.

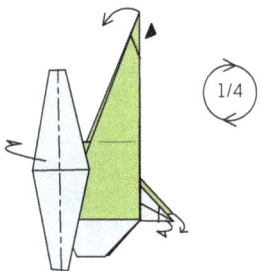

28. Reverse fold the tail. Mountain fold the wheels, Mountain fold the propeller. Rotate the model.

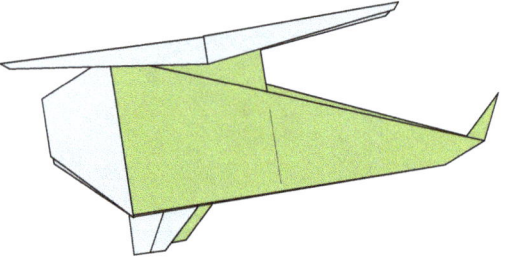

29. Completed *Chopper*.

Satellite

A multi-piece version of this *Satellite* was devised for a private Christmas tree decoration job, for a family in the telecommunications investment business. The piece for the dish was folded from a corner of a square, to allow for the other sections to be folded all from the same sheet. Folding this is a bit harder than it looks, as the body section is completely enclosed.

satellite

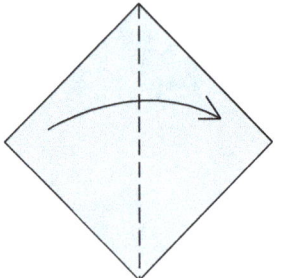

1. Colored side up. Valley fold in half.

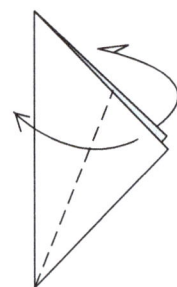

2. Valley fold the sides to the edge.

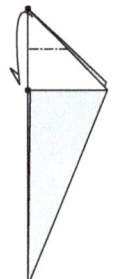

3. Mountain fold to the colored corner behind.

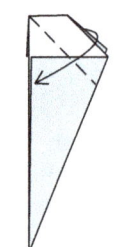

4. Valley fold along the angle bisector.

5. Unfold the pleat.

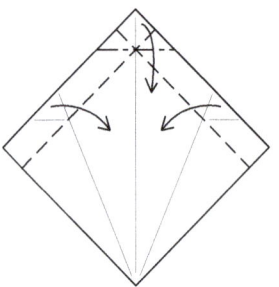

6. Collapse down.

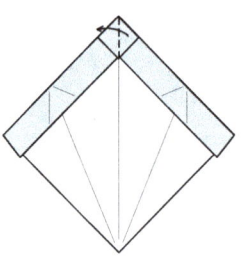

7. Swing over one flap.

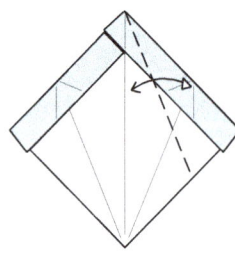

8. Precrease along the angle bisector.

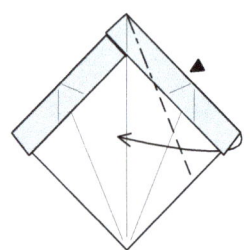

9. Reverse fold.

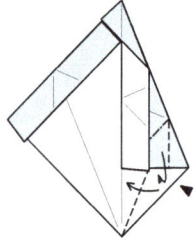

10. Swivel the edge in.

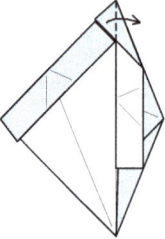

11. Swing the flap back over.

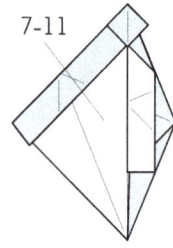

12. Repeat steps 7-11 in mirror image.

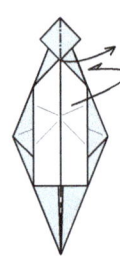

13. Mountain fold the model in half while pulling out the top corner.

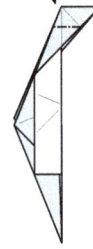

14. Open sink the top flap in half (precrease first).

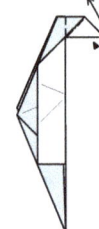

15. Squash fold the flap up.

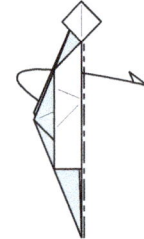

16. Swing the layers from behind back over.

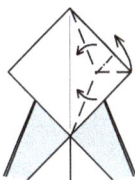
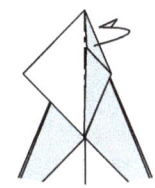
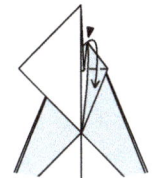
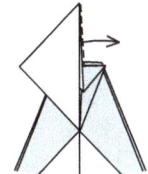

17. Rabbit ear the corner up.

18. Swing one layer through.

19. Reverse fold the corner.

20. Swing the layer from behind back out.

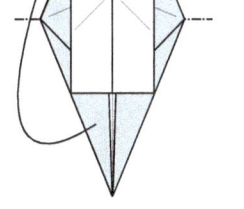
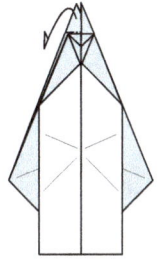
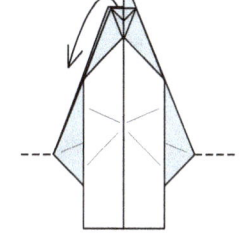

21. Repeat steps 17-19 in mirror image.

22. Mountain fold the flap up.

23. Mountain fold to align with the folded edge.

24. Swing the flap back down.

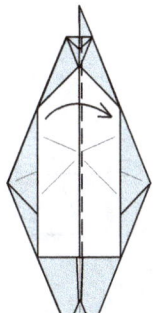
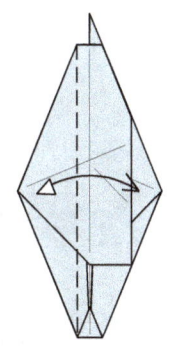
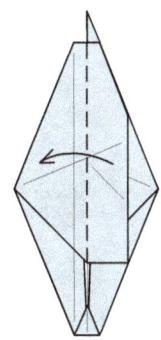
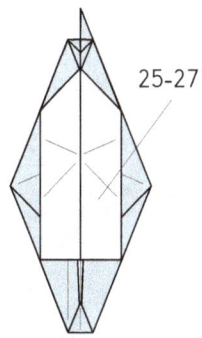

25. Swing over one layer.

26. Precrease.

27. Swing the flap back over.

28. Repeat steps 25-27 in mirror image.

satellite

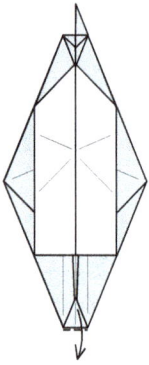

29. Swing the tip down.

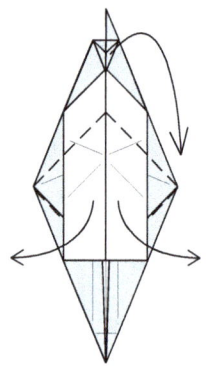

30. Valley fold down while swiveling the sides outwards. Note in the next step how the creases align with the folded edges.

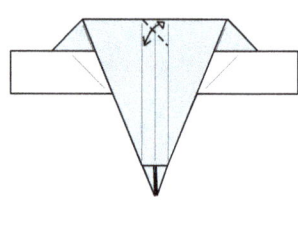

31. Lightly precrease.

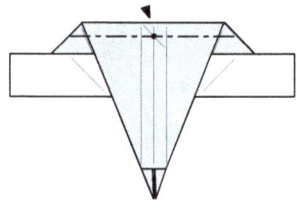

32. Closed sink through the indicated intersection.

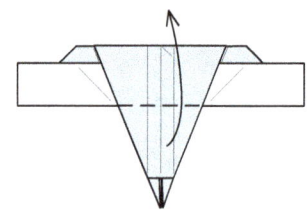

33. Lightly valley fold up.

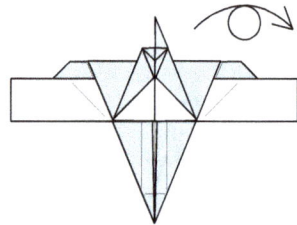

34. Turn over.

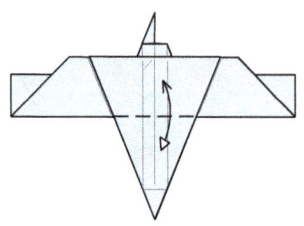

35. Lightly precrease.

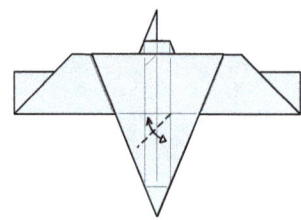

36. Lightly precrease.

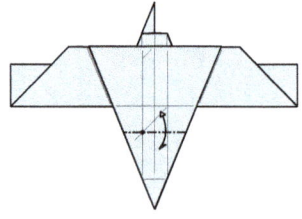

37. Precrease with a mountain fold.

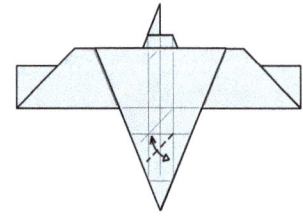

38. Lightly precrease.

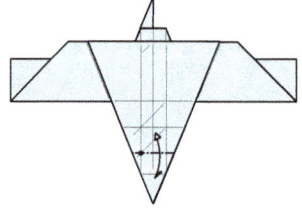

39. Precrease with a mountain fold.

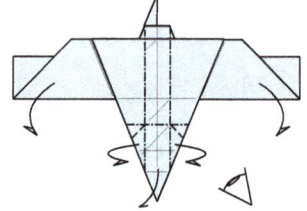

40. Fold down the sides (do not crease sharply) and collapse the front down.

satellite

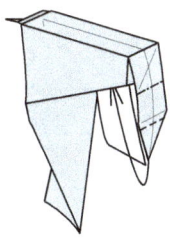
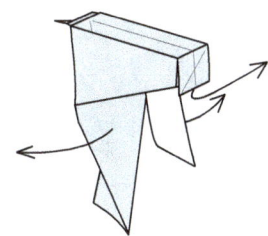
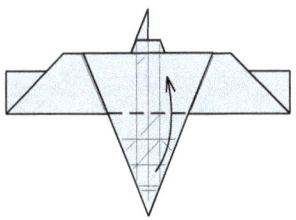

41. Tuck the flap inside. The tip will lie flush with the top of the model.

42. Open out the last two steps.

43. Lightly valley fold up.

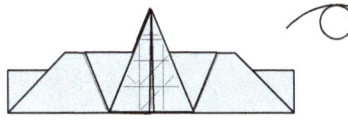
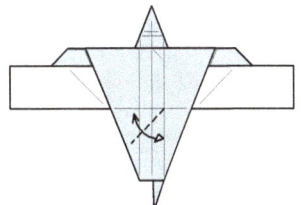

44. Turn over.

45. Swing the flap back down.

46. Lightly precrease.

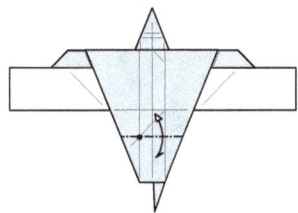
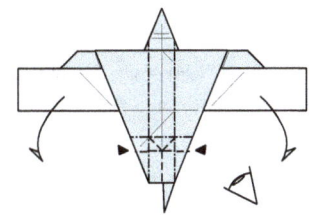
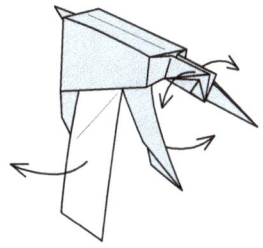

47. Precrease with a mountain fold.

48. Swing down the sides while rabbit earing the front.

49. Undo the previous step.

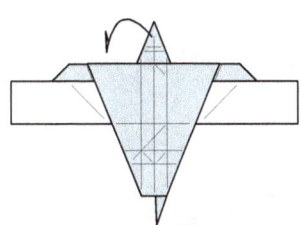
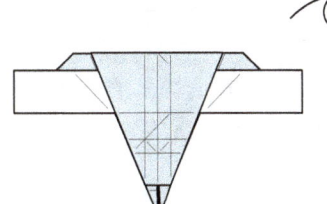
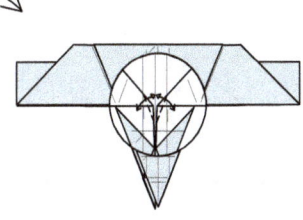

50. Swing the back flap down.

51. Turn over.

52. Precrease the hidden corners along the angle bisectors.

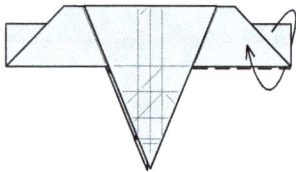

53. Wrap around a single layer.

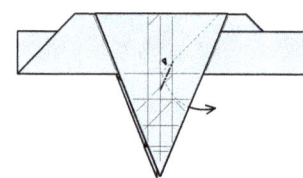

54. Reverse fold the hidden corner along the existing crease.

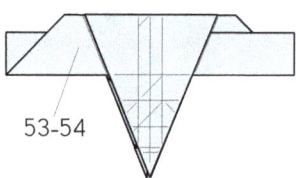

55. Repeat steps 53-54 on the other side.

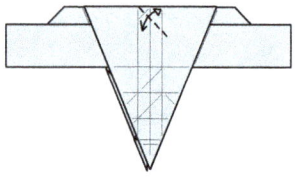

56. Lightly precrease.

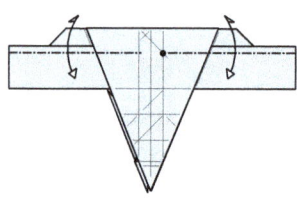

57. Precrease with mountain folds, using the indicated intersection as a guide.

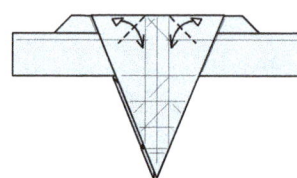

58. Precrease.

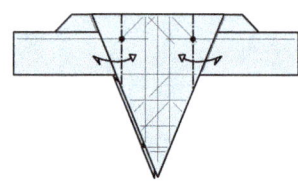

59. Precrease with mountain folds.

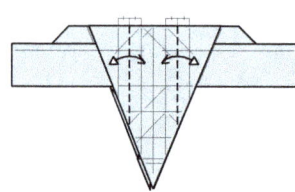

60. Precrease.

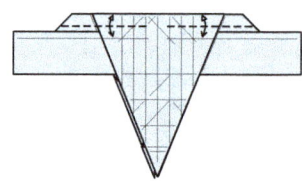

61. Precrease the sides towards the horizontal crease.

satellite

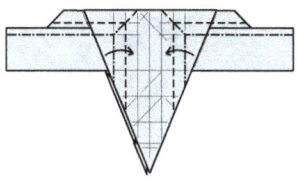

62. Collapse the sides inwards.

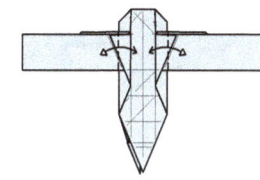

63. Precrease through all layers.

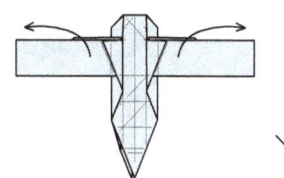

64. Unfold to step 62.

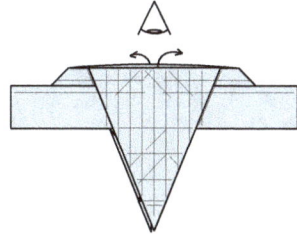

65. Pull apart the sides, making the central single layer as flat as possible.

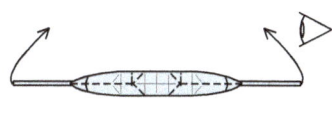

66. View from previous step. Rabbit ear the sides up, allowing the central section to become boxlike.

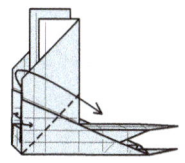

67. View from previous step. Valley fold the flap down, allowing the side edge to spread apart (mostly) flat.

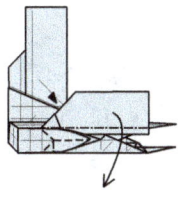

68. Squash fold the flap down, inserting a rabbit ear.

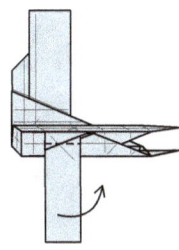

69. Valley fold the flap up at a right angle.

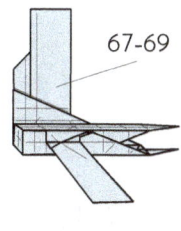

70. Repeat steps 67-69 on the other side.

151

satellite

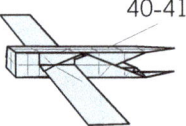

71. Redo the folds from steps 40-41.

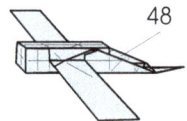

72. Redo the folds from step 48.

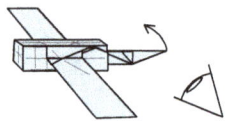

73. Pull out a set of pleats from each side.

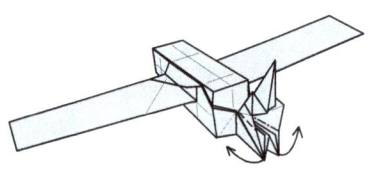

74. Pull out the trapped sides at right angles. A hidden valley fold will be formed at each side.

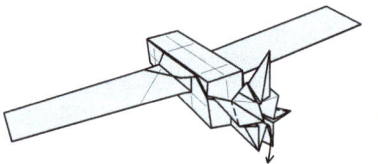

75. Spread out the pleats.

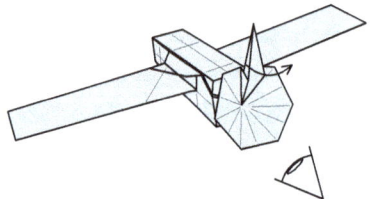

76. Swing the center flap to one side.

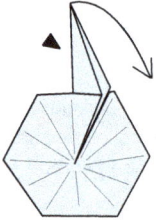

77. Reverse fold.

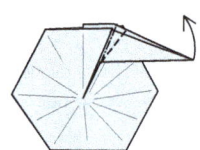

78. Pleat the flap up.

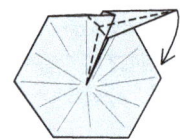

79. Rabbit ear down.

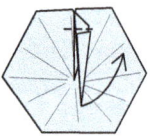

80. Point the flap outwards.

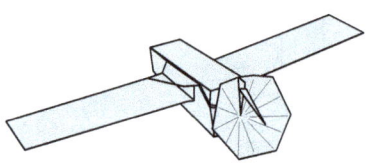

81. Completed *Satellite*.

Spaceship

Designing this *Spaceship* was a personal challenge from fellow origami expert Jeremy Shafer. He had already devised his own version and noted that having sections that sprouted from a "Y" shaped formation was difficult to fit onto the symmetry of a square. Some sections in this version are very thick and can make the closed sink on the fuselage a bit tricky. The sequence to form the engines does succeed in distributing the layers quite elegantly.

spaceship

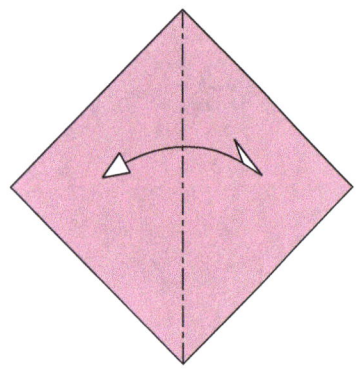

1. Precrease with a mountain fold.

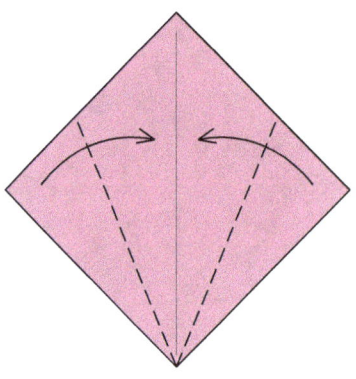

2. Valley fold the sides to the center.

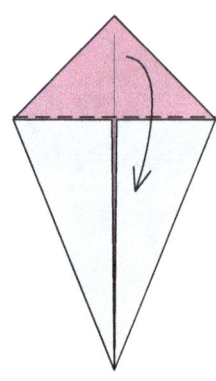

3. Valley fold down.

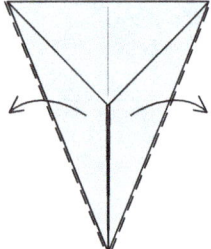

4. Unfold the sides.

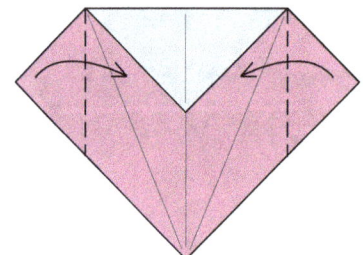

5. Valley fold the sides inwards.

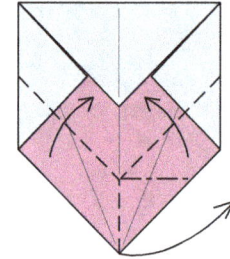

6. Rabbit ear the bottom.

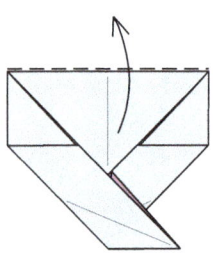

7. Unfold.

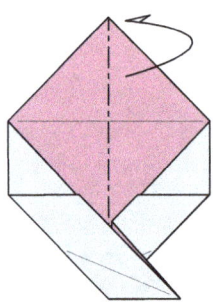

8. Mountain fold in half.

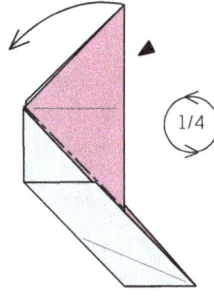

9. Reverse fold and rotate 1/4 turn.

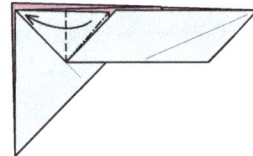

10. Pull out the original corner.

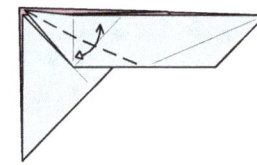

11. Precrease along the angle bisector.

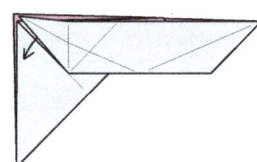

12. Pull out the corner.

spaceship

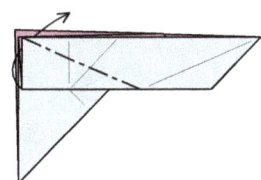

13. Reverse fold.

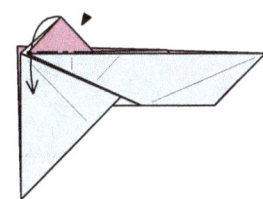

14. Reverse fold back down.

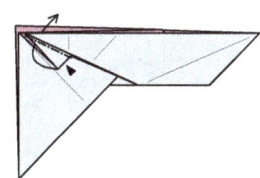

15. Reverse fold again.

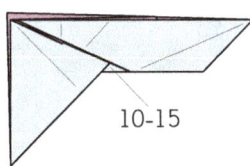

16. Repeat steps 10-15 behind.

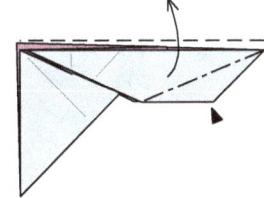

17. Raise the top layer while squash folding.

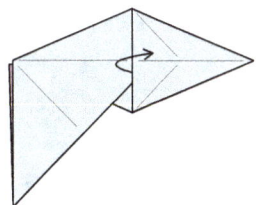

18. Wrap around the hidden corner.

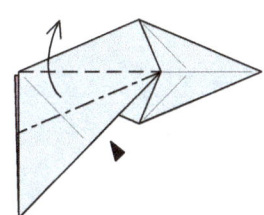

19. Squash fold.

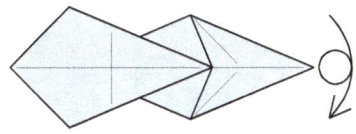

20. Turn over.

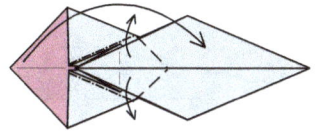

21. Spread apart the sides and squash down the center flap.

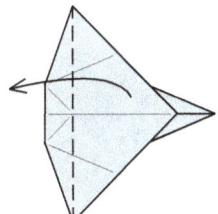

22. Valley fold.

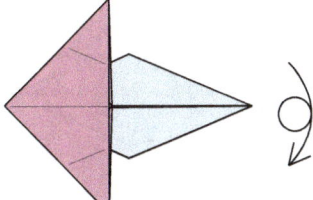

23. Turn over.

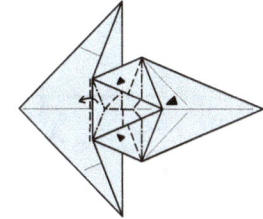

24. Spread squash, while folding the resulting center ridge to one side.

spaceship

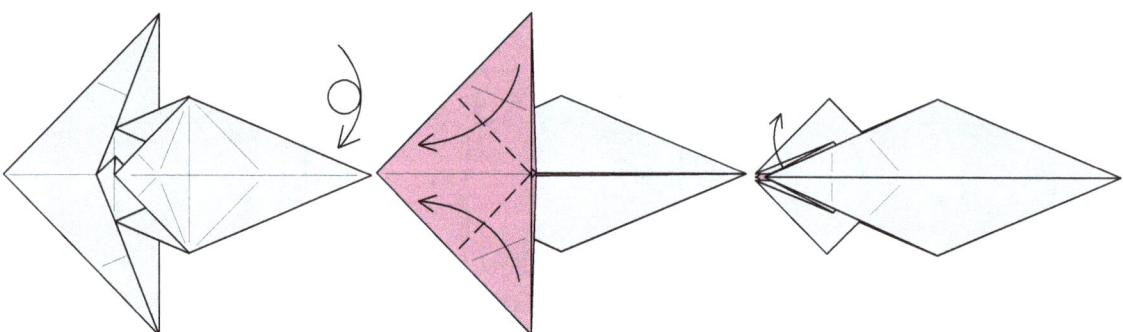

25. Turn over.
26. Valley fold the large flaps over.
27. Undo the series of reverse folds.

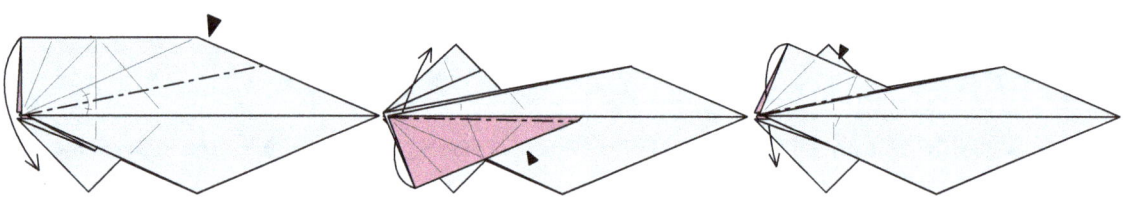

28. Closed reverse fold along the angle bisector.
29. Reverse fold back up.
30. Reverse fold down.

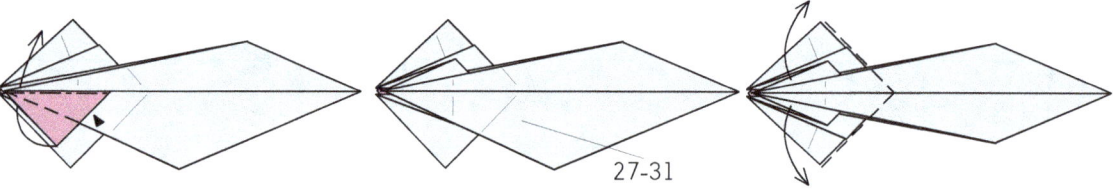

31. Reverse fold in and out along the existing creases.
32. Repeat steps 27-31 on the bottom.
33. Swing the flaps outwards.

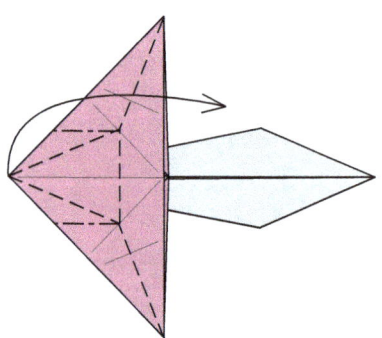 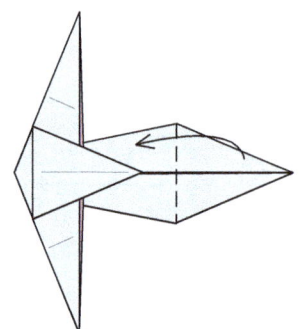 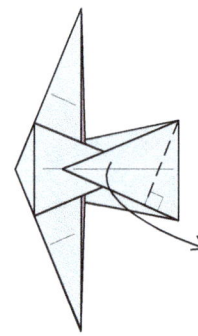

34. Using the angle bisectors, collapse the flap over.
35. Valley fold.
36. Valley fold down.

spaceship

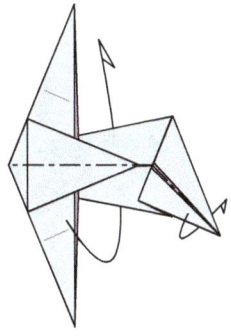

37. Mountain fold in half while swiveling the front flat.

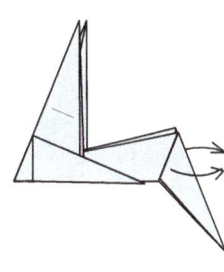

38. Slide out a single layer at each side.

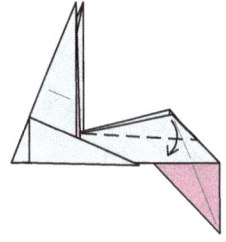

39. Valley fold down.

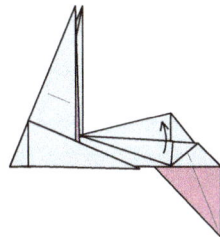

40. Unfold.

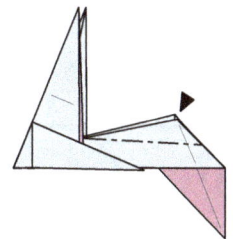

41. Sink triangularly.

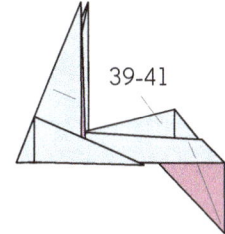

39-41

42. Repeat steps 39-41 behind.

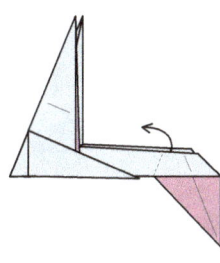

43. Reverse fold the center flap as far as possible.

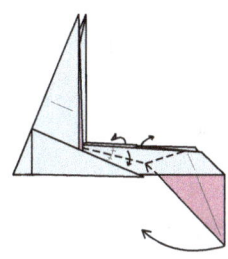

44. Valley fold the sides down, allowing small squashes to form and the colored flap to crimp inwards.

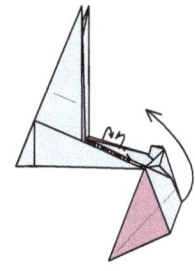

45. Crimp the flap upwards.

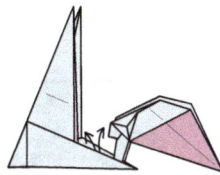

46. Slide a single layer up at each side.

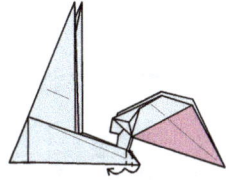

47. Outside reverse fold the corner over and over.

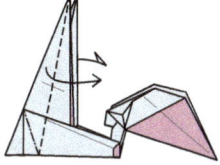

48. Crimp the outer edges forward.

157

spaceship

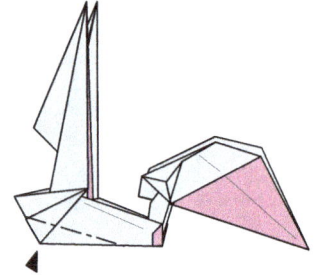

49. Carefully closed sink the corner.

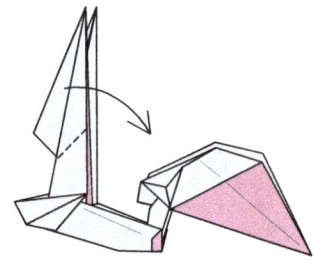

50. Valley fold the cluster of flaps over.

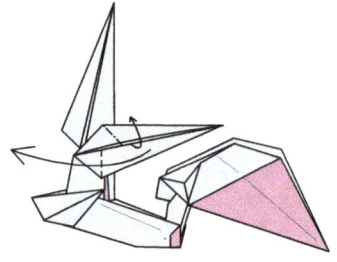

51. Swing the flap over while pulling two layers up.

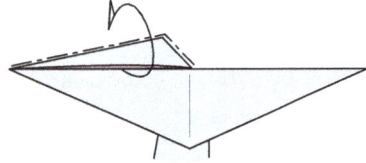

52. Wrap around two layers.

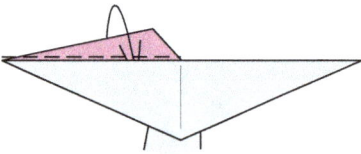

53. Tuck the flap into the pocket.

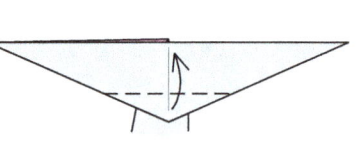

54. Valley fold up as far as possible.

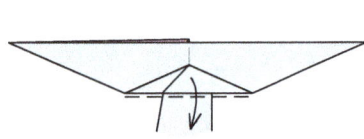

55. Unfold.

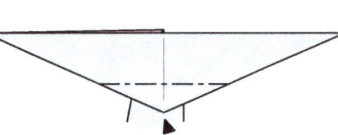

56. Closed sink along the existing crease.

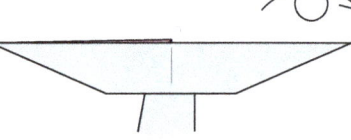

57. Turn over.

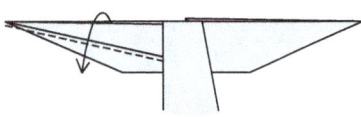

58. Swivel down two layers.

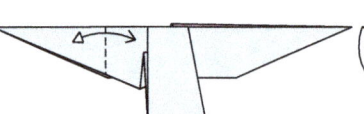

59. Precrease, aligning with the corner behind.

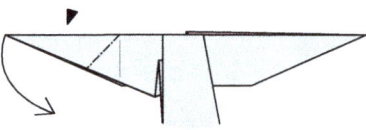

60. Reverse fold, distributing the thin center layers behind.

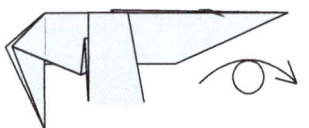

61. Turn over.

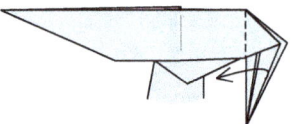

62. Open out the flap.

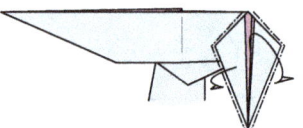

63. Wrap around one layer at the left and two layers at the right.

spaceship

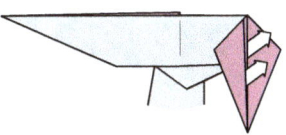

64. Unsink the two small flaps.

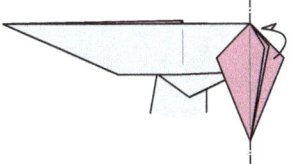

65. Mountain fold the back layer.

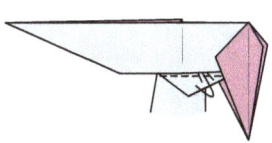

66. Valley fold the protruding corner inside.

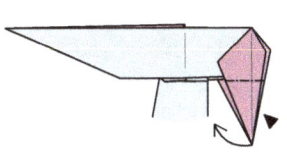

67. Reverse fold.

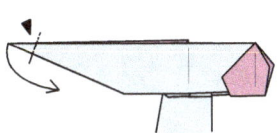

68. Reverse fold the tip.

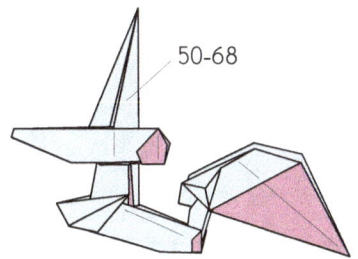

69. Repeat steps 50-68 behind.

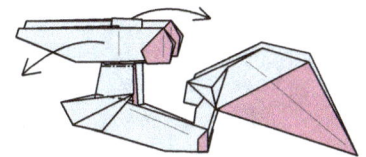

70. Pull the flaps outwards.

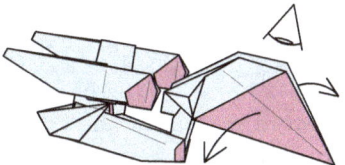

71. Spread apart the front flap.

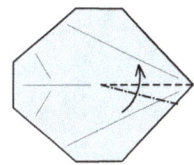

72. View from previous step. Form a pleat, allowing the flap to become convex.

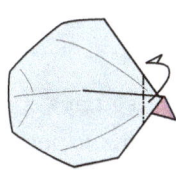

73. Mountain fold.

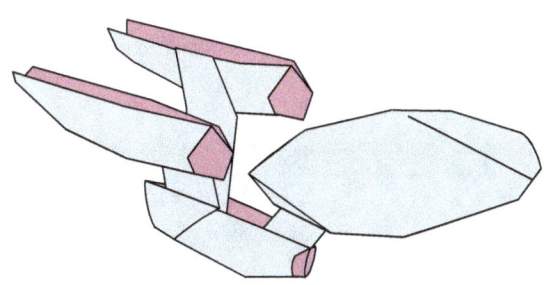

74. Completed *Spaceship*.

159

Materials and Methods

In theory, the only things required for origami is a piece of paper and a pair of hands. In practice, however, you will want to have the right materials for the project at hand. For initial practice attempts, you will want to use papers that are easy to fold, but not necessarily of presentable quality. The two most popular practice papers are commercial origami paper (sometimes sold as kami) and American foil. Both papers are available colored on one side, and white on the other. American foil is preferable as it holds its shape more easily. These papers feature a thin layer of decorative foil that helps your model hold its shape. Most of the origami supply houses sell a 10" version as their largest size, but some thinner wrapping paper can be used if you are looking for something larger. Japanese foil is thinner, and generally easier to fold than the American variety, albeit more expensive. Kami is better for those who have trouble with reverse folds and sinks. Both types of papers will yield adequate results, but almost invariably, more decorative choices will make your models look better.

For display-worthy efforts, you will want to use papers and methods that heighten the result, possibly at the expense of ease of folding. Such methods include foil-backing and wet folding, which includes the related technique of back coating. Both approaches allow the paper-folding artist to use material combinations to create interesting effects.

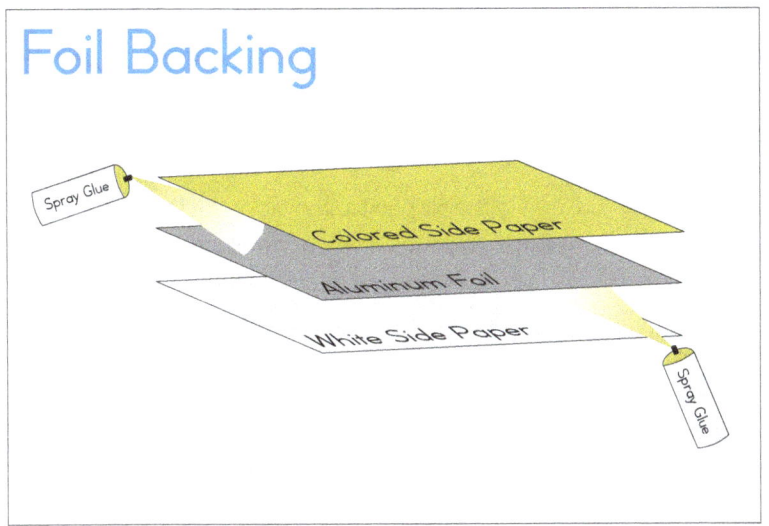

Foil Backing

Foil backing is a great way to utilize nonporous materials, and papers with patterns that could get ruined with water (such as newsprint). Foil backing is the process of adding a layer of aluminum foil (yes, the same material you can find at virtually any grocery store) to paper, to give the resulting material unique folding characteristics. A common backing choice is tissue paper, which further enhances the folding properties of the foil (this combination is also known as "tissue foil"). Regardless of the backing material, the metal-like quality allows folds to instantly stay where they are placed. Spray adhesive is used to bond the layers together. This is also known as artist's adhesive or photo mounting spray, and it contains the same glue found on adhesive tape. You can find this at most art supply stores, but you will find it much cheaper at a hardware or office supply store. While you can usually use 3M's Spray Mount, some projects (typically involving very thick papers) will require something like 3M's Super77 Spray Adhesive. All work should be done in a well-ventilated area, as the glue is toxic. You will also want to protect your floor with newspaper. Place a sheet of foil on the floor. Leave the shinier side up first and use as the surface for the main color. In most cases, the foil will be the limiting factor as far as size is concerned, so use as large a sheet as necessary. Spray the glue onto the surface of the foil according to the manufacturer's directions.

If you have a choice of nozzles, use the one with a finer mist. When spraying, be sure to cover the entire surface area of the foil, while paying special attention to the edges. After spraying, you should give the glue about a minute to get tacky.

The next step is to apply your paper to the tacky surface. Start by adhering the bottom edge of your paper to the bottom edge of the foil. Then start working your way upwards until the foil is completely covered. You can also use a baker's rolling pin to apply the paper. Another variation is to start at one corner and work your way to the opposite corner. Try several methods to see which feels most comfortable. For thicker papers, it might be easier to simply drop the paper onto the foil. When you are done, rub out any wrinkles, and then apply another layer of paper on the other side.

To get the largest possible square, cut along the edge of the foil, which should be visible through the layers of paper, provided your papers are translucent enough. If you wish you can also tear through the foil, which is surprisingly accurate (and fun), provided you are using thin enough paper. First, score the paper, unfold, and turn over to leave the resulting crease in mountain fold formation. The paper can easily be torn in this position. Of course, you won't get the largest possible square this way, but it is easier to be accurate.

A rotary cutting board is recommended when tearing is not possible, or you cannot see the silhouette of the foil through your backing paper. While a traditional guillotine cutter might suffice, spending an extra $100 or so on a rotary cutter is worth the investment for the serious paperfolding artist. These can be purchased at better art supply stores or photography supply stores. A pair of scissors can be used when a paper cutter is not as convenient.

If you wish to make a square that is wider than your piece of foil, there is a way to accomplish this. First, you must adhere two (or more) strips of foil together. If you spray along the edge of one piece and attach the other piece along that edge, the results are remarkably seamless. Most likely, the paper you will want to use on the surface will be smaller than the foil piece you have prepared. There is a way around this hurdle as well. First, you should fold your foil in half. The resulting surface area should now be small enough for your paper. Before you use any adhesive, place a sheet of newspaper between the fold to avoid getting any glue on the inner layers. You can now adhere your papers on each side of the foil. When you are done with the gluing part, use a scissor to cut along the folded edge. After you unfold your piece, rub out the crease, and the seam will almost disappear. You can repeat the same process for the other side.

When folding larger models, you might find certain portions to be flimsy. While wire is traditionally used to add rigidity, I have found stuffing layers of foil to be even better. You can fold a piece of foil over upon itself a few times to make it many layers thick. This can be stuffed between the layers of the parts of the model that need more rigidity.

If you are using tissue as the backing paper, where the properties of the foil are at their most extreme, you are in for a radically different folding experience. By themselves, foil and tissue make for flimsy and weak folding materials, but together you have one of the strongest and most resilient materials around. Also, when you make a crease, it will hold very well. It will hold so well that it is difficult to change its direction (i.e., valley to mountain). This makes procedures that require precreasing, such as sinks, difficult to perform. You can unfold the paper after precreasing, rub out the creases must be changed, and replace them with new folds that are in the right direction. Unlike commercial foil paper, you can rub out unwanted creases without leaving a trace.

While it is true that foil backing will make folding your model more difficult for most if its stages, its properties are fortuitous at the end of a model's folding sequence. If your model has many layers, it can easily be flattened. In extreme cases, a hammer can work wonders. After your model is as flat as you desire, you can shape and pose it any way you wish. Your model will hold that shape forever, until you decide to reshape it, or someone or something inadvertently reshapes it. The latter scenario is obviously undesirable. If you use a slightly thicker paper (such as the Japanese papers), you will lose some of the malleability but will have a much more solid looking model, due to its increased thickness. It can still be bent out of shape, but is acceptable if being displayed in a controlled environment.

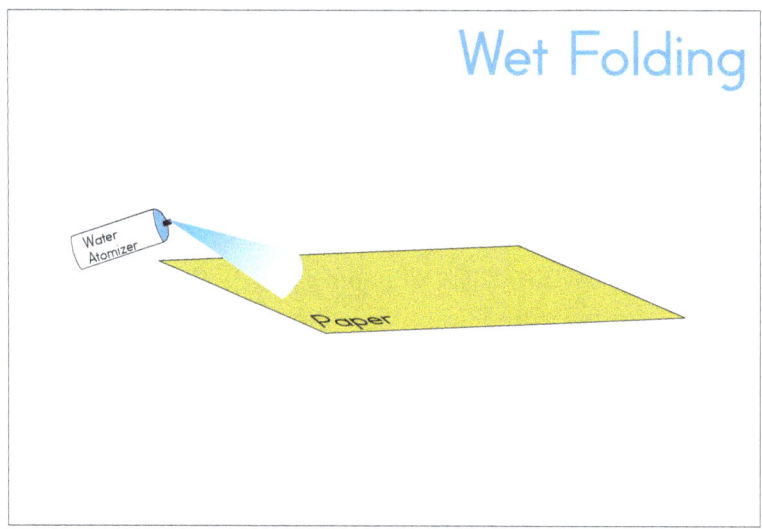

Wet Folding

Foil backed paper looks great in person, but the camera lens often picks up the foil through the backing, even when the backing paper seems to be dense enough. This might be okay for some subjects, but to have a less reflective look, wet folding techniques are more effective. The process might be slower, but the results are more permanent.

Wet folding involves lightly dampening your paper during the folding process, so when it finally dries it will retain its shape. When paper is wet, the sizing (glue-like substance) that holds the paper fibers together is loosened. Once the paper is dry again, the sizing will hold the paper in its new position. Taking advantage of this property of paper enables the folder to hold shapes that seem to defy gravity. Not all papers contain a lot of sizing, so you might have to add a methylcellulose paste to your paper before folding. To do this, you first add the methylcellulose powder (which is sold at many art supply stores) to water and mix the compound until it is syrupy. You can use about a teaspoon for each cup of warm water. This paste can now be brushed onto your paper with a standard painter's brush. After the paper is dry, it will be even easier to wet fold. To speed up the drying process, you can use a table fan.

When wet folding it is important to realize your paper will expand, often unevenly. This makes accurate folding much more difficult. Also, reference fold crease lines become difficult to see while paper is wet. For these reasons, you may prefer to delay wetting the paper until key folds are in place. When you are ready to wet the paper, it is important not to allow the paper to get soggy. By using an atomizer's mist sparingly, a leathery texture can be obtained from the paper. These spray bottles can be found at many perfume sections; try to find one with as fine a mist as possible.

Holding your model in position while drying can be a creative challenge. Tools that work include twist ties (the plastic-coated ones that are often used for electrical wire packing), portable clamps, and painter's masking tape. As an example, you can wind a twist tie around the legs of your insect model, bend them into the desired position, and secure them to a flat surface with masking tape. After further moistening your model with your atomizer, it will retain its stance after it is dry and the bindings have been removed.

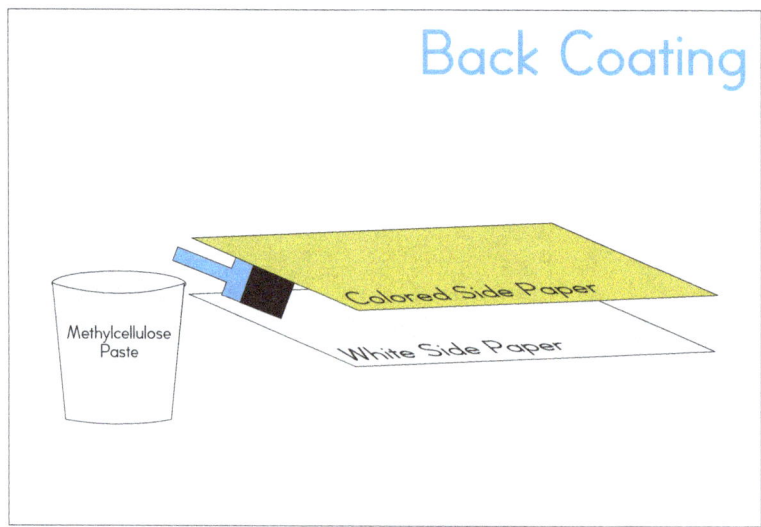

Back Coating

A related technique to wet folding is back coating. Since most specialty papers are monochromatic, the two-toned effect in many origami models is lost. You can use methylcellulose paste to adhere two complementing colors of paper together. Brush the paste on one paper, being sure to work on a smooth surface, as the paper will pick up any texture from your working surface. Apply the second sheet on top, brushing it into place. You can cut your square once it is dry, using a table fan to expedite the process. Again, a rotary cutter is recommended. The materials you chose to mate together should both be porous and fibrous enough to stay together, otherwise you might have to resort to foil backing.

Papers that work well include the Unryu variety (both regular and soft) from both Japan and Thailand. These papers might be labeled as containing mulberry or kozo fiber, but other fibers will work as well. You can also try Yatsuo papers from Japan, which are made from kozo and sulfite pulp, and have a much smoother look than the Unryu papers. These and other fine art papers can be found at better art stores and via mail order. You can expect to pay about three to four dollars for a 25" x 37" sheet.

Other important paper considerations include weight, which is how a material's thickness is described. To give you a gauge of what this means, standard copy paper is often at 20 Gr/M2 weight. Of course, you will double your thickness if you are bonding two sheets together. Try to keep the total thickness under 80 Gr/M2. When dealing with lighter colors, you might have to work with thicker papers just to get the right opacity (but you can mate them with lighter weight darker papers if you are trying to avoid additional thickness). As a test, you can hold the paper against a black surface to see how well it eclipses its backing. Sometimes, having the contrasting color show through is a good thing, as your color choices will seem to blend a bit. One thing you would like to avoid is having your paper bleed (having the dye run) when wet. The most temperamental colors tend to be reds and black, but it is a good idea to test out a sheet first if possible.

Dry Wiring

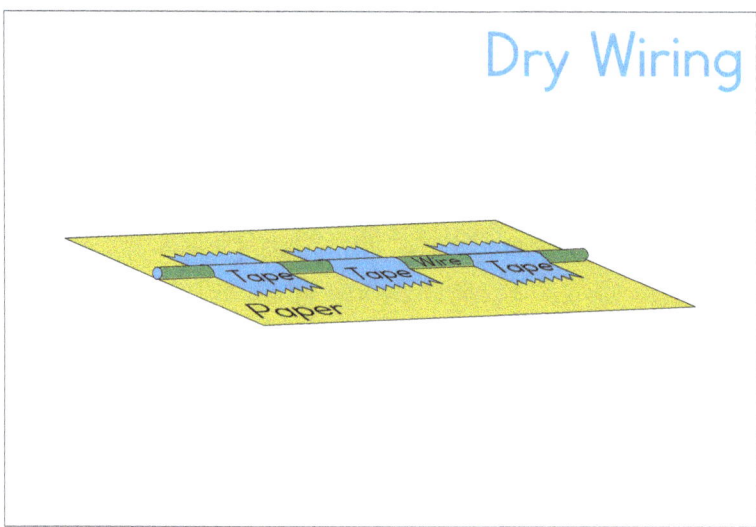

Both wet folding and foil backing will give your models a sculpted look. Sometimes is preferable to have a crisper look, where the paper looks less molded and more folded. Simply folding your paper without any of these special techniques will sometimes work, but for most models (especially those that are very complex), will have sections that will gradually spring apart. The solution is to strategically add wire to these troublesome sections.

For most models, florists wire will suffice. 26 gauge is a good thickness for most scenarios, and 22 gauge can be used where more strength is needed (lower numbers correlate with thicker gauges). The wire typically has a PVC coating (often green) that can be secured simply with a few pieces of scotch tape. For some heavier duty situations, PVC glue is useful. It can be cut with a pair scissors, but heavier gauges might be best trimmed with a wire cutter.

The wire has a palpable thickness, and it can sometimes be a challenge to avoid having it bulge through the surface layers of your model. It is best to lay the wire along a fold line that is on the underside of your model. In rare cases, you can cover the wire with multiple layers of aluminum foil to cover up the bulge.

It will be necessary to unfold and refold your model, adding wire as you feel it is helpful. Of course, this adds to the challenge of folding, but when done well, the results are worth it. As with foil backing, the final model can get bent out of shape, so special care is needed when storing. With enough experimentation, you should be able to conceive the perfect material for any model.

www.ingramcontent.com/pod-product-compliance
Lightning Source LLC
Chambersburg PA
CBHW081721100526
44591CB00016B/2460